Boat Modeling
the Easy Way

Boat Modeling the Easy Way
A Scratch Builder's Guide

H. H. "Dynamite" Payson

International Marine
Camden, Maine

Published by International Marine

10 9 8 7 6 5 4 3 2

Library of Congress Cataloging-in-Publication Data

Payson, Harold H.
      Boat modeling the easy way : a scratch builder's guide / H. H.
"Dynamite" Payson.
          p.   cm.
      Sequel to: Boat modeling with Dynamite Payson.
      Includes index.
      ISBN 0-87742-320-2
      1. Boats and boating—Models.   I. Payson, Harold H. Boat
modeling with Dynamite Payson.   II. Title.
VM298.P385   1992
623.8'201042—dc20   92-38474
                                                              CIP

Questions regarding the content of this book should be addressed to:

      International Marine
      P.O. Box 220
      Camden, ME 04843

Typeset by A & B Typesetters, Inc., Bow, NH
Printed by Malloy Lithographing, Ann Arbor, MI
Illustrations by Doug Alvord
Design by Edith Allard
Edited by J. R. Babb, Jane Crosen, Thomas P. McCarthy
Production by Janet Robbins

To Phil Bolger

Contents

Acknowledgments

To the designers, Phil Bolger, Alan McInnis, Arthur Herrick, Bob Steward, Tom Bernardi, and Bill Garden; to the captains, Ken and Ellen Barnes, Doug and Linda Lee, and Bernard Raynes; and to all my friends for their help in making this book possible, my eternal thanks: Amy, Peter Spectre, Doug Alvord, Jay Hanna, Nancy Pomroy Stone, Helen and Edgar Post, Tim Payson, Neil Payson, and the IMP crew.

Introduction:
Boat Modeling the Easy Way

If you've ever wanted to build a beautiful boat model, but didn't know where to start, here is the easiest, fastest, most accurate way I know of. This is my variation of the old lift, or bread and butter, method. Lift models are built by stacking horizontal wooden slices representing the height elevations of waterlines that the architect uses to determine a boat's shape. Why is building a model this way so easy? Instead of laboriously transferring measurements from the plans to wood, you just cut up the architect's plans and use them for templates right through the whole process. And what could be faster and more accurate than tracing around the architect's original drawings?

Using this simple method, there's no mystery—no lofting, no springing of battens, no guessing at what the boat's shape is supposed to be. You're guided every step of the way, always working to a point of reference, a line that is always there to guide you.

I'm excited about this method because it eliminates all this hemming and hawing about getting started. If you want to begin a boat model, all you need is a set of plans—either enlarged from this book to whatever size you want (most any photocopy shop can do this for you; enlargement percentages are listed on each set of plans), or with full-size plans which you can buy from me—a pair of scissors, a can of spray adhesive, and some tempered Masonite to stick the cut-up plans to, and I can have you starting on your goal in just a few minutes.

This book includes a fleet of boats Phil Bolger has designed just for lift modeling, including the handsome Gloucester inshore lobsterboat *Laura B.*; a pretty Friendship sloop, *Lisa*; *Mite*, a sharp-looking Maine harbor tug; a turn-of-the-century low-power day cruiser, *Alice*; a plank-on-edge Victorian English cutter, *Foam*; *Snow Leopard*, a sleek torpedo-sterned runabout; and *We're Here*, the Gloucester fishing schooner from Kipling's wonderful old book *Captains Courageous*. There are also lines (from the actual boats) and instructions for building two sardine carriers: *Pauline* from Thomaston, Maine (designed by Roy Wallace, lines taken by Woodin & Marean), and *William Underwood* from Dorchester, Massachusetts (designed by Eldredge-McInnis, redrawn by Arthur R. Herrick, Jr.).

Here's how it works: Each plan shows the views of the boat—the hull profile (viewed from the side), the deck plan (viewed from above), and the body sections (viewed from the bow or stern). Each waterline lift is laid out for either solid or hollow hull construction. By cutting to the centerline, you can build a solid half model to hang on the wall; or if you have a dite more skill and patience, you can build a hollow half model or a full model that you can put on your mantel or even sail. It's your choice; the plans are adequate for all three options. We'll go through the whole process of cutting out the templates and laying up the lifts for a half hull step by step in Chapter 1, so no matter which model you decide to build, be sure to read this chapter.

Here's the whole building process in a nutshell: The hollow full model is built in two halves. First the lifts are stacked and glued. The profile shape is traced on each half, then cut on the bandsaw. The two halves are glued together, and the lift ridges are carved down to take off everything that's not a boat. The deck template is laid on the hull and marked around; the hull is then trimmed right to the line. With the deck and profile views established, the width of the backbone/keel at the rabbet line is marked on the hull, with two parallel lines on each side of the hull's centerline running along the hull's length to the top of the stem. The backbone is cut out and slipped onto the hull. With the deck shape precisely cut, the profile precisely cut, and the backbone in place, the body templates show how much is to be taken off at each station. You can see the lines at all times.

Why glue two halves together instead of making the model whole? First, it saves on material, because you don't need wide, expensive boards. The glue lines are better because you avoid the boards' natural tendency to curl. Most important, this method is designed to make modelmaking easy—you can always see what you're doing.

What's so new about this method? Nothing; just a different approach. This idea of building models using waterline lifts has been around since architects put down the first hull lines on paper. But it all changed when my friend Peter Spectre and I had a crack at making the Friendship sloop lift model *Amy R. Payson* for *WoodenBoat* magazine. Both of us have boat backgrounds—we know the pointy end from the back end—and are fair to middlin' woodworkers with a fair amount of tools. But neither of us had ever before made a lift model, especially a model in this class. Working together, paying no attention to how lift modeling was supposed to be done, we devised the simplest, fastest, and the most accurate hassle-free approach for putting a hull together I've ever seen. Now I'm hooked!

How much talent and experience will you need? Lots of people are turned off from the idea of building either a boat or a model when they look at the plans, with all those curved lines going in all directions seemingly out of control. But think plumb and square, and you've got it, because that's how every good boat worth her displacement ever came to be: plumb and square right on the architect's drawing board, and plumb and square in the builder's shop. All you need to do is keep things plumb and square while you're laying up the model. It's no different than starting to build a house. You'll be surprised at how much will come to you simply from starting in.

The Building Jig

Since plumb and square is the name of the game, the first thing you'll need is a right-angle jig long enough for your model, built from braced-off boards. For one or a few models, a jig built of ¾-inch boards would be OK; 2-by planks would be better. The jig should be a little wider than half the beam, a little higher than the greatest depth, and a good 6 or 8 inches longer than the hull. It must be perfectly square; brace it well to keep it that way. At the jig's center, square off a plumb line and a horizontal line, and the jig is ready for the job.

You can also make a jig welded from aluminum or steel. I had one made out of aluminum because wood has a tendency to go out of shape during dry and moist periods, and since I plan on building models for a long time to come, I didn't want to have to check the accuracy of the jig every time I used it.

Templates

This method uses Masonite templates for the most part because they're much easier to trace around for the large, complex shapes typical of hull lifts. Take a paper template that you've cut from a photocopy or blueprint enlargement of the plans in this book (or a tracing of the full-size plan), give it a shot of spray adhesive, stick it down on a piece of ⅛-inch tempered Masonite that's smooth on both sides (buy a whole sheet; you'll want it for template material), saw it

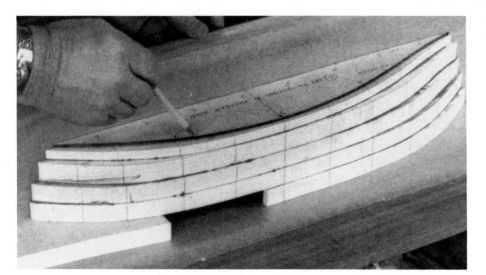

The building jig: keeping things plumb and square.

out, and you've got it: instant template. In addition, because this stuff is stable, you can save the templates for posterity. Who knows, perhaps one of your kids or grandkids will want to build a model someday. You can make a storage case cheaply and easily from 1/8-inch prefinished lauan office paneling; pack the templates in the case, and they'll be there waiting.

You might want to try using thin aluminum for your station and transom templates or where flexibility is a helpful feature. I'm talking about the thin aluminum sheets used by newspapers as plates for printing. These come in 2-foot-by-3-foot sheets, are recycled and reused, and I get them for free from my friendly local newspaper printer. You can cut them with ordinary scissors, yet the aluminum is durable—much better than cardboard if you want templates that will be used again. The thin aluminum wins out for station templates, in my opinion, because the templates are so thin, it won't matter which side of the station line you hold them when checking for accuracy as you carve the hull.

Woods

Let's talk for a minute about woods. Basswood, sugar pine, and the ordinary house-construction grade of finish pine are common woods for modelmaking. I generally use what I can get handily and locally, but that doesn't mean you must. Any fine-grained, stable wood will do.

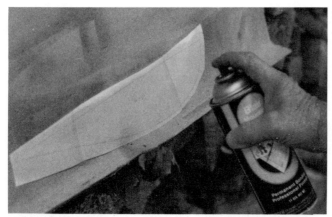

Clockwise, from upper left: Gluing rough-cut template to Masonite. Storing lift templates for posterity. Template boxes labeled and ready for your grandkids.

Basswood sizes from hobby shops run from $1/32$ inch $\times$ 4 inches $\times$ 2 feet up to 2 inches $\times$ 4 inches $\times$ 2 feet. This is well within the size range of almost any model you're likely to make for your home; in fact, a "miniature lumberyard" of this wood in different lengths and thicknesses is nice to have around, if you get into building models. Basswood cuts easily and is nice to work with, having a very stable grain. Its only fault, as far as I can see, other than its high price at hobby and mail-order outlets, is that it can have hidden blemishes—-dark grain that suddenly appears, or quick changes in color right where you don't want them. Of course, this is only a concern if you want to give the model a clear finish. Other than that, I'm all for basswood, even considering its price—but I'd recommend you shop carefully. For example, at this writing one mail-order hobby supplier prices one piece of basswood planed $3/8$ inch $\times$ 4 inch $\times$ 2 feet at a whopping $3.55, which makes for an expensive model.

Pine from a local lumberyard—ordinary finish pine for house construction—is cheaper than that, so I sometimes use it. I get the best grade, .1, which at this writing is $2.75 per board foot for $3/4$-inch finish pine. Use only kiln-dried wood that the moisture and sap has been cooked out of to avoid splitting and checking later on. Make sure the grain is straight, and as free from knots as you can get it. Since you aren't likely to find kiln-dried clear pine at your local lumber supplier in $3/8$-inch thickness, you use $3/4$-inch pine, which is readily available, and cut the lifts down to $3/8$-inch thickness on your table saw, using a hollow-ground planer blade (you don't need an expensive thickness planer); this is described in Chapter 1. Actually, pine corner boards a full 1 inch thick, if you can find some, would be a good way to go; you could easily get two lifts from one cut, since there'd be plenty of room for even a fairly thick saw kerf. If you can't find the 1 inch, $3/4$ inch will do.

Another source is specialty lumberyards. I've found that at A. E. Sampson and Son (P.O. Box 1010, Warren, ME 04864, tel. 207-273-4000) they sell rough "four-quarter" (and other thicknesses) random-length basswood for $1.85 a board foot (at this writing). I can get six $3/8$-inch $\times$ 3-inch lifts out of one 2-foot cut (a square foot is 12 inches long, 12 inches wide, and 1 inch thick), which is pretty economical! Of course, that doesn't take milling or shipping costs into consideration. Even then, I'd wager, you would save by buying from a specialty lumberyard like Sampson's. Besides that, they'll ship anywhere in the country—great if you live in some out-of-the-way place. For the $3/8$-inch lifts, you can do the milling yourself: Plane the rough four-quarter to $7/8$ inch; this leaves $1/8$ inch for a saw kerf (using a planer blade), with room to spare. Sugar pine, at this writing, sells for $1.98 a foot at Sampson's and is a delight to work with.

Tools

Basic power tools for making a half or full model consist of a bandsaw and a table saw.

For cutting out the lifts you'll need a bandsaw with a $3/8$-inch, skip-tooth blade. This is the best blade for rapid cutting with the least amount of dust to blow around your shop. These hardened skip-tooth blades are sold by Olson Catalog Sales, Route 6, Dept OCS-R, Bethel, CT 06801. Ask for their catalog. If you don't have a bandsaw, you can cut the lifts out with a saber saw—before resorting to this, though, I'd hunt hard for a friend with a bandsaw, because it's so much easier and more accurate. Also, if you can afford it, some kind of power scroll saw would most definitely be worth your while, especially for cutting the sharper curves in the lifts. You can live without one, but if you plan to build several lift-type models, a scroll saw will save you a lot of time.

To rip the lift sections accurately, if you're resawing them from thicker stock (see Chapter 1), you'll need a good table saw—and I mean a good one: no pressed metal tops, no sloppy miter gauge slots. You want one with a cast metal, machine-ground table. You'll need a sharp, hollow-ground planer blade, which will give you a saw cut as smooth as if it had been planed. (If you have a thickness planer, naturally you'd use this instead of your table saw.)

For hand tools you'll need a 1-inch chisel, a $^7/_8$-inch or 1-inch gouge with an inside bevel, a standard low-angle block plane, a spokeshave, a 10-inch rasp, an 8-inch mill bastard file, and 60-, 80-, 100-, and 220-grit sandpaper for shaping the hull.

For sanding in areas with a concave curve, like the tuck (near the sternpost), you'll need a sanding fid—a cone-shaped sanding block with a comfortable handle, about 10 inches long, tapering from $^1/_2$ inch at the top end to $1^7/_8$ inch near the handle. You could make one yourself from an old oar with its grip intact; just cut it to length, taper as shown, cut a slit for holding the sandpaper, and you'll have a great sanding fid (see page 8).

Long, flexible sanding battens are good for final fairing of the hull. Make yourself a good assortment of these by cutting strips of $^1/_8$-inch or $^1/_{16}$-inch aircraft plywood, 12 to 15 or so inches long—whatever bends around the hull easily—$^3/_8$ inch, $^1/_2$ inch, and $^3/_4$ inch wide. Spray-glue them on one side, and stick on sandpaper of various grits—60, 80, and 100, finishing with 220- and 320-grit. Glue blocks at each end for handholds, and away you go!

And of course, any builder of boats big or small can't have too many clamps. Get yourself a bunch of small clamps—you'll find plenty of uses for them in modelmaking. Most of the mail-order model supply houses carry them.

Buy yourself a miniature hand drill—also called a "pin vise"—and a selec-

A collection of useful handtools.

tion of drill bits numbered from 61 to 80 (in thousandths), and you'll have all the drills you need for everything you'll put on one of these models. If you're going to do much modelmaking, a drill gauge from 61 to 80 and a micrometer will save you a lot of time and guesswork.

And, of course, a Dremel tool with all its accessories is the number one miniature power tool to have for boring, sanding, and countless other operations. For turning small parts such as horns, search and running lights, barrels, life preservers, and what have you, a Dremel lathe is adequate.

You'll need a pair of dividers for scribing lines. I use a sliding-clip depth gauge for scribing in tight corners, such as marking the height of a floor for a pilothouse. This gauge is small enough to work in close spaces where you couldn't begin to use a carpenter's combination square, and it's light—just right for delicate work. You could get by with a simple stick marked for depth, but this handy gadget has a stop on it so you can work quickly and accurately. You can pick one up at most any hardware store or hobby shop. Mine is 6 inches long, ½ inch wide, is marked off in that many inches, and even comes with a pocket clip. I made one alteration on mine, however: the sliding clip slid too easily and was prone to sliding unnoticed while scribing, which won't do—so I gave the clip's grips a few light whacks with a hammer to stiffen them up a little. The gauge works fine now and can be trusted.

There are a few other special tools for modelmaking: A magnifying glass is handy for reading plans. A jeweler's ball-peen hammer is great for heading over brass wire or driving small pins. A miniature modeler's plane does the job for fine hand planing. Extra-fine needlenose pliers will help you hold onto small parts. And a drill stand for your Dremel tool allows precision boring and router work. Micro Mark (340 Snyder Ave., Berkeley Heights, NJ 07922, Model Expo (P.O. Box 1000, Industrial Park Drive, Mount Pocono, PA 18370), and other hobby shop catalogs will sell this and all the other miniature tools you'll need.

Above all, buy yourself an architect's scale rule. It's as easy to read as an ordinary rule (see "Measuring to Scale," below), so don't let the idea of owning one scare you. Every plan should show the scale the architect has drawn his boat on. When in doubt whether a measurement is real inches or scale inches, or should you want to add one of your own, this simple device puts you in control and removes all the guesswork: simply lay your scale rule on the plans, and see for yourself. I get more calls than I should from builders wondering how to measure something on their plans. When I ask if they have an architect's scale rule, the answer is always "No." Buy one and save us both time.

No question about it, the more tools you own and know how to use, the better modeler you're going to be. What a pleasure it is to just grab the right tool for the job and do it! Frustration comes from trying to make do with inferior tools when you know there are tools out there to do anything you want.

Glues and Fastenings

You'll need artist's spray adhesive, such as Blair's or 3M Spra-ment, to glue the plans to the templates and make an assortment of fairing battens (see Chapter 1).

As for the hull itself, if you're planning to build a model that floats,

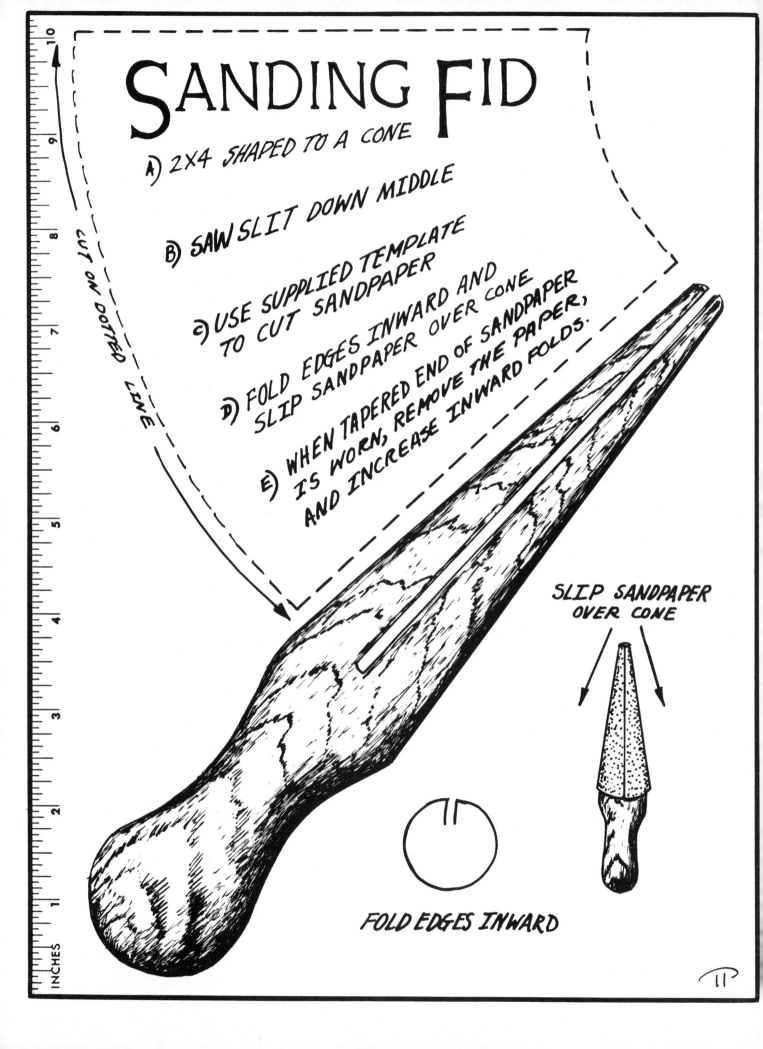

SANDING FID

A) 2×4 SHAPED TO A CONE

B) SAW SLIT DOWN MIDDLE

C) USE SUPPLIED TEMPLATE TO CUT SANDPAPER

D) FOLD EDGES INWARD AND SLIP SANDPAPER OVER CONE

E) WHEN TAPERED END OF SANDPAPER IS WORN, REMOVE THE PAPER, AND INCREASE INWARD FOLDS.

CUT ON DOTTED LINE

INCHES

SLIP SANDPAPER OVER CONE

FOLD EDGES INWARD

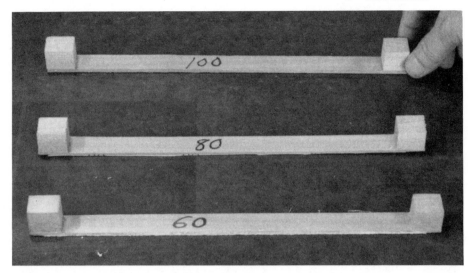

Sanding battens marked for 60-, 80-, and 100-grit paper.

Weldwood plastic resin dry-powder glue mixed with water works fine for gluing the lifts together. If your model will spend its life ashore, you can use carpenter's wood glue, such as Franklin Titebond. It's a quick-grabbing glue, and joints need only be held together for a few minutes—even in your hands. It isn't waterproof, however. If soaked for a few days your model will come apart, but for mantelpiece projects it's perfect. Thirty-minute epoxy is great for gluing the lifts because it allows time for repositioning if you notice one out of kilter. At the moment, I like using slow-setting epoxy mixed with Cab-O-Sil as a thickener. Whatever glue you choose, tongue depressors make handy glue spreaders.

For delicate work, where Weldwood or Titebond is too thick, I use quick-setting epoxy. I also use thin "superglue" (cyanoacrylate, also called CA glue; one brand is Krazy Glue), and damned carefully. Instantly bonded fingers are no fun. If it happens to you (as it did to me), resist the urge to rip them apart. Roll them apart, or holler like hell for your spouse to dump fingernail polish remover on your stuck fingers. After that experience, any tiny parts that needed gluing I impaled on a pin. The advantage of using this water-thin glue is that you can clamp together a joint and the glue will penetrate it, no matter how tight it is. This saves trying to align joints in a panic while glue is setting, and there's no glue to wipe up. It sure does stink, but a fan behind you helps, or you can pay top dollar for the stinkless variety.

By the way, if you're going to do much modelmaking, you'll want a supply of ³/₈-inch (#6 ribbon), ¹/₂-inch, and ³/₄-inch (#12 pleating) brass dressmaker's pins, if you can get them. These are smaller (less than 20 thousandths) than common pins, which are too large for delicate work. The small brass pins can be cut, sanded down, and, because they don't rust, left in your work forever—a big timesaver. Brass dressmaker's pins can be purchased by the pound or half-pound from Newark Dressmaker Supply, 6473 Ruch Road, P.O. Box 20730, Lehigh Valley, PA 18002.

A pound will probably last you a lifetime of steady modelbuilding, but they're much cheaper bought this way than from model supply houses and sewing shops, where you can pay up to a buck or so for a tiny packet of 50 or 100 pins. Since I'm apt to lose or drop that many in the course of a project, I don't mind being oversupplied. To keep the pins handy, I stick a bunch of them in a chunk of Styrofoam, and pick them out one by one with needlenose pliers when I need them. By the pound or by the piece, I wouldn't want to tackle modelmaking without them.

Painting and Finishing

Because the choice of paints, sealers, varnishes, and how to apply them depends a lot on what you like to use and have on hand, I haven't listed these with the materials and tools you'll need for each model—other than the suggested or designed color scheme for finishing each model.

Floquil scale-model paints are a good place to start, especially for painting small parts by hand. They work well, are flat in appearance, and look good even when touched up later. Because they have pigments ground to scale size, they don't obscure fine detail. Floquil paints come in a wide selection of "Railroad" colors and are found in almost any hobby shop. You can mix the colors if you like—for example, you can add a touch of gray to black or white, or a drop of black to red, to get a flatter color. They're not inexpensive, at $1.79 (at this writing) for a small 1-ounce bottle, but they're convenient for small jobs. If you decide to go that route, plan to buy their thinners, retarders, and all the rest; otherwise, if you find fault with their paint and you've thinned it with kerosene, you won't have a leg to stand on. If you have no hobby shop near you, write to Micro-Mark for their catalog. They carry the full line of Floquil products— along with everything you'll ever need to start in the model business.

Floquil's thinner formula is called Dio-Sol. It says on the can it's also used for cleaning paintbrushes used for Floquil, but I found it doesn't clean brushes anywhere near as clean or as fast as lacquer thinner, which you get by the gallon at an automotive store (ask for the cleaning kind, which is cheaper than the more refined type). A note of warning here: Be sure the lacquer thinner has dried out of your paintbrush before using the brush with Floquil or any other oil-based paints, or you'll see your paint job curdle before your very eyes. And for sure, don't try to thin Floquil paints with lacquer thinner. After I got over the shock of spoiling a paint job by not waiting for the brush to dry, I decided I still liked the idea of starting each paint job with a perfectly clean dry brush. (Drying time for a ⅜-inch to ⅝-inch flat brush is only a few minutes.)

I didn't have very good luck with these paints for hand-painting a hull or other large areas, because they'd dry too fast and pile up with an unsightly ripple effect, even when thinned. Maybe the first coat would be successful, but then, without changing anything, the paint, out of the same bottle, would suddenly pucker up and look like curdled milk. Spraying these touchy paints offers less trouble, so I'm told.

All the colors are nice, but that stuff is a bit sophisticated for my tastes. These days I generally stick with what I can stir up at home myself from regular paints. I mix my own red bottom paint from Pettit International orange and D-Rusto red primer to whatever shade I want. It's flat and looks like the real thing. I have also used off-the-shelf spraypaints. You can get good results, too, with an airbrush, but I've found it's usually not worth the extra time and trouble it takes to mix the paint and clean up, unless you're after a color that you can't find in a can.

If you use your own concoctions of oil-based paints, you can still get the desired flat effect. When using gloss, use a generous amount of paint and sand the last coat with 320-grit sandpaper, or with a rag dipped in oil and pumice powder. Or you can put a bit of talcum powder in gloss paint to flatten it; I stumbled on this one. As for paint piling up and dragging, that happens for me with any kind of paint, no matter what I do. It's hard to keep a wet edge all the time so the paint will continue to flow without brush marks. For this reason I no longer try to lay on the perfect coat, but put it on as fast as I can, as evenly as I can, and hope to get on enough so that when it's sanded, the color is solid.

I've found that the shellac-based sealer B-I-N makes a great primer and a finish coat anywhere the color scheme calls for white, such as cockpit and deck. Put on two or three coats, one after the other (it dries fast), then sand it down with fine sandpaper for a flat but smooth finish. I used B-I-N as a primer on many of the models in this book, and for a finish coat on the Friendship sloop *Lisa*'s hull.

Last but by no means least are the easy-to-use acrylic water-based paints—which you can find in many stores in a wide variety of colors.

For sealing the hull before painting, you can buy special sealer concoctions, but at a special high price, which I see no point paying when a coat of shellac, varnish, or B-I-N will do. For filling any uglies before painting I like "Pic and Patch," a white water-based putty that you can get from mail-order hobby shops like Model Expo, Micro Mark, and others. It is fine enough for the smallest uglies and has a long shelf life. Putty the hull before sanding the sealer coat; this ensures the putty a good grip, which it wouldn't have if you tried puttying over a missed dusty spot from sanding the hull first.

To round out your supplies you'll want a good-quality paintbrush, fairly wide—about ½ or ⅝ inch at the ferrule, and 1 inch or so at the business end. Err on the side of a little larger rather than smaller. This size works well for painting a 2- or 3-foot hull, allowing you to put paint on fast enough so laps don't dry out. It's a mistake to paint a model by hand using a small brush; the job goes so slowly that the paint dries between strokes, thus ensuring a poor paint job. Of course, air brushing is the best way to put on paint in most instances. But that means acquiring another skill and buying an airbrush, and that takes time and money. Hardly worth it for one or two models.

You'll also need narrow masking tape for masking off the waterline and boottop. It's a good idea to stock up on several widths of the fine drafting tape, ¼ inch, ⅛ inch, and 1/16 inch, using the wider tape along straight areas and the narrower along curved areas at the stern. You can find these narrow widths in most stationery or art supply stores, or you can by pin striping from auto stores; I use the drafting tape made by Charrette, 44 Brattle Street, Cambridge, MA 02138. This tape comes in its own protective envelope and should be kept there when not in use to avoid collecting dust, which is an enemy of clean sharp waterlines: the edges of the roll of tape tend to pick up dust and debris that you may not see, but will spoil the looks of your model, leaving a ragged-looking waterline when you peel off the tape. You can cut your own narrow tape from ordinary wider masking tape, using a razor knife and a good straightedge to cut narrower widths on a piece of glass, being careful to trim off the outside edge, which is bound to be dusty.

For finishing things bright on a full model, I like to use varnish thinned down 30 to 40 percent with turpentine, and add a dollop of Japan dryer to help it set up. Thinning varnish is the secret to a good varnishing job. My work, using varnish dipped right from the can, used to look as if someone had dumped a load of gravel on it, but no more. Using thinned varnish, most everyone can get a professional-looking job. Or, right out of a can, you can spray fast-drying Minwax clear satin polyurethane. It dries evenly, leaving no gloss spots. Two applications will give you a beautiful, somewhat dull sheen. It's also great stuff to spray on half models and their backboards. Usually, though, I'll finish a half model with three or four coats of tung oil, applied with a rag or brush. If the last coat looks too glossy, I dull it by rubbing with a rag soaked in tung oil thinned 50 percent with turpentine and a bit of pumice powder.

Lettering Transom Names

For putting a name and port of hail on your model, "Zippy-Sign" transfer letters are the way to go. You can get an unbelievable selection of style and size, in white or black. I found them in black at a local stationery/art supply store. White letters were harder to find (though model suppliers have them), so I ended up with Letraset Instant Lettering, which my son Timothy found for me in Boston. You can order transfer lettering from Charrette in Cambridge, Massachusetts, or from a good artist's supply store. The letters come on a translucent backing sheet, and what you do is rub the letters off the sheet onto the hull. They're easy to put on—and easy to take off if you make a mistake. The proper way to apply them is to lay out guidelines for them on the hull, then hold the whole sheet in place while you rub the letters, one at a time, onto the hull. You can buy a special applicator for rubbing the letters on; it consists of a rounded metal tip on one end and a burnisher on the other. There's also a special eraser with which you simply "pick up" (erase) any misplaced letters (an ordinary eraser doesn't work as well, having a tendency to smudge). On flat areas, I've found that with a broken-off razor blade inserted in a wooden handle you can lift off the letters with better results than with using an eraser.

Before you lay out the letters, mark the centerline of the transom, using the transom template; this helps in centering. For curving the home port, you can trace the top of the transom template. There are all kinds of ways of doing it, but curving the letters slightly along with whatever curve your model has on her transom looks nice. It isn't always easy to get them spaced right. When you lay out the letters, you must consider the rake of the transom, and the viewing angle—don't get the letters too close vertically, or they'll look too close together when viewed from above the stern. You can also use the guide marks and spacing on the sheet of transfer lettering to help you align and space the letters.

Fittings, Parts, and Rigging

For wire rigging, and for specific parts to scale—parts that are hard to make, such as steering wheels, propellers, small cleats, blocks, anchors, cowl ventilators—write to Bluejacket ShipCrafters, Order Dept., P.O. Box 425, Stockton Springs, ME 04981 (800-448-5564). Send $2.00, and ask for their catalog.

As for finding miniature sailors to scale, I came to the conclusion—after much hunting around and head-scratching—that my best bet was to remodel the tiny toy spacemen, baseball players, etc. that can be found in the kids' toy section of most department stores. I use a Dremel tool to grind away their unsalty trappings, then paint or glue on the right kind of cap, beard, and clothes. (For more details, see Chapter 4, the section on outfitting *Mite*'s pilothouse.)

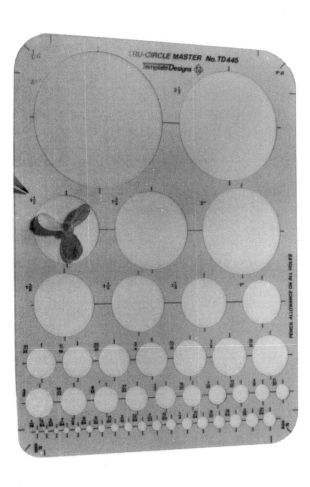

A circle template is handy for sizing propellers and portlights, among other things.

Other Designs

Once you learn this easy, straightforward method of building a scale-model hull, you'll be free to apply it to almost any design and build any waterline lift model you like. Once you see that you can make a decent hull, chances are you'll be motivated to keep on going. Whether it's a schooner, a tug, or whatever, this method will work on any architect's waterline drawing that has a plan view of the deck (that's looking at her from directly overhead, or from a fish's view below), a hull profile, which shows the boat's true height and shape viewed from the side, and a sectional view, looking fore-and-aft at the shape for each station. Those three views must be kept in mind. The templates are then cut out of the plans of each of these views and worked together to make a perfectly fair hull that looks exactly like the architect's drawing.

The Smithsonian Institution and Mystic Seaport Museum have plans available to the public at moderate cost. Write to the Smithsonian Institution, National Museum of American History, Division of Transportation, Room 5010, Washington, DC 20560. If you're mostly interested in small craft, write to Mystic Seaport Museum, Boat Lines, P.O. Box 6000, 06355-0990. Also at Mystic (same address), the Ships' Plans Department has collections of lines plans of larger vessels. And you can find plans in all kinds of books and magazines, old and new; some of these you'll need permission to copy, others you won't (although

1/4" = 1:0" SCALE

1"	1/32" −
2"	1/32" +
3"	1/16"
4"	3/32" −
5"	3/32" +
6"	1/8"
7"	5/32" −
8"	5/32" +
9"	3/16"
10"	7/32" −
11"	7/32" +
12"	1/4"

3/8" = 1:0" SCALE

1"	1/32"
2"	1/16"
3"	3/32"
4"	1/8"
5"	5/32"
6"	3/16"
7"	7/32"
8"	1/4"
9"	9/32"
10"	5/16"
11"	11/32"
12"	3/8"

3/4" = 1:0" SCALE

1"	1/16"
2"	1/8"
3"	3/16"
4"	1/4"
5"	5/16"
6"	3/8"
7"	7/16"
8"	1/2"
9"	9/16"
10"	5/8"
11"	11/16"
12"	3/4"

1/2" = 1:0" SCALE

1"	1/32" +
2"	3/32" −
3"	1/8"
4"	5/32" +
5"	7/32" −
6"	1/4"
7"	9/32" +
8"	11/32" −
9"	3/8"
10"	13/32" +
11"	15/32" −
12"	1/2"

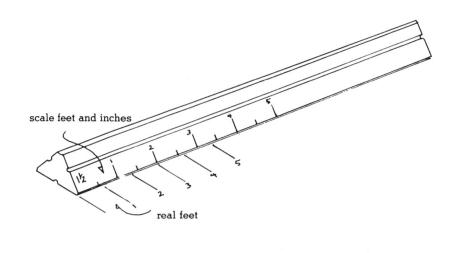

scale feet and inches

real feet

A simple chart for no-sweat scale conversions.

few architects will care if you're just making a model for personal use). If the scale of the plans won't suit for modelmaking, you can take them to a blueprint store or photocopy shop and have them blown up or reduced down, so you can make just the size model you want.

You can follow the same basic methods for laying out the plans. If you want to make a hollow model, cut the waterline lifts out solid to the centerline first, then stack them on edge (like a deck of cards) offset by about an inch, lined up on their stations, and mark the shape of one from its neighbor. Peek down between them, and you'll be able to see how much wood needs to be taken off for a telescoping fit, yet leaving enough for gluing (leave the bottom lifts solid). The idea is to have enough wood left in the hull after carving to shape.

It's so simple! But you won't know until you try.

Measuring to Scale

Because many of the boats in this book are built from full-size boat plans, I've often given the dimensions for the full-size boat, which are on the plans. Where the scaled-down dimensions worked out neatly at the scale I built the model, I've mentioned these. But because many of them are such improbably accurate dimensions as 17/64, you'll probably find it easier to use an architect's scale rule.

Like a computer, the architect's rule automatically converts real inches to scale inches (as long as you remember to use the correct scale), with absolutely no mental gymnastics on your part. This makes it easy to build a model to any scale you want from any plans for which dimensions are given. Just roll the rule over to another scale, and build away.

On page 14 is a conversion chart for 1/4", 3/8", 1/2", and 3/4" scales. Though none of the models in this book is 1/2" scale, I threw it in for good measure in case you ever run across the need. Conversion from scale to real inches or vice versa is right before your eyes and so simple. For instance, 6" at 1/4" scale is 1/8" in real life; 3" is 1/16", and so forth.

Building at larger scale such as 3/4" is easier yet, because 6" = 3/8" and so on. Set your saw blade 3/8" from the fence and you've sawed 6" at 3/4" scale. Nothing to it, but perhaps enough to keep you awake.

You can also simply calculate the scale you want. Here's an example of how it works. Suppose you want to build a model at 3/4 inch = 1 foot scale, like the *Laura B.* Since 3/4 inch divides into 12 inches 16 times (12 / 3/4 = 16), the model is one-sixteenth the size of the real boat. So, where just the full sizes are given, divide by 16 to get the corresponding size for the model.

It's all really quite simple; just thinking about it will probably keep you from nodding off in your chair, and may even help ward off early senility.

Alternate Ways of Expressing Drawing Scales

1/32"	1:384
1/16"	1:192
1/8"	1:96
3/16"	1:64
5/32"	5:384
1/4"	1:48
3/8"	1:32
1/2"	1:24
3/4"	1:16
1"	1:12
1 1/2"	1:8

Building the Basic Half Model
Laura B.—A Gloucester Inshore Lobsterboat

Materials Needed

- one-half 4' × 8' sheet of ⅛"
  tempered Masonite (smooth both
  sides)
- 12 running feet of 4" × ⅜"
  basswood or pine
- 4' × 4" × ¾" basswood or pine
- 2' × 4" × 1/16" aircraft plywood
- spray adhesive
- Weldwood plastic resin glue,
  epoxy, or carpenter's glue
- ⅜" #6 brass ribbon pins
- 1" #18 brass escutcheon pins
- full-size plans
- 27" × 8" × ¾" or ½" mahogany, Spanish cedar, pine, or
  whatever you have available

Tools Needed

- table saw
- bandsaw, jigsaw, or sabersaw
- vise
- clamps
- gouge with inside bevel
- spokeshave
- block plane
- 10" mill file
- sanding fid
- sanding battens
- combination square
- scissors
- #3 pencil
- masking tape

We'll build a hollow half model of the *Laura B.* as an example of how this lift method of modelmaking works. Then in Chapter 2 we'll go on to build the full model, with two halves put together and finished. Should you feel elated with your success, the *Laura B.*'s plans are adequate for building her full-size for lobstering.

Getting Started

These plans were drawn at a scale of ¾ inch = 1 foot (before being reduced to fit on a book page), and should be enlarged to that size, using the enlargement percentage shown on the plans. If you're too lazy to run down to a photocopy shop that does this, you can order the plans directly from me. Be sure to number all the stations on each template before cutting them free of the plans. You don't need to transfer any measurements in this easy modeling procedure, but you do need to know how all the stations line up, so they must be clearly marked. This is the whole idea of this kind of modeling. When you trace the templates on the wood, you'll need to make sure all the station marks are on them. This follows right straight through the building process.

Cut out all the waterline lifts and body section templates from the plans leaving plenty of paper all around, making no attempt to cut close to the lines. Leave the insides of the lifts solid for now—that is, intact to their centerlines. This is to keep the paper templates from edge-setting (going out of shape) on the Masonite, which they'd probably do if cut out now to their hollow lines, thus spoiling the shape of your model. Then lay your sheet of tempered Masonite on sawhorses and arrange the paper templates for the best layout for sawing them out. One at a time, spray-glue the back side of each cutout. A piece of thin cardboard pinned or taped upright against a wall or door at a convenient height makes a good "backboard" for spraying; turning up the bottom edge of the cardboard will form a wide lip to set the cutouts on. Give each cutout a shot of spray adhesive, put it back where it belongs on the Masonite, and smooth it out with your hands or a roller. Stick the middle down first, then work toward both ends.

Cut the templates out of the sheet of Masonite, leaving plenty of room around them; then saw them out right to the line, as accurately as possible. That's why we didn't cut to the line in the first place; there's no point in doing it twice. With the plans glued to the Masonite, it's safe to cut their skinny hollow shapes now. For a solid half model, simply lay the centerline of the hollow template on the edge of the board, and mark around only the outside of the template; ignore its inside shape.

A bandsaw or a scroll saw would be nice for this job, but if you don't have either, a sabersaw or Skilsaw would do. Set the body section templates aside for now; we'll use them to check the hull's shape later, as we carve.

Next cut out the hull profile, deck, and keel templates. Cut the hull lift profile free from the keel very carefully along the rabbet line, right from the top of the stem through its length. (On the real boat, the rabbet is a beveled recess cut into the backbone to receive the plank ends. In building the model of *Laura B.*, we'll take a shortcut—we'll glue the keel on, using the rabbet line as a guide for its width.)

The skeg can be extended to suit (made solid, if you wish; see "The Keel" in Chapter 2, on building the full model), or made "as is" with a metal strap set on its top serving as bearing for the rudderpost.

Leave plenty of paper forward of the stem and under the keel so it won't edge-set when it's glued and stuck to the Masonite. After cutting out the keel template, check for accuracy by laying it against the hull profile; this way, you leave nothing to chance. You can cut out the section templates now or wait until you are ready to carve the hull. The procedure is the same as making the lift templates. Stick them to Masonite or thin aluminum.

The deck is a large piece of paper, so you're not likely to edge-set this or the hull profile. Cut out the transom and the rudder, and that does it for cutting out the templates for this half model.

When tracing the lift templates onto your lift stock, mark their ends 1/4 inch longer and saw 1/16 inch wider to allow a safety factor in alignment and carving. Station marks and numbers are already on the templates, so transfer to each wood lift and number them before cutting them out to make the model.

Square the station lines all around the lifts. You'll use one amidships station line as a reference point to align the lifts when you stack them.

Note that the hull profile lifts for this model vary in thickness. Lifts 1, 8, 9, and 10 are 3/4 inch thick; the others are 3/8 inch thick. If you'll be resawing the 3/8-inch lifts from thicker stock, first you'll trace the templates onto the wood,

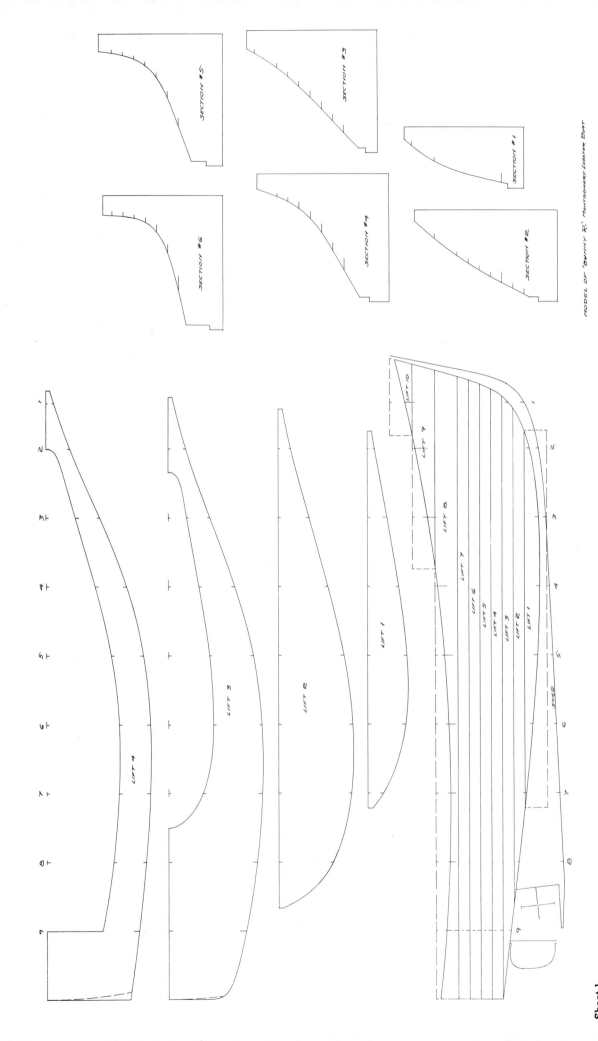

Sheet 1

Enlarge 323 percent for full-size plans.

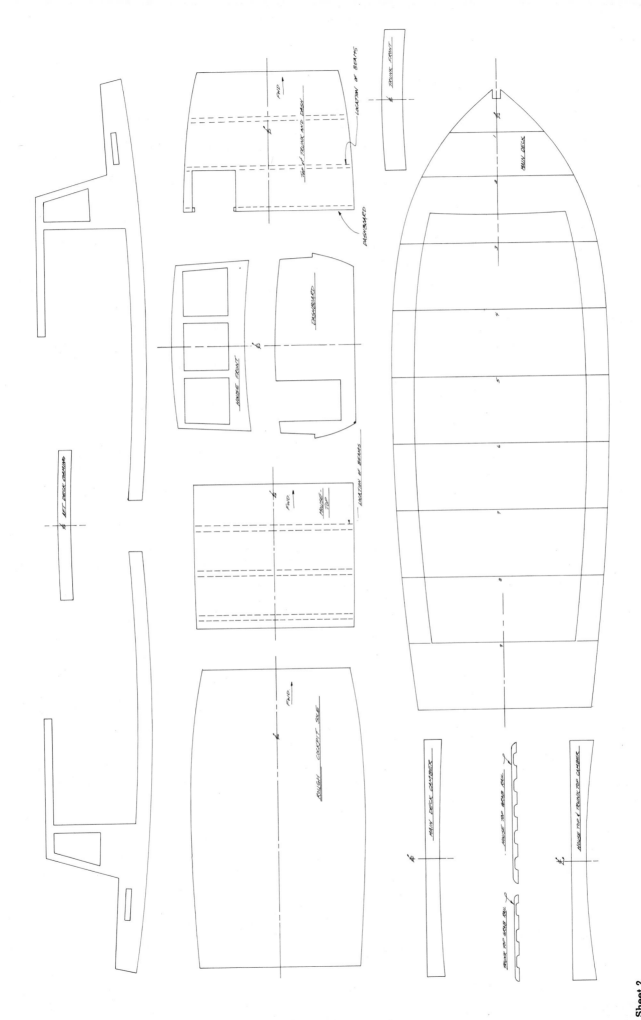

Sheet 2
Enlarge 323 percent for full-size plans.

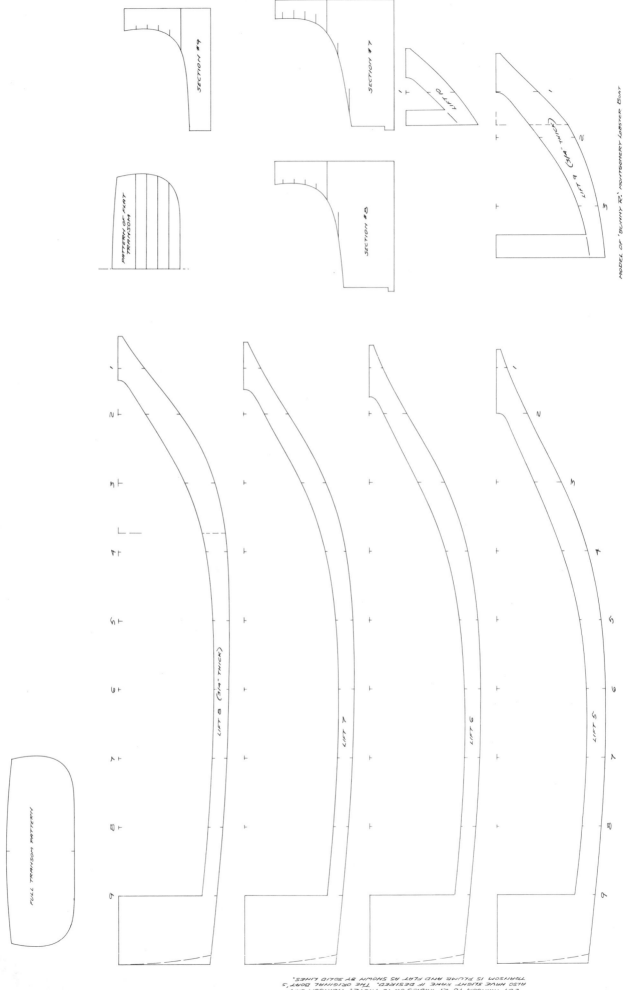

Sheet 3
Enlarge 323 percent for full-size plans.

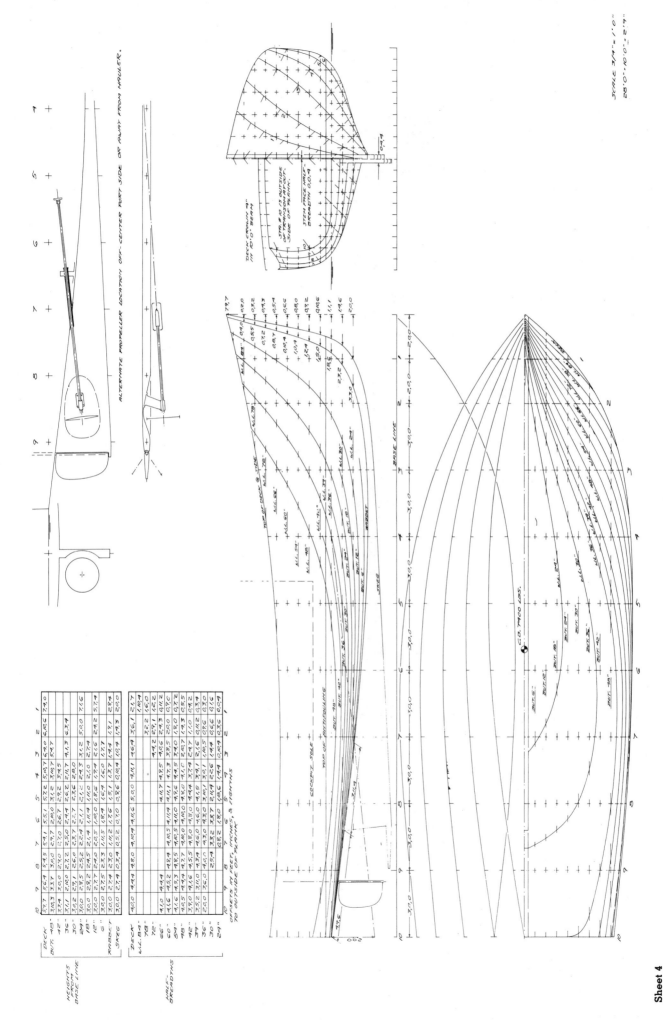

Sheet 4
Enlarge 323 percent for full-size plans.

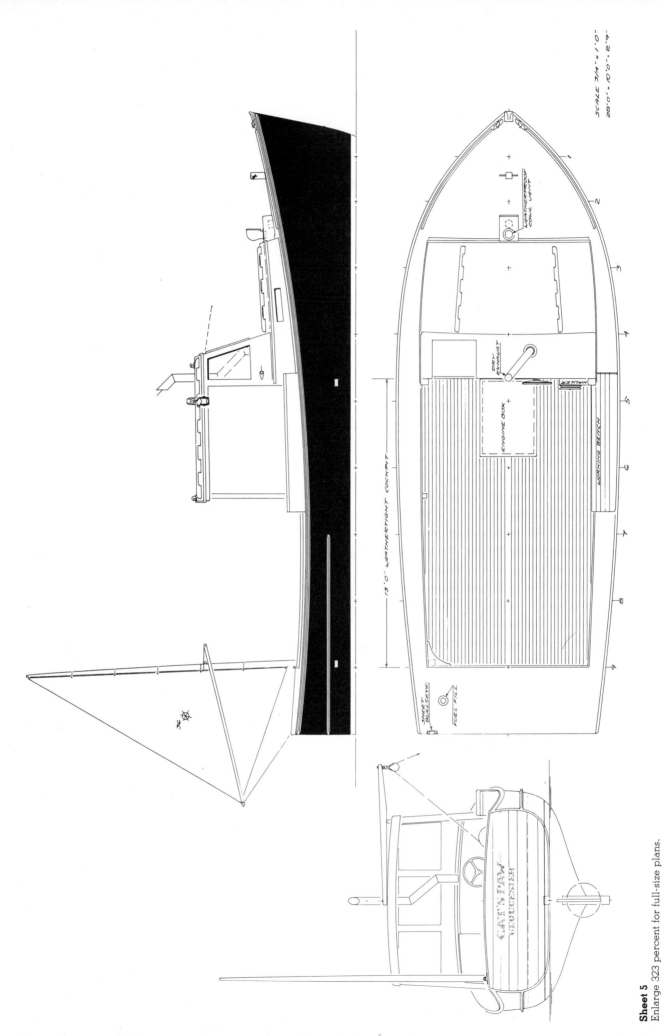

SCALE 3/4" = 1'0"
29'0" = 10'0" = 2'9"

13'0" WEATHERTIGHT COCKPIT

WEATHERPROOF
COWL VENT

DRY EXHAUST

ENGINE BOX

HAULER

WORKING BENCH

SHEET BULLSEYE

FUEL FILL

Sheet 5
Enlarge 323 percent for full-size plans.

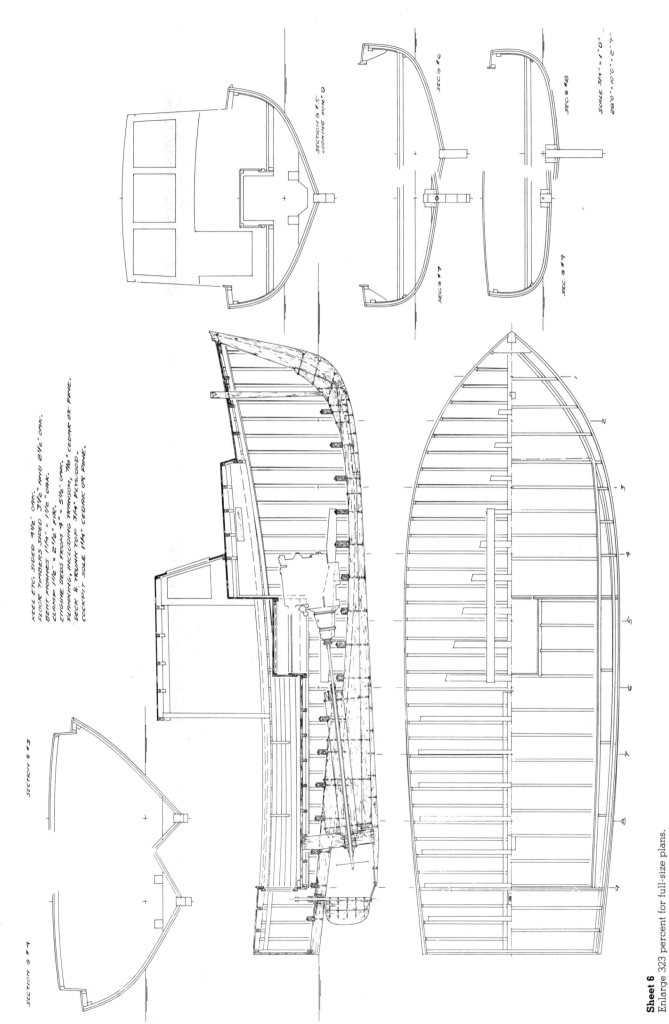

SECTION @ #5

SECTION @ #4

SECTION @ #3

SECTION @ #5
LOOKING FORE'D

SEC @ #6

SEC @ #7

SEC @ #8

SEC @ #9

SCALE 3/4" = 1'0"
28'0", 10'0", 2'9"

KEEL ETC. SIDED 4½" OAK.
FLOOR TIMBERS SIDED 3½" AND 2½" OAK.
BENT FRAMES 1½" × 1½" OAK.
CLAMP 1½" × 2½" FIR.
ENGINE BEDS FROM 4" × 5½" OAK.
PLANKING INCLUDING TRANSOM, ⅞" CEDAR OR PINE.
DECK & TRUNK TOP 3/4" PLYWOOD.
COCKPIT SOLE 1¼" CEDAR ON PINE.

Sheet 6
Enlarge 323 percent for full-size plans.

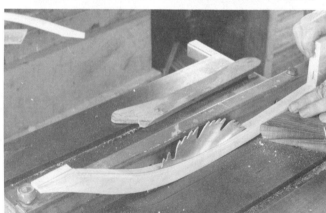

Clockwise, from upper left: Making templates: gluing plans to
Masonite. . . . Tracing cut-out templates onto lift stock. . . . Cutting
out lifts on bandsaw. . . . Cutting down lifts to desired thickness;
notice safety "fingers," top. . . . Matching lift scrap thickness to
those on plan.

then cut the lifts out on your bandsaw. Then you'll resaw the lifts to the desired
thickness on your table saw, using a hollow-ground planer blade and a set of
wooden "fingers" (a slotted push-stick, also called a feather stick) to hold the
stock steady against the fence. This takes some skill and patience, so don't
hurry. If some get slightly tapered all is not lost. Accuracy returns when the hull
profile is laid on the stack of lifts for carving.

Whatever wood you use (see the Introduction), match the thickness to that
of the hull lifts shown in profile. If you're resawing Lifts 2 through 7 down to 3/8
inch from thicker stock, run a test strip through the table saw first to check for

accuracy. Cut out a scrap piece as close as you can get to ³/₈ inch, whack it into six pieces, and set them on edge right on the hull profile drawing to see how close you are (discount glue thickness). If all together they're slightly more in thickness, fine; if they're under, run some more scrap through your saw or planer and try again until you're sure they're thick enough. The idea is that if there is more wood there than you need, you can get everything back to proper size again when you lay the cut-out hull profile template back on the stack of lifts. If your stack of lifts isn't high enough, you're going to get shortchanged when it comes to carving: you'll find the amount of wood doesn't quite fill out the hull profile.

When you run the scrap pieces through, make sure each has a factory-planed edge on one side. This is the way your wooden lifts are going to be after you put them together, so this is the way your test scraps must be. Don't take anything for granted—Murphy never sleeps. If you use a planer blade to saw both sides of the scrap wood you use for a test, your results will be different. The same goes for the saw fence and depth of cut of the blade: Once they're set, don't change them. With a set of wooden "fingers" and a good-cutting hollow-ground planer blade, you're in business. You don't need a thickness planer. (Of course, the small thickness planers do a great job for this kind of thing. Mine is a 10-inch-wide-capacity Ryobi, and I wouldn't want to be without it. At 58 pounds, it's portable and well worth the price for the job it does.)

At this point, if you're planning on a clear (bright) finish for the half model, you might decide that a mahogany boottop waterline would look good and would be easier to do as part of the lifts than by scribing one on later. If so, let it be the top part of Lift 4. A strip of mahogany or walnut—any wood of contrasting color—will do it. Cut a strip ¹/₈ inch thick for the boottop, then put it with the ³/₈-inch Lift 4 and run them through the saw again, still set for a ³/₈-inch cut.

Laying Up the Lifts

Pick the glue of your choice—Weldwood dry-powder, Franklin Titebond, or epoxy, fast or slow curing—and get ready to lay up the lifts. First, use masking tape to attach some waxed paper on your right-angled jig (see the Introduction) to keep the lifts from sticking to it, and dry-stack the lifts on the jig, aligning each lift at Station 5 to the jig's plumb line. Note that Lifts 9 and 10 are short lifts, so you'll need to slide two pieces of ³/₄-inch scrap pine under Lift 8 at the aft part of the hull and another piece under Lift 9 at the bow (don't glue them) so the hull sits level on the jig. In other words, the lifts should line up horizontally straight through all the stations.

Beginning at the top of the stack, trace the shape of each lift onto the next one underneath (this shows where to spread glue). Unstack the lifts; then, starting with lift 10, spread glue in the penciled areas and restack. It's a lot like buttering pieces of bread. Align Station 1 of Lift 10 with Station 1 of Lift 9, then with Station 1 of Lift 8. Then pick Station 6 to line up the rest of the lifts.

With hollow lifts, very little clamping pressure is needed, especially if the model is to be painted—that is, if you picked good, straight-grained wood to make the lifts from in the first place. Weighting the lifts slightly is often enough for good glue joints; I use scrap lead to weight them down once the last lift is in place, and tack or wedge any wayward ends to the jig's back. Wipe off excess

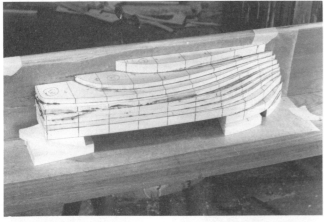

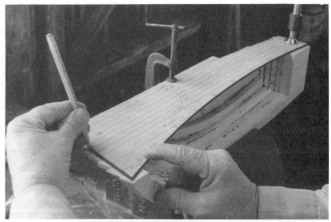

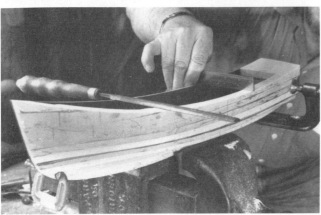

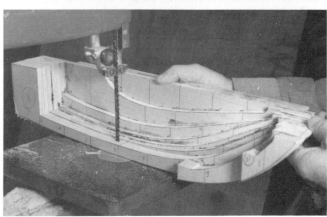

glue from the lifts, since it's easier to do now than later. A chisel works well for getting in close to the lift lines, and for scraping the glue away.

If weighting doesn't do the trick, or if you plan to finish the model bright and the glue lines will show, clamp a piece of wood along the edge of the jig, and wedge the lifts down slightly. Of course, there are a number of ways to do it. At the moment I like using slow-setting epoxy mixed with Cab-O-Sil as a thickener, because this gives about two or three hours for readjustment. (Epoxied joints love to creep, so keep checking alignment.) Titebond sets up in a few minutes, so I wouldn't use it unless I was certain I wouldn't have to readjust the lifts.

Let the glued lifts sit long enough to harden. A Weldwood glue layup at 70 degrees sets up enough to work on in about four hours, since you won't be putting much strain on the joints. If you can get this far into making a lift model, you're well on the way.

If you notice some slack spots in the seams after you remove the half-hull from the jig, you can fill these spots now. Just mix up some more glue and work it into the seams with a putty knife made from part of a razor blade stuck in a wooden handle.

Now, with the glue set, you're ready to trace the hull profile. Clamp the hull in a vise and carefully lay the hull profile on the stack of lifts, Waterline 4 matched to Waterline 4 and Station 6 to Station 6, and clamp it here. Trace around the profile onto the lifts. This is the beauty of using the templates, and building a half hull. If, between cutting and gluing them, your lifts had grown slightly more than you wanted, you can see exactly how much deviation there

Clockwise, from upper left: Lifts stacked and aligned. . . . Tracing hull profile to trim around hull and sheer. . . . Cutting the sheer with a bandsaw; if you're inexperienced, do it by hand with a spokeshave. . . . Using a square to check sheer.

was when you lay the hull profile template on, and you can regain accuracy when you cut the profile to shape.

With the hull profile still clamped in place, take your combination square and snug it against the profile sheer with the tongue touching the inside of the hull, and place a dot. Keep sliding the square along, until you have a series of dots close together (about ½ inch apart) locating the sheer on the inside of the hull. This very accurately transfers the sheerline of the template to the hull and is extremely easy to do. Remove the template once you're done spotting in the sheer.

Now you're ready to cut the sheer. To remove the excess wood fast, tilt your bandsaw slightly—2 or 3 degrees off plumb—or tip the hull slightly so that the blade toes out from the line. This is so that when you saw along the dots you marked, leaving them by about ¹/₁₆ inch, you'll saw the unseen outer sheer higher than you marked on the inside of the hull; in other words, your sawcut will be higher on the outside of the hull than the inside. You'll take this extra wood down to the dotted line when fairing the sheer. (I recommend freehand cutting of the sheer with your bandsaw only if you're extremely confident from experience; if in doubt, take the sheer down by hand making a series of cuts across the sheer with a handsaw, then chiseling the cuts out and finishing with a low-angle block plane, a spokeshave, and a half-round mill file.) Cut around the whole hull profile, trimming square across right to the centerline profile at bow and stern but leaving the sheer in between a dite high.

When you get to building the full model in Chapter 2, it's at this point that you'll glue the two mirror-image half hulls together.

Fairing the Sheer

Now put the hull right-side up in your vise, clamp the hull profile template back on again, and work the sheer down from the higher outside to the penciled dots inside, squared flat across to the sheer of the template. Fair the higher outside of the hull just until it blends into the dots, and the sheer will be right on the money. Eyeball the dots as you take the sheer down, rather than looking much at the outside of the hull. A sanding block (a piece of 60-grit sandpaper stapled to a flat board long enough to span the hull's width) also helps in the last stage of fairing the sheer. Now you have the profile shape of the sheer.

When satisfied with the sheer, and with the hull profile still in place, draw the station marks across the sheer, then lay the deck template on them with its centerline aligned to that of the hull, and mark around it. A word of caution here: With all these lift models, you'll notice a slight discrepancy between the length of the template and the length of the hull. This is because the plan was drawn on flat paper, and you are now asking it to accommodate the longer curved sheer (the more rocker the sheer has, the bigger the discrepancy). The way to get around this is to line up the forward part of the deck template with the first station, trace it to Station 5, then pull the template aft a hair until the aft stations match and trace back to Station 5. Stretching the template ¹/₁₆ inch or so amidships this way means nothing to the accuracy of the model. Once you get to carving, you'll trim the side of the hull at the sheer to conform to the deck shape.

Let's talk about the transom a moment. You can leave it flat across, or you can curve and rake it to suit your taste. Whichever you decide, finish the top of the transom and stern deck flat across. Using the template provided for its shape with its waterlines matching those of the hull, mark around for the general shape of its face. Cut the face of the transom flat across now, then curve and rake it later, if you want to, after you've carved and faired the rest of the hull. There will be only a slight difference in the flat or raked version.

To this point you have the profile, the sheer, and the deck (plan view) well established. This is quite a lot of shuffling templates around, but have you noticed . . . you kept your rule in your pocket and yet were guided every step of the way?

Carving the Hull

Mark the half-width of the keel along the stack of lifts from the top of the stem through to its end. With the keel width drawn on the hull and the deckline of the hull at the sheer established, you need only to shape the hull at each section in between the keel (rabbet) line you just drew and the deck plan view of the sheer. For this, the body templates guide you. You can't miss.

Now you're ready to carve the hull. But first, you need something to hold the hull upside-down in the vise. Cut a piece of scrap wood 3/4 inch by 2 inches by about 9 inches, stick one end down to the bottom of the lifts at the centerline with five-minute epoxy, and stick a couple more supports at a right angle from it, landing on the lifts for bracing. Put the hull in your vise, and start carving.

Here the reason becomes apparent for marking and numbering the station lines across the deck: When you carve the side of the hull away at the sheer to meet the deck plan, the station marks begin to disappear. For sure, don't lose the station marks at the sheer and on the bottom, because you'll want these for guides when you use the body templates. You don't have to constantly redraw the station marks on the hull as you cut them away, but they must be kept at the sheer and keel rabbet. If you lose them, they're easily replaced using the appropriate templates.

A gouge with an inside bevel, a spokeshave, and a rasp all work well to remove excess wood from the hull (the sharp lift ridges) fast. For outside curves like the turn of the bilge, be careful, because it's easy to take too much off. Work the concave area of the bow and the stern area for practice, then work Stations 5 and 6 down fairly close and go in both directions from there.

Hold the body templates square to the hull against their corresponding stations and work all the stations down a little at a time, as evenly as you can. For each station, visualize, while holding the template, what that section is going to look like. Look a little and cut a little, working all the stations gradually down together until the body templates fit between the keel rabbet and the deck plan view. It's quite likely wood will be left high between stations, so even them out and finish fairing the hull by sanding with homemade fairing battens, described in the Introduction under "Tools."

Keel, Deck, and Finishing

Measure the keel's half width off the plan (it's a strong 1/8 inch). Mark the keel's shape from the template on 3/4-inch-thick wood, if that's what you have, cut its profile shape on a bandsaw then saw its 1/8-inch thickness on a table saw, slip it

Clockwise, from upper left: Marking half width of keel on rabbet line. . . . Gluing in scrap hold for vise. . . . Begin carving with gouge, but finish fairing with your sanding fid. . . . Fitting the keel. . . . Finished half model on backboard, ready for your mantel.

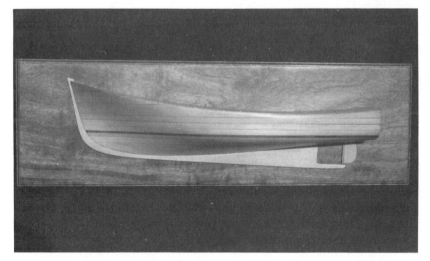

over the hull, and take off any high spots that the keel shows up. If the fit is tight, take just the slightest amount off the hull and the inside of the keel with a mill file or sandpaper. Mix up some five-minute epoxy, and spread it on the hull out to the rabbet line. Lay a piece of waxed paper on your jig or some flat spot, lay the hull on it, and slip the keel onto the hull. Putting the glue on the hull instead of on the keel pushes the glue away from you to the inside of the seam and against the waxed paper (with quick-drying glue, this will help you avoid a panic cleanup).

Since this is a hollow half model, it wouldn't look like much without a deck. First you'll need a sheer support. Using the hull profile for a pattern, cut a piece of wood about ½ inch thick and about 1 inch deep, the same shape as the sheer. Cut the top off the support used to hold the hull in the vise, and slip this sheer support for the deck in and glue it to the support and to each end of the hull. Using the deck template for a pattern, cut a piece of ¹⁄₁₆-inch aircraft plywood for the deck (a bit oversized) and glue it on with five-minute epoxy, clamping it to the sheer support. You can hold the outboard edge of the deck down with masking tape, which does the job very well—luckily, since there's no good way of clamping. The deck dresses up the top of the model nicely, and its dark inner veneer (this stuff is three-ply) looks great with a natural finish against the lighter-toned basswood.

The backboard is 28 × 8 inches and should be planed to a thickness of ½ inch, left squared, or fancy routered—all look good. Finish it with a few coats of thinned varnish and two coats of fast-drying spray Minwax clear satin polyurethane, which gives an even, beautiful sheen and makes you look like a pro.

For finishing a half model, I usually use tung oil; three or four coats look nice. Tung oil is extremely easy to apply with a rag or brush, and you can control the finish to get the effect you want. Each added coat means a higher gloss, so if you get more gloss than you want, you can dull it by rubbing with a rag soaked in tung oil cut about half with turpentine and a little pumice powder. Or, as you did with the backboard, use two coats of Minwax.

So, there you have it—one way of building a hollow half model. Of course, a solid half model would be less than half the work but heavier for hanging on the wall. With a solid model, the sheer would be a bit harder to cut since you'd be cutting across about 4 inches of solid wood, but the basic method is still the same and prepares you for making a hollow full model.

Whichever method you use, the important thing is, "Go for it, and get at it!" I'll tell you, though, in all fair warning—you might get as addicted to modelmaking as I am.

Fed up with removing balky spray can covers? Try this: Remove the cover, and with a knife cut away the locking ring at the bottom edge of the inner circle. You can't really see it, but run your finger around the inside of the lip and you'll feel it. Cut away a little at a time until you get the locking power you want.

Building the Full Model

Laura B.—A Gloucester Inshore Lobsterboat

Materials Needed

- one 4' × 8' sheet of ⅛" tempered Masonite (smooth both sides)
- 24' × 4" × ⅜" basswood or pine
- 8' × 4" × ¾" basswood or pine
- 2' × 1' × 1/16" aircraft plywood
- Weldwood plastic resin glue
- spray adhesive
- ⅜" #6 brass ribbon pins
- acetate, .025 to .035 inch
- rudder, wheel, shaft, and assorted fittings
- full-size plans

Tools Needed

- table saw
- bandsaw, jigsaw, or sabersaw
- vise
- clamps
- Dremel tool with accessories
- razor saw
- gouge with inside bevel
- spokeshave
- block plane
- 10" mill file
- sanding fid
- sanding battens
- combination square
- scissors
- narrow masking tape
- #3 pencil

This 28-foot lobsterboat was designed by Phil Bolger for inshore lobster fishing, and built by Dave Montgomery of Montgomery Boat Yard in Gloucester, Massachusetts. *Laura B.* is a nice-looking boat, with her pronounced sheer and bow flare. (Joel White reviewed her in issue No. 77 of *WoodenBoat* magazine.) She'd be a good boat not only for lobstering, but for just puttering around in, without costing an arm and a leg to run and maintain. Because she's easily driven, she's low powered, with a six-cylinder Ford truck engine that pushes her about 8 knots cruising speed; she also carries a riding sail to hold her head-to-wind when hauling. Her beam of 10 feet—about one-third of her length—was the trend back in the 1940s and '50s; later lobsterboats gradually became beamier as the fishing fleet needed more room to handle their ever-increasing volume of lobster pots.

She's a skeg boat—that is, planked in to the keel, which makes her easier to build than a planked-down boat. With all that keel outside supporting their hulls, skeg boats had a tendency to survive winter haulouts better than planked-down boats, with their very slim keels. My own 26-foot lobsterboat, built in Friendship, Maine, by Sid Carter in 1946 and used by me for 10 years, is still fishing, with the help of a layer of fiberglass—not bad, when 20 years of life was figured as average for lobsterboats. Keeping them in the water, and keeping the fresh water out of them, was their best means of survival.

Laura B. shows a high sheer forward, which Bolger says makes her easier to plank in the flared bow area. The full-size version, which you can build from the plans provided if you're ambitious, is planked with ⅞-inch cedar or pine. The frames are 1¼-inch oak, and her cockpit floor is 1¼-inch cedar or pine.

Getting Started

To build the full model of the *Laura B.*, follow the instructions in Chapter 1 for building the half model, right up to the section "Fairing the Sheer." Cut out the lifts for the half hulls as "mirror images"—just flip the templates and plans over when you trace them—and lay them up on your jig, one half at a time. Before you stack and glue the lifts, be sure to pair each half-lift with its mate on a flat surface to ensure that they're identical. If they aren't, make them so, using a block plane, a spokeshave, or a rasp—whatever it takes. It should take you only a few days, according to your skill. To make the best use of your time, you can begin by just cutting out the waterline lift templates; the body section templates can be cut out later when the hull halves are joined together while you're waiting for the glue to dry. The same goes for the deck plan, which is cut out of the building plans.

Note that waterline lifts 9 and 10 have doglegs sticking out to the centerline. These hold the lifts at the proper distance from the jig during layup. they're cut off later when the glue dries.

Before marking the hull profile on the lifts, put each half-hull in your vise and sand the hull free of glue buildups, fairing the centerline a bit. A sanding belt cut in half and stapled to a board works great for this.

It's easier to scribe the keel width on each half before you join them, though it can be done later as well. Chances are the keel rabbet may have to be re-marked during the carving process anyway.

After you've finished cutting the profile all around both hulls, mix up some glue and stick the half hulls together, matching the lift lines, station lines, and profiles exactly, paying special attention to Station 6 and Waterline 4. For a gap-filling glue, just mix it a little thicker, if you're using Weldwood dry-powder glue; if you're using epoxy, add enough Cab-O-Sil for the right consistency. Clamp the two halves together, saw out two wedges of scrap and tack one on each side to give you something to clamp onto.

Now work the sheer down flat across, just as I described in Chapter 1 ("Fairing the Sheer") for the half model. Also, mark and number each station across the deck, and trace the deck template across the sheer. When you carve the hull, you'll trim the hull sides to conform to this shape. Finish the transom flat for now; you can curve and rake it later, after carving the hull.

Carving the Hull

To hold the full hull upside-down in the vise, a scrap piece of 2 x 4 will serve nicely. Cut off the length you want, place it on end in the hull, and glue a

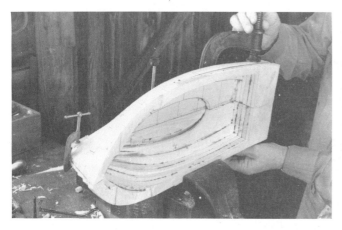
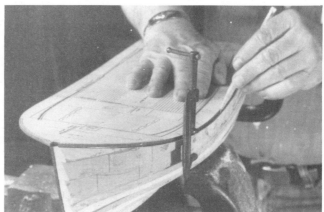

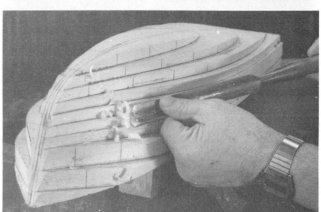

Clockwise, from upper left: Clamping the two hull halves; notice scrap wedge under forward clamp at bow. . . . Tracing the deck template across the sheer. . . . A scrap 2 × 4 will hold inverted hull in vise. . . . Carving the hull; go easy around the turn of the bilge. . . . Using a body template to check shape.

couple of cross-ties across it and to Lift 3 or 4. I use five-minute epoxy for this because it's plenty strong and takes about as long as I can wait to get to the carving. When the hull is finished, a chisel cuts it all free.

Mark the keel's width along the full length of the hull, and you're ready to carve. The keel is 4½ inches wide in the full-size boat; use your scale rule to figure the dimension at ¾ inch = 1 foot scale.

A gouge, a block plane, a spokeshave, and a rasp are what you need for taking down the sharp edges of the lifts and shaping the hull. The flared section at the bow is going to be the hardest to carve and will take the most delicate touch. I'd use a gouge with an inside bevel and a cone-shaped sanding fid with 60-grit sandpaper for the rough shaping—and, of course, the body templates. This is a good place to start, because there's plenty of wood there to remove between the lifts. Go a little easy around the turn of the bilge, because it's easy to flatten the turn here with a few misplaced cuts. Now's the time to dig out the body templates—not that you use them yet at this stage for actual carving, but it helps to look at them for each area you're going to carve so as to practice your eye before you get there with your gouge.

While carving the hull, don't work in just one area—carve as far as you dare to go, then go to another part of the hull. A spokeshave and a block plane work best on straight places—both of these tools take excess wood off fast. Take care to leave the keel rabbet line well clear until you get down to the final nitty-gritty of finishing; you'll then cut carefully right to the line and slip the keel onto the hull. (I don't recommend putting the keel on first, because it would be in the way of carving and could easily be damaged.)

You'll find that as you carve the sides of the hull away, the station marks at the sheer and on the bottom will begin to disappear. You don't have to keep redrawing the station marks on the hull, but you'll need to keep them at the sheer and the keel rabbet. Just slip the keel template on the hull to reestablish the stations along the keel, and the deck template on to mark the stations along the sheer. Hold each body template square to the hull against its corresponding station and work the stations down a little at a time, as evenly as you can. Look and cut, working all the stations down together until the body templates fit between the keel rabbet and the deck plan view. If you're using rasps, be sure to stop well clear of the final shape of the hull, otherwise you'll risk cutting too deep.

From here on, use mill files and sandpaper to fair down any high spots left between stations. Final fairing is best done with the homemade fairing battens described in the Introduction, finishing with at least 100-grit sandpaper—go as fine as you want.

Before you add the keel, now is a good time to lop off the transom, and curve and rake it to suit or cut it off plumb and square as the plan shows. No more than a couple of degrees' rake is enough to take the curse off the dead-flat transom. The reason for doing this now, before putting on the keel, is that with the bottom being dead flat at the stern, it can rest on your bandsaw table for steadying the cut. Put the keel on first, and that advantage is gone.

The Keel

Let's talk about the keel for a minute, since it's next. Note that, as designed, the aft, skeg portion of the keel is angled and there's a metal strap connected to it to support the rudderpost. Make it that way if you want, but I chose to make the model's skeg solid (Maine style) all the way aft past the rudderpost and stick a brass plate on it with a hole in it to accept the rudderpost. I'd do it in real life, too, if I were building her full-size, because it's also stronger and looks better. That metal strap arrangement is OK in Massachusetts, where I'm told there are few rocks to bump over, but here in Maine where rocks abound this could get wiped out in one pass over a ledge. Most of us Mainers who are unfortunate enough to run aground with the tide going just don't sit there and pray—we try to do something about it. In most cases we'll try backing down, which usually doesn't work since the pull of the wheel sucks you down harder. The other brutal way, if you happen to know that it's a flat-topped rock you've hit, is to "gun her" and hope you go over it. This is the reason I prefer a good, stout chunk of oak for the skeg, with nothing to catch when sliding over something. I'm also less likely to break it off on this model.

The same goes for the snatch block attached to a support on the house roof (canopy). Though this likely works on sandy bottom, it wouldn't work here in Maine. Here you could find yourself with no house if the trap you were hauling got hung down. So, like the rest of the lobstermen in Maine (and I was one for 30 years), I'll take the liberty to rig this lovely little lobsterboat my way.

If you want (and it's much easier than joining pieces), you can cut the keel (really, the whole backbone) from skeg to stem all in one piece, out of pine or basswood or some hardwood. Sure, the cross-grain on the nearly vertical part of the stem is delicate, but if you are careful in the sawing and handling, the advantage of not having to bother with joint alignment when putting on the keel is worth it. Using the keel template, I sawed the keel profile on my bandsaw from 3/4-inch pine to its outside shape first, then saturated the outside with thin superglue so it would enter the end-grain of the stem to help minimize breaking.

I then sawed the piece again well clear of the inside shape, then ran it through the table saw to the required real-life thickness of 4 1/2" at 3/4-inch scale, same as sawing the lifts' thicknesses. Then I sawed to the inside shape on my scroll saw, leaving the stem head high and notched so it would hook over the deck sheer. What a pleasure it was to slip this on in one piece! Once the keel is glued, you'll find that the grain is good at the stem for fairing the stem to the hull (after determining its face from the body plan drawing).

Before gluing the keel on, bore the rudderpost hole, or you can bore it from the outside bottom of the skeg later if you forget. You could leave the keel off until later after the deck is on, but the kid in me says, "Do it now," since adding the keel springs the model to life. I think this is one reason I was never that impressed with half models mounted on a board with no keel on them: sort of like a plucked chicken with no head or feathers.

With the hull all faired and the keel on, now's a good time to seal the hull with something. A thinned, about 50-50, application of shellac and alcohol makes a good sealer, as does most anything else.

Deck, Cradle, Cockpit, and Carlins

Deck beams are next. A couple of them are all you need—one for the forward end of the cuddy to bear on, and another one between it and the bow for the deck to bear on.

There's no crown, or camber, to these deck beams; this is a different approach than we'll use in building the sardine carriers *Pauline* and *William Underwood*. For the *Laura B.*, we'll put the deck beams in flat across and crown the deck. The 3/16-inch deck is cambered athwartships with a crowning board, which is shown on Sheet 2 of the plans. Cut the crowning board template out of the plan and stick it on some Masonite same as the lifts. I used this same method when building the Friendship sloop *Amy R. Payson* (described in my first modelmaking book, *Boat Modeling with Dynamite Payson*). The thicker deck allows you to glue in the coamings without putting additional backing under the washboards. (The washboards, also called covering boards, are deck planks that run fore-and-aft along the sides of the cockpit in an open boat, to keep spray out.)

Instead of using 1/16-inch aircraft plywood as was used for the half model's deck, I edge-glued 3/16-inch × 1¼-inch × 22-inch pieces of cedar that I happened to have lying around, then traced the deck template onto the glued pieces and cut a bit outside the lines, which gave me a planked deck I could put on in one piece, extending right out to the end of the stern. After springing the deck in place and gluing it, camber the deck by matching the crowning board's centerline to that of the deck. Keep cutting down the outer edges of the deck until the crowning board and the deck match transversely. Another nice feature of the thicker deck is that with the amount of bow flare this boat has, you'll need a vertical surface to lay her gunwale against. This provides it nicely without having to twist the gunwale or leaving an area underneath to be filled with glue or putty.

Before putting on the deck, there are a few more things to do. Since the 2 × 4 carving support is no longer needed, chisel it out, and make a working cradle for the model out of 3/4-inch scrap using the body templates for Stations 4 and 7 as patterns for the arms—the pieces that support the hull. On the waterline hull profile drawing (Sheet 1) draw another waterline below the keel, taking into consideration how much depth below it you want for how high the model is going to sit. Measure in between the stations for how long to cut the filler block, and you've done it all in a few minutes, without any guesswork. I let the 3/4-inch board thickness of the body stations come forward of Station 4 and aft of Station 7. You'll probably need to do a little sanding or reshaping of the cradle to suit the hull shape. To prevent damaging the hull, put some strips of masking tape or glue pieces of felt on the cradle where the hull bears.

Next, let's get ready to build the platform—the lower deck that goes in the cockpit of an open boat—and the house. Start by cleaning up the lifts inside where the ceiling goes under the washboards, first with a ball cutter on a Dremel tool, then with a disc-sanding attachment. If you find the ceiling (the inside sheathing of the side of the boat) between the platform and washboards is a bit rough for painting, don't fool with it. Scribe-fit 1/32-inch or 1/16-inch aircraft plywood to fit, and glue the pieces in place, using clamps.

We'll put the platform in next. You can cut it quickly and neatly out of 1/16-inch or 3/32-inch aircraft plywood. We won't use any elaborate framing for this model—we'll just put in five carlins, then glue the platform to the top surface of Lift 4, which Bolger has left conveniently wide. The length of the platform can run full-length clear to the bow, or it can stop at a bulkhead at Station 5, where the platform in a lobsterboat usually stops so as to give headroom down below in the cuddy. One carlin should be placed at the extreme aft end of the cockpit to support the platform there, and another aft bulkhead, made of something thin like aircraft plywood (about 1/16-inch), should be glued against the end-grain of the lifts as a way of covering them rather than trying to make them smooth for painting. Another carlin should go just before the cuddy bulkhead; place the three others in between. A fast way to cut and fit the carlins is to start out with a stick 3/8-inch square, long enough to make the five carlins. With dividers, measure across each station, mark each one's length on the stick, number each according to station, then cut them off like link sausage and glue them in. They don't have to be accurate for length.

Of course, instead of using aircraft plywood, you can lay the platform and

Clockwise, from upper left: Scribing washboards. . . . Crowning the deck. . . . Leveling hull to build house. . . . Putting up the house sides. . . . Clamp the forward section temporarily in place while you put the carlins in the canopy.

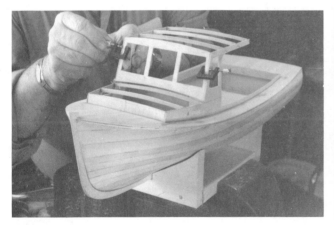

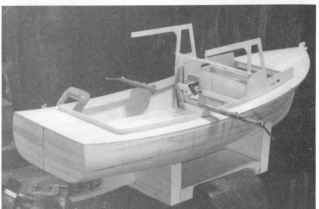

the ceiling using strips. It would look good, and for some people it's worth the time. Sometimes I'll do it this way, if I'm in the mood for fiddling with detail. Some folks prefer doing the detailing on a model. As for me, I'm mostly interested in getting the hull lines as accurate as I can. That's the part I like the most—seeing the lines spring to life, and finishing the hull.

Now that the platform is in, the deck and washboards are next. Note that the construction plan view of the deck (Sheet 5) shows the washboards pinched in at their ends at the aft end of the cockpit. I wouldn't want that on the real boat, because when sliding a lobster pot along the coaming and toerail the pot would get pinched, since the laths on the old wooden lobster traps were put in parallel. At the forward end of the cuddy the washboard is pinched again, not allowing toeroom for safety when putting the boat on the mooring. So, for both reasons, I'll make the washboards parallel to the sides the whole length. I like the way the house sides tumble in; this is a good safety feature when putting her on the mooring, because it keeps your body weight inboard. I'll make the washboards the same width to scale as at Station 6 on the full-size boat, which is 12 inches—a good, reasonable width.

Fitting the deck in one piece is easy, since it's wide enough to span the width and length of the hull. Simply lay the deck on the hull, clamp it in place, aligning the stations you marked across the deck with those on the hull, then trace the shape of the hull around the bottom edge of the deck. To scribe the inside edge of the washboards, fit the deck snug to the hull sides everywhere, then scribe a line 3/4 inch (this is 1 foot at 3/4 inch scale, remember?) in from the outside edge the whole length of the cockpit. Take off the deck and cut out the opening from the stern deck to the forward end of the cuddy, glue it back on, then crown the deck using the crown template.

The House

There are a couple of ways of building the house. You can make a plug first and build around it, using the hull profile and plan view templates. (This is how we'll build the house on both the sardine carrier *Pauline* and the tugboat *Mite*.) But for the *Laura B.*, I wanted to build the house the way my friend Bill Makinen (master boatbuilder) built the house on my 26-foot lobsterboat back in the early '60s—right in the boat.

Watching and helping Bill was an inspiration for me. My boat was hauled up for the winter among the other boats at a small yard, and was setting far from level. Bill dug out his declivity level, perched himself on a nearby hill, aligned the bubble of his level with that of the boat's waterline, and locked the adjustable bubble in place. Next he showed up with a bunch of boards and went at it, all without a word of explanation.

You won't need a declivity level for putting on this house, but, like Bill, who wanted to know how the boat set as a point of reference for building the house, you'll need to know how the model sets.

Note that the hull profile (Sheet 6) shows the bulkhead square or vertical to the platform (ignore the engine box), so you'll need to level the hull fore-and-aft by laying a level (a small, cheap plastic dime-store level is OK—mine is 9 inches long) on the platform. Mark where the cuddy bulkhead comes across the platform, stand your level on this line, and plumb up from it, marking both sides of the ceiling.

Cut out the profile view (Sheet 2) of the house side from the forward end of the cuddy clear back to the aft end of the coaming where it butts against the stern deck. Make a template of this and spring it in; I made the coaming a dite higher. Cut out the forward section with the three windows, and deduct from its sides the thickness of whatever you're going to make the house sides from (1/16-inch aircraft plywood works perfectly). Use the bottom curve of the forward section for the crown of the carlins (transverse cuddy and canopy supports). Cut the plan view of the cuddy top clear back to the bulkhead, allowing for a slight overhang of the canopy over the side supports and top carlins when finished (cut its sides to allow for the thickness of the house profile). Use this pattern to cut the cuddy top out of 1/16-inch aircraft plywood. Glue both sides of the house in after locating the ends at the right height. Put in the carlins—three in the cuddy area, with one against the bulkhead and two in between. The top of the canopy, which flows with the curve of the hull's sides, also gets three carlins. Maintain the cuddy's width and shape by leaving the forward three-window section temporarily in place while you put the carlins in the canopy. Then slip it out, apply glue, and slip it back in, with its bottom resting on top of the cuddy. Then put in the canopy top.

So I didn't mention how to fit the bulkhead? Cut out the bulkhead (Sheet 2, see dashboard) and remove the thickness of the house from its sides. It's unlikely that you'll hit the height of the platform and the inside thickness of the ceilings exactly, so make a template of the area from the platform to up under the washboards, using both bulkhead templates, and fit the bulkhead all around. Check the top of the height where it meets the sides of the house, and you've done it. Actually, you can make the lower part of the bulkhead template first, then work the tapered upper part to the house sides later.

Put some flat trim around the topsides of the house to catch the edges of the canopy top (house top, see Sheet 2) and glue it in place. Add some half-round around the top edge of the cuddy, add the grabrails, and you're done with the house for now.

Toerails, Guards, and Finishing Details

Now for the toerails, guards, and towing bitt.

First, make the bitt (also called a bollard) 1/4 inch square to the height shown. Put a brass pin in it and embed the bitt in the deck with five-minute epoxy; note that the bitt sits plumb on the foredeck.

I made the toerails and guards from maple. Cut the toerails 2 feet × 3/32 inch square or to suit, and run them from the stem to the end of the transom. Since the toerails run the whole length, you'll need waterways (cutouts to allow water to drain off the deck); five of them will do it. To locate them, level the model fore-and-aft, and pick the lowest spot on her washboards (deck). Use dry heat to bend each toerail—around your stovepipe, if you have one, or around a lightbulb—until it conforms to the deck at the hardest bend (forward).

Bore tiny, tight holes for #6 brass ribbon pins (or their equivalent) to hold the toerails in place. At the lowest point of each rail, mark the first waterway, then mark two more on each side of it, 2 1/4 inches apart on centers. Then remove the rail and cut these waterways in, with the rail *off* the boat. (This will require some careful handling, because cutting the waterways in before installing the toerails weakens them for bending—but it's worth the risk, compared to the extra care needed when cutting them in with the toerails installed.) Round the top corners of the toerails slightly, fit their forward ends to the stem, and fasten them just a hair inboard of the edge of the deck with the 3/8-inch brass pins. Make sure the rails fit snugly; you can sand their inboard undersides slightly so they'll lay better without "cocking off." Give them a shot of superglue, cut the heads of the pins off, then drive the pins flush and sand them off. (If you're using softwood for the model, you can drive the pins down with their heads on, then set them and fill them if you want.)

Guardrails and quarter guards are made ⅛ inch thick or thereabouts and beveled about 23 degrees top and bottom—nothing fussy. The best way to make them is to cut a strip of wood ⅛ inch thick by ¾ inch or so wide, bevel both edges on your table saw, and saw the guards off each beveled edge to whatever width you want. For this you need a hollow-ground planer blade that's tiptop sharp.

You'd think you would follow the same pre-bending procedure as for the toerails, but for these pre-beveled guards it won't work, for the same reason that a piece of half-round won't follow around a curved surface without "cocking off." So, fit the ends of the guards flush against the stem, bore a hole for a brass pin, put some glue on the guard, and nail it home. Wait until the glue dries, and spring the guard around the sheer, boring and nailing as you go.

Quarter guards—these run along the sides, from the transom to Station 7, serving as fenders—are no trouble. They measure 9 real-life feet or 6¾ inches at ¾ inch scale, with their lower edges 14½ real-life inches above Waterline 36. Make these to scale the same shape as the others, and put them on. In fact, they were so easy to do, I noticed mine weren't on—of course—until after the model was finished. Add protection strips to the stern deck, and you're done with as much as you need for woodwork. Saw these five strips about ³⁄₃₂ inch square, round their ends, and put them on 1⅛-inch centers parallel to the centerline, with their forward ends kept back about ⅛ inch from the coaming. Their aft ends are kept back a tad from the end of the stern.

You can keep going if you want to by adding hauling protection strips on the side, and a muffler for a dry exhaust—though there's nothing wrong with a pipe out through the stern (real simple, just call it a "water-cooled exhaust"). I intentionally dispensed with the engine box. It's your choice whether to add a riding sail. Though they do help somewhat to keep a boat heading into the wind, most boats don't have them.

The rudder and the wheel are next. The wheel is 1⅛ scale inches in diameter; you can get one this size from almost any mail-order supplier. The propeller shaft on the real boat is 1¼-inch brass rod or tube. Install the shaft and wheel first, then bore a hole up through the skeg into the underbody of the hull (also called the horn timber) for the shaft to bury in. Groove the forward face of the rudder to accept the rudderpost, then bore a couple of holes small enough for a couple of brass pins through the rudderpost. Shove the rudderpost up through the hole, place the rudder on the post so it clears the top of the skeg, and pin it.

For boring pinholes in round brass, I have a set of "V-blocks" to hold the stock in place while I prick-punch the holes. For measuring the size drill, I use a micrometer, and for actually boring the holes I use my Dremel tool mounted in a Dremel drill press, a combination I would not want to be without because of its versatility. For instance, you can be boring freehand with the Dremel tool and decide you have to bore a precise hole straight through something. For this, you stick the Dremel in a perfectly aligned support on the drill press (the same idea as sticking a gun in a holster), hand-tighten one screw, and you're in business. When done, loosen the screw, and you're back freehanding again, all in a matter of seconds.

With the rudder ready to hang and the wheel and shaft ready to slip in, it's painting time. You can be as fancy or as plain about this as you want. Painting the inside of the house is a good job for my airbrush so I use it for this and sometimes for the rest of the model as well. Though on the outside of a hull, where it's easy to get to, an airbrush doesn't seem worth it.

Color Scheme

Deck, light buff
Canopy, cuddy top, and shelf, light buff
Cuddy bulkhead and ceiling, white
Coamings, toerails, guards, boot-top, white
Lettering, white
Hull topsides, medium dark green
Bottom, red

Waiting for high tide.

But first you'll need to strike the waterline, now that you've sealed the hull. Looking at the lines drawing, right below the table of offsets, you'll note that the antifouling bottom paint comes to 3 inches above WL 36. This line, designated as WL 39, is the boat's waterline. So, find a level spot and level the hull fore-and-aft and athwartships, and go to it. A boottop always looks nice if you want to do the extra masking . . . and would be 2 scale inches higher than WL 39.

You can use thin acetate for the window glass, from .025 to .035 inch thick—thinner is better if you can get it. No acetate at all looks great, too. And you never have to clean them. On the full-size boat, the window directly ahead of the steering wheel should be able to open; this is faked on the model—one piece of acetate backs all three openings. For fitting the glass, place a piece of paper on the inside of the house against the window opening. Mark its shape with a *sharp* pencil, lay the acetate on your tracing, cut it out slightly larger then the opening. Carefully apply superglue from a needle with the tip of its eye ground off—it acts the same as a soap-bubble pipe, and you can put the glue where you want it—just a tad will do it, and stick the acetate in the house.

For *Laura B.*'s name use 18-point Clarendon bold white transfer lettering.

A bait barrel, bait iron, lobster crate, gaff, winch-head, davit with snatch block, steering wheel, chocks, and of course a riding sail (mizzen) all add to the boat's looks. A lobster trap or two sitting on her stern deck would help also, but these things can all be added later—some of them bought, some of them made. The barrel was easily turned on my Dremel lathe. The baiting iron, 20 inches long overall in real life, is 1¼ inches overall at ¾-inch scale. For a lobster crate, I made a scale model of one I used to use lobstering that measured 29 inches × 20½ inches × 12 inches and held 100 pounds of lobster, which was all I could haul by hand over the side of my boat. Like the real thing, the ¾-inch-scale crate has rope beckets (handles) in each end with glue on them so they'll stand out proud for easy grabbing.

I can still hear it now from the late Ralph Rackliff, an old, crusty lobster fisherman I went up alongside one day. Looking at my near-empty lobster crate, the old salt said, "My God—overhand knots in the ends of your beckets?" I replied, "Yeah, sure, what else?" The old salt said, "Double wall knots, of course." I asked, "How do you do that?" He replied, "Tie a single wall knot, and follow the tucks around again." This was new to me, but looking at his crate I could see the advantage he was talking about, plus the beauty of the double wall. Before this on-the-spot, out-in-the-middle-of-the-bay lesson, I'd always stopped off the end of a three-strand rope with a wall and a crown, remembering—from somewhere—the admonition how to do it: "To tie a wall and then a crown, first tuck up and then tuck down."

Fishermen had simple but effective ways of sorting out things that had to be right and that really mattered. Hauling traps all day long with a winch-head that was either too low or too high could be an aching problem at the end of the day. When I asked the late Lyle Drinkwater, a Spruce Head, Maine, fisherman, what was the best hauling height for the horizontally mounted winch-head I was about to install, he shot right back with a universal answer—and I see no other way to put this: "Pecker high."

Pauline, "Queen of the Fleet"
A Maine Coast Sardine Carrier

The headline of the August 1948 edition of *Maine Coast Fisherman* reads, "Bottle of Sodapop Helps Launch Carrier, *Pauline*"—surely one of the most unusual launchings along the coast.

The 83-foot sardine carrier *Pauline*, built at the Newbert & Wallace yard in Thomaston for the Lubec Canning and Manufacturing Co., was ready to be launched. The tide was just right, but there was no sponsor. Marjorie Hunter, the 12-year-old daughter of the yard's outfitter-machinist, Roy Hunter, was asked to do the honors, and she eagerly agreed.

With Marjorie standing ready with a pop bottle wrapped in an undershirt, the holding boards were cut. Marjorie swung her pop-bottle, which thumped against the hull but failed to break, and fell from the shirt. But *Pauline* was in a hurry and didn't stay around for another try. She went on down the ways, unchristened by the customary champagne, but a fine boat nonetheless.

Back in the 1940s and '50s, in the heyday of the Maine herring-fishing industry, the Newbert & Wallace yard built a fleet of these beautiful, seagoing boats, with their narrow beam and canoe sterns, ranging from 70 feet to *Pauline*'s 83 feet on deck. They were common sights all along the coast of Maine, nosing in and out of remote coves, calling at weirs and stop seines for herring destined for the sardine plants at Rockland, Boothbay, or Belfast.

Pauline was built with hard pine planking over oak frames and powered with a 171-horsepower Buda diesel. I had seen her from my lobsterboat in her heyday running through Muscle Ridge Channel on her way for a load of herring or returning loaded deep. Slim, low, and graceful, she was the epitome of function, always slipping along easily, loaded or light. She was known as the "Queen of the Fleet," both for the amount of fish she carried and for her loving upkeep by her skipper, Henry Dodge, and her mate, "Swede" Carlson, during her last 19 years as a workboat.

Like many things, the herring industry is no longer what it used to be. I had heard *Pauline* was hauled out at North End Shipyard in Rockland for conversion into a passenger-carrying cruise boat for the summer tourist trade by her new owners, Captains Ken and Ellen Barnes of Camden. When I found her, she was stripped to the deck, her pilothouse lying on the ground, and her two masts beside it in a tangle of rigging, in preparation for being fitted out for her new role in life.

I was lucky to get her lines so I could build a model of her. Talking to her designer/builder, Roy Wallace of Thomaston, now 89 years old, I learned he had no lines for her, nor for any of the other sardine carriers he and the crew at Newbert & Wallace had built. He would take lines off a half model, lay them out full size, build the boat, then paint over the lines. It was a stroke of luck that Ken and Ellen had needed *Pauline*'s lines and had the naval architects Woodin & Marean of Wiscasset take them off while she was hauled out.

I started on the model of *Pauline* in the middle of November and finished her up about three months later. That length of time is about the limit of my attention span. It wouldn't have taken that long, except that I had only hull lines to work with. I spent a good many hours driving back and forth to Rockland, filling in the blanks—measuring all the stuff taken off her, then reducing it to ⅜-inch scale to match the scale of the hull lines.

Building her model was a labor of love—it had to be; I don't know what else would get me up at 5:30 in the morning, day after day, and headed for the shop in the middle of January! Not only did I learn a lot in the process, but I've recorded a bit of history.

Materials Needed

- 21 running feet of 4" × ¾" kiln-dried pine or basswood
- one-half 4' × 8' sheet of ⅛" tempered Masonite (smooth both sides)
- 4' × 1' × 1/16" aircraft plywood
- spray adhesive
- Weldwood plastic resin glue
- superglue
- ⅜" #6 brass ribbon pins
- assorted rigging supplies (for ⅜" scale): six 7/32" blocks, four single, two double; 6' of three-strand nylon rigging, .020 inch; three eyebands; one spool of 23-gauge brass wire
- assorted fittings (for ⅜" scale): one ⅛" brass propeller shaft; one length of ⅛" aluminum tubing for Cape Anne stovepipe; one lifering; four chocks; four deck cleats, two mast cleats; one mast collar; three 3/16" pipe ventilators; one 1½:" kedge anchor; one 7/8" steering wheel; acetate for windows; one 1½" propeller; one ¼" bell for pilot house; one mushroom vent; ¼" deck plate
- full-size plans

Laying Up the Half Hulls

Making the hull was easy. I ran the lines through my blueprint machine, cut them out with scissors and stuck them to Masonite with spray adhesive, and used these as templates for the lifts. I did the same with the profile, backbone, and deck plan. I started cutting out the templates one day, and the next day had both halves of the hull laid up by 9:30 A.M. The trick is to pick one station, and line up all the lifts using the views right off the architect's drawing board. This way, you keep your rule in your pocket and let the plans do the work.

Begin by cutting the paper waterline lifts out, numbered from 1 to 9 (see Sheet 3 and Sheet 4). Following the same basic steps described in Chapter 1 for building the half model of *Laura B.*, cut out the paper waterline lifts, then glue them to the sheet of Masonite. You can lay out all of the parts for making *Pauline*'s hull at once—all nine waterline lift templates, the body templates, the deck view, the hull profile, and the backbone. Take the lift templates to your bandsaw (or use your sabersaw if you absolutely must), and cut right to the lines.

I'll assume you're going to make a hollow full model, so I'll describe the procedure for it. You can follow these same instructions for the half model, finishing it off with or without the bulwarks and backbone—though to my eye, a half model looks more dressed up with a backbone and a rudder, which are easily added.

Lay your lift templates on your wood and trace around them. The lift ends should be cut a bit long to compensate for slight error (accuracy comes back when the hull profile is marked on the glued-up stack). The right-angled leg sticking out on Lift 9 holds the distance of the lift out from the centerline of the building jig; you'll cut it off after the half hull is glued up. Be sure to mark the station lines on each lift, and number them.

When sawing out the lifts, leave the line by $1/16$ inch on the outside of the lifts, and saw to the line on the centerline. The inside cut isn't the least bit fussy. On the profile view of *Pauline's* hull, you'll see that the lift heights are all $9/16$ inch. To run a test for accuracy, the same idea as described in Chapter 1, set your table saw for $9/16$-inch thickness, saw a piece of scrap wood and cut it into nine pieces, put them together, and lay them on the profile drawing to see how close you've come. If you have a thickness planer, naturally you'd use it instead of your table saw. If the scraps run a bit thicker, fine; if thinner, reset your saw and run them again. The idea is to get them close, but they don't have to be perfect. If you cut these lifts on your table saw, saw them with a planer blade, and use a set of wooden "fingers" (a slotted push stick) for holding the lifts against your saw fence.

Pauline's hull at $3/8$-inch scale will be 31 inches long, so you'll need a good-sized jig. Find a plank 2 inches × 8 inches × 6 feet (house framing stock is fine), make sure it's straight, without twist or cup, and cut it in half. Make a bench with the back exactly square to it; draw a centerline at 18 inches squared to both pieces. Cover the area of the jig where you'll be gluing the lifts with waxed paper held with masking tape. Mix up some Weldwood glue or use the glue of your choice, and start laying up one half of the hull. Station 5 is the key station for alignment. Lay Lift 8 on your jig with its Station 5 aligned with the centerline on your jig. Slip Lift 9 (the bow) under Lift 8, aligning it with the marks for station 8; slip a piece of scrap the same thickness as Lift 9 under the stern end of Lift 8. Now slip Lift 9 out from under Lift 8, glue it, and slip it back in again with the "dog leg" against the jig, and away you go. Place Lift 7 on Lift 8 and so forth, right through to the last lift (Lift 1). As these lifts are glued together you can check their alignment both vertically and horizontally with the centerlines on your jig. If they vary a little, it won't hurt a thing as long as you remembered to saw their outsides $1/16$ inch or so larger.

You don't need to do any clamping while laying up the lifts—that is, if you picked good, straight wood to make the lifts from in the first place. I weighted them down with some scrap lead when the last lift was in place, and temporarily tacked some of the ends that didn't want to lay in snug to the jig's back. Wipe off excess glue from the lifts, since it's easier to do now than later. I found that a chisel worked well for getting in close to the lift lines, and for scraping the glue away. Dip the chisel in water and wipe it regularly with a rag with Weldwood dry-powder; if you're using epoxy, wipe the chisel with acetone or lacquer thinner.

Let the glued lifts sit long enough to harden. A Weldwood-glue layup at 70 degrees sets up enough to work on in about four hours, since there's no strain on it, though directions on the can call for 12 hours. You'll need to lay up the

Tools Needed

- table saw
- bandsaw, scroll saw
- $7/8$" or 1" gouge chisel
- vise
- clamps
- block plane
- spokeshave
- sanding battens
- sanding fid with 60- and 100-grit sandpaper
- rasps
- Dremel tool with drills from #61 to #80
- needle and riffler files
- rattail files
- 10" mill file
- combination square
- #3 pencil
- scissors
- narrow masking tape

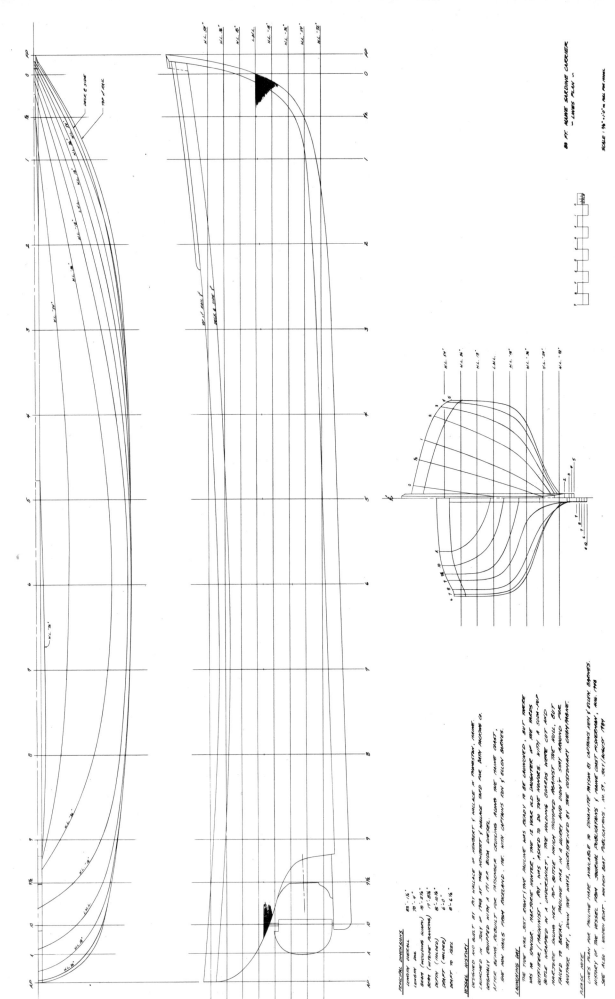

Sheet 1
Enlarge 323 percent for full-size plans.

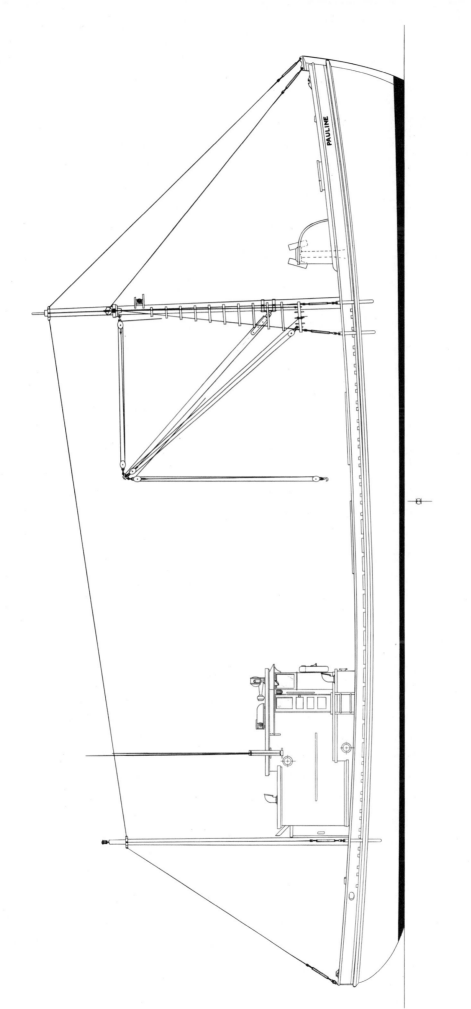

PAULINE

83 FT. MAINE SARDINE CARRIER
– OUTBOARD PROFILE –

SCALE : ⅜" = 1'-0" = FULL DIMENSIONS.

Sheet 2
Enlarge 323 percent for full-size plans.

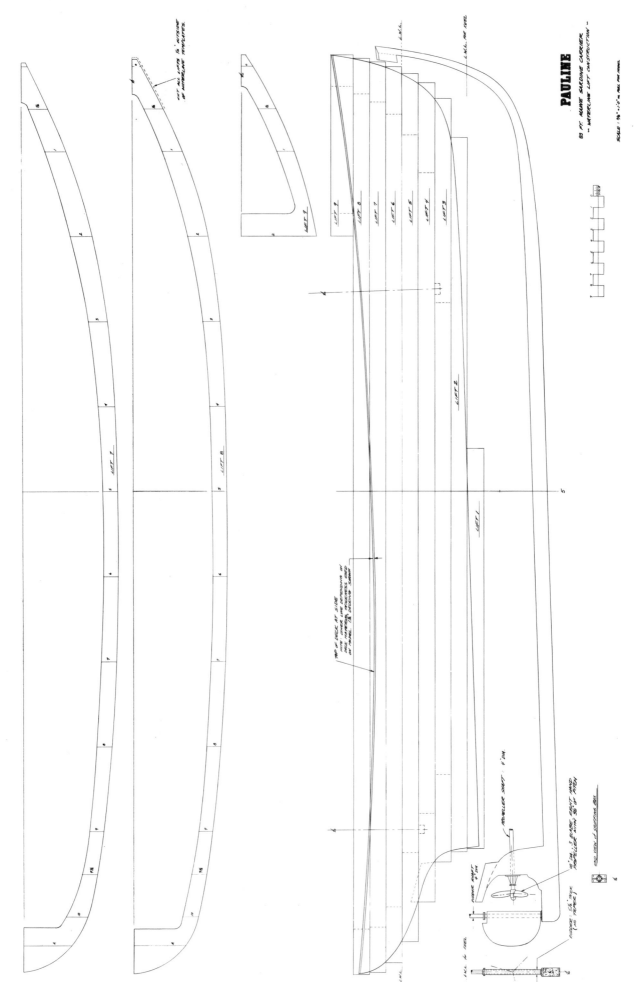

Sheet 3
Enlarge 323 percent for full-size plans.

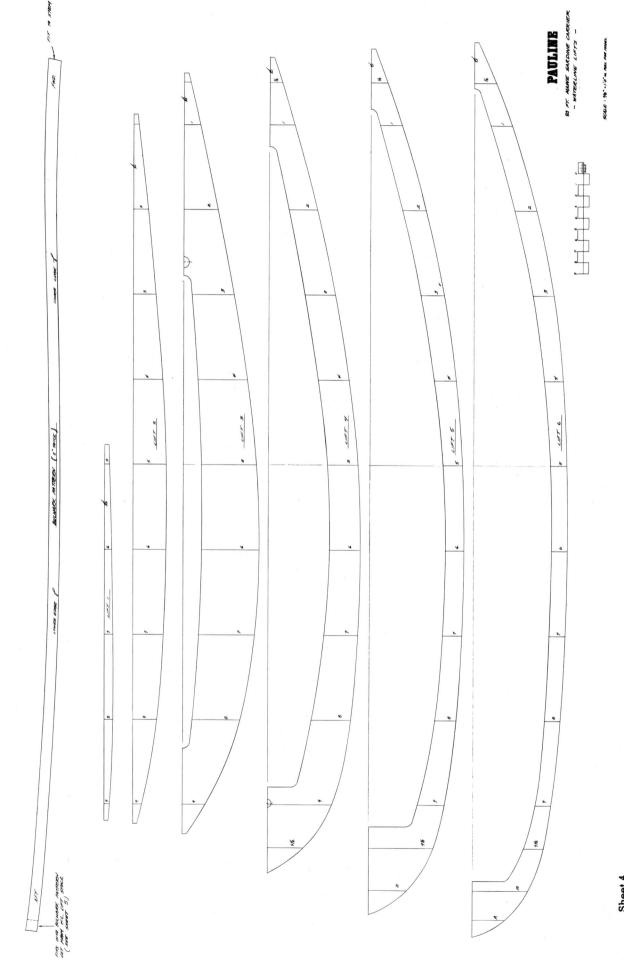

PAULINE

83 FT. MAINE SARDINE CARRIER

~ WATERLINE LIFTS ~

SCALE : 3/8" = 1'-0" IN FULL FOR MODEL.

Sheet 4

Enlarge 323 percent for full-size plans.

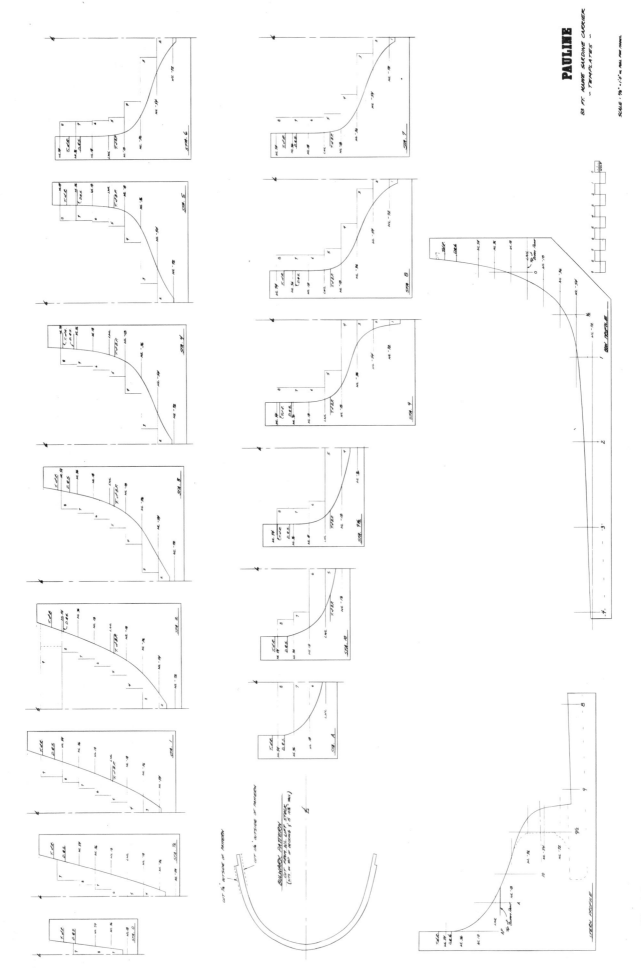

Sheet 5
Enlarge 323 percent for full-size plans.

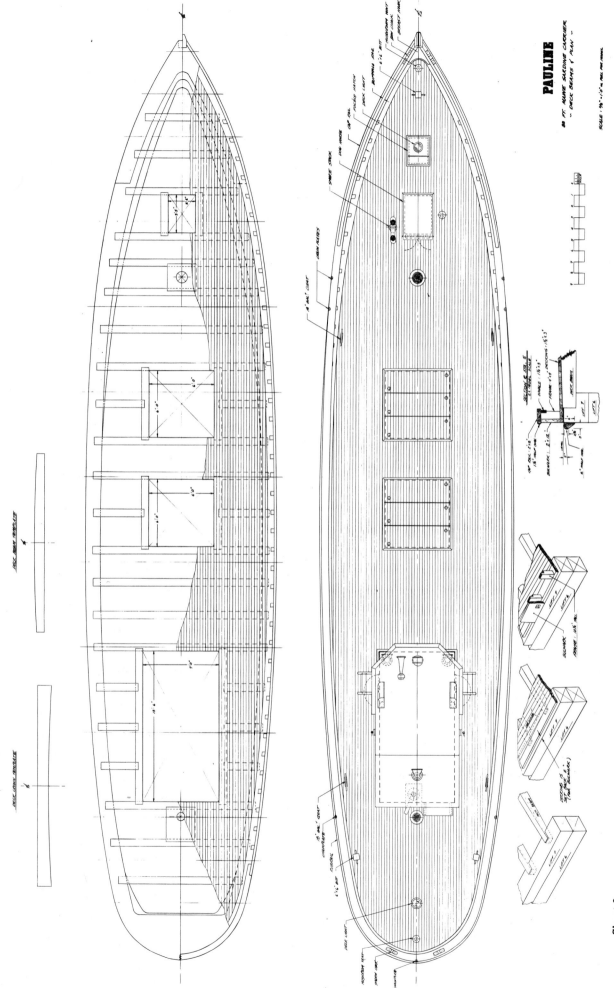

Sheet 6
Enlarge 323 percent for full-size plans.

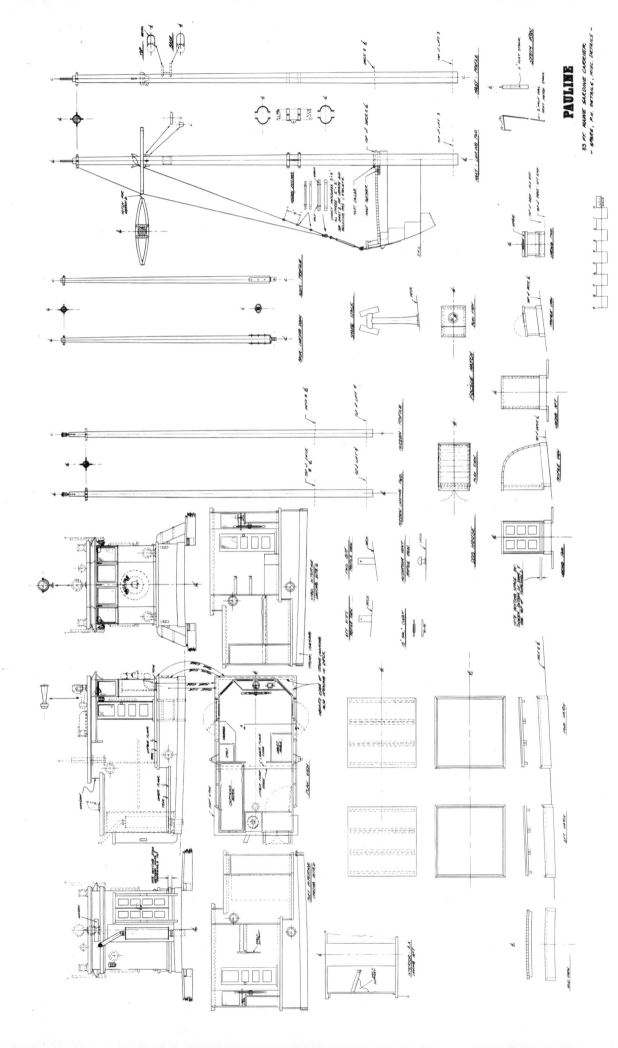

PAULINE

83 FT. MAINE SARDINE CARRIER.
— SPARS, PH. DETAILS, MISC. DETAILS —

Sheet 7
Enlarge 323 percent for full-size plans.

other half of the hull anyway, so it makes sense not to hurry. This may seem obvious, but . . . don't forget to make the halves "mirror images" of each other. All the lifts are traced the same way and flipped upside down for the second half hull. This means watching Station 5 closely during the layup. When you're laying out the template, mark across its face for Station 5 and any others that are out of sight.

If you notice any slack spots in the glue joints, mix up a fresh batch of glue and work it into the seams with a putty knife you can make for the purpose, using part of an old razor blade stuck in a wooden handle.

When you're satisfied that the glue is hard, carefully lay the hull profile template on the port half. Match Station 5 on the template with Station 5 on the hull; likewise match the waterline on the template with the waterline on the hull. Clamp the template to the hull and mark all around it.

Now for spotting in the sheer. With a combination square, square the sheer profile to the inside of the port half of the hull, spotting it along with pencil dots every $3/8$ inch or so. This is done by resting the square on the profile template and touching the tongue repeatedly at various points. Repeat this for the starboard half. With the sheer and profiles marked on each hull, you're ready to cut them to shape. You can do it by hand, or freehand on a bandsaw if you trust your sawing. If you do it freehand, hang on to the model tightly to avoid tripping the blade while sawing *Pauline*'s uneven lines, be very careful not to make sudden moves or shifts in position. Saw the port half out first and leave a strong $1/16$ inch all around. Set your table or tip your model so the blade *toes out* from the line everywhere—the idea is to leave the sheer higher on the outside of the hull than on the inside as you cut along the dots. This extra wood is then taken down to the dotted line when fairing the sheer later. Bandsawing is certainly the easiest and fastest way to do it, but it is not without risk. If the risk seems unacceptable, use a coping saw to cut around her stem and stern, then put it in the vise and cut down her sheer and along her bottom with a drawknife, spokeshave, and block plane.

If you're worried about cutting too deep along the sheer with your drawknife, or worried about splitting out along the grain, make transverse cuts every inch or two apart and work the excess wood off that way. Finish working her ends at the sheer along her centerline right to the line. This puts her lines in profile at the exact height at her extreme ends and eliminates guesswork as to how she is supposed to look at these crucial points. Square her profile ends across, outboard from the centerline, leaving the outside of her sheer along the outside of her hull a bit high for now.

Make a saw cut for the rudderpost and shaft hole, and file them out with a small rattail file. Repeat for the starboard half. To use the template from the starboard half, mark the waterline and Station 5 with a razor saw. There will be some slight irregularities along the centerlines of the glued lifts because that is the nature of wood, but don't let it disturb you into doing excessive fairing and sanding. To do so would decrease the overall beam of the boat when the two halves were glued together, and that for sure you don't want to do. Just a few swipes across the lifts with coarse 60-grit sandpaper are enough to take off any glue buildup from laying up the lifts; a sanding belt cut in half and stapled to a board works well for this. Let a stiff mixture of glue take care of any irregularities when you glue the two halves together. Before putting the hull halves together, make sure their profile shapes are cut right to their lines. It's best to use square cuts out from the centerline; you can't get in trouble that way.

Before joining the hulls mark the width of the backbone along the hull with

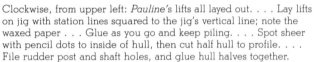

Clockwise, from upper left: *Pauline*'s lifts all layed out. . . . Lay lifts on jig with station lines squared to the jig's vertical line; note the waxed paper . . . Glue as you go and keep piling. . . . Spot sheer with pencil dots to inside of hull, then cut half hull to profile. . . . File rudder post and shaft holes, and glue hull halves together.

a combination square. If you forget you can wait until the halves are joined and the hull's sheer is faired (see The Backbone, below).

Mix up some Weldwood glue to a fairly stiff consistency, put the port half in your vise with her side down, and spread on plenty of glue. Carefully mate the starboard side to it, matching waterlines and Station 5 lines. You might want very slight pressure from some small clamps. It's hard clamping the top of the bow area, because the clamps want to slip off, so saw a couple of wedge-shaped pieces of scrap and tack them to each hull for the clamps to bear on. Glue will seep into the rudderpost and shaft holes, so ream them out two or three times until you're satisfied that no more glue is seeping in. Let the hull cure while you think about the next step, which is to finish working down the sheer.

Fairing the Sheer

Put the hull right-side up in your vise. No special cradle is needed, though this might be a good time to make one, while the glue is hardening. (If you do make one now, use the body templates for Stations 4 and 7, following the instructions in Chapter 2. You can see how far they should be apart by looking at their location on the hull profile.)

Back to fairing the sheer. If you cut the hulls right, leaving the wood high on the outside of the sheer, when you look down the centerline you should see wood rising outward on both halves. This slight slope is good, because it shows the wood is there to take off. If it isn't, you're in trouble. Assuming it is, with a block plane start working the sheer down to the penciled dots, always with the plane canted slightly inboard. Work the sheer on both sides of the hull together toward the ends. When you have both sides as close as you dare to the dots, start at the stern centerline and work square across to the outside of the sheer, blending it into the sheer previously faired along the dotted lines. For a short distance at both ends, from the centerline outboard along the sides, there are no sheer lines because they got buried when the hull halves were put together, so let the higher outsides you left guide you. Work them down carefully, fairing them square across the centerline with a straightedge and sanding board.

Make the sanding board 3/4 inches × 3 inches × 17 3/4 inches. Cut a 3-inch x 21-inch 60-grit sanding belt in half, or cut down a larger sanding belt to that width (longer length is OK). Bring the belt up over the ends of the block, and tack or staple them. Starting about amidships and working both ways, sand across the sheer, taking off the higher outboard edges. Finish cutting the sheer down to the penciled dots, then work the ends down until all the dots flow in together. Step back now and then to take a look at what you're doing. Your eye here is better than any measurement will ever be. The sheer should be flat across to the centerline everywhere.

When satisfied that you have the sheer as good as you're going to get it, lay on your deck pattern and align its centerline with that of the hull and Station 5. Too short by about 1/8 inch from the bow? That's because the deck in plan view drawn flat on paper is a dite shorter than in its curved profile view. As described in Chapter 1, shift the template to the bow station marks and trace the shape back to Station 5, then move the template to the stern stations and mark back to Station 5. That 1/8 inch you stretched the template amidships means nothing to the accuracy of the model. Cut the deck outline in plan view, right snug to the line. With a block plane, spokeshave and fair the line with 60-grit sandpaper glued to a fairing batten.

The Backbone

Turn the hull upside down, and mark the width of the backbone along the hull. On the full-size boat the keel is 9 inches in cross section, so on the model you'll need to draw two parallel lines a little over ¼ inch (4½ real inches at ⅜-inch scale) apart on each side of the centerline. Each line would then be a strong ⅛ inch from the centerline, running from the rudderpost to her stem head, each half the distance of the keel's width to scale from the centerline.

Trace the backbone template on a board, or cardboard—anything with some room around it—and lay waxed paper over the tracing. Using the template, make the backbone in two pieces with the joint between Stations 1 and 2. Lay the backbone back on the tracing with the waxed paper over it, and glue its two parts together right there. (You could also make the whole backbone one piece, if you want.) Let the glue harden, then slip the backbone onto the hull. If the fit is tight, take just the slightest amount off the hull and the inside of the backbone until they fit like a glove. This means a few swipes with a mill file or sandpaper, no drastic alterations needed. Don't glue the backbone on now, because it's apt to suffer damage when carving the outside of the hull, which is next.

Carving the Hull

For carving you'll need something rugged to hold the model in the vise to allow freedom to work all around it. Cut a 2 x 4 about 8 or 9 inches long, and glue it in the middle of the hull; also glue a couple of scrap pieces for cross braces, landing on the lifts.

Next, get a ⅞-inch or 1-inch gouge with an inside bevel, a spokeshave, a block plane, and a sanding fid with 60- and 100-grit sandpaper, and you're in business. (The sanding fid is great for working the hull in close to the rabbet line along the keel, where it hollows for most of its length.) Remove the excess wood—the sharp lift ridges—from the hull, then hold one of the body templates square against the hull on the corresponding station (you have marked the stations on the hull along the keel and sides). Visualize, while holding it there, what that section is going to look like. Do this for each station: look and cut a little, working all the stations down together gradually until the body templates fit between the keel rabbet and the deck plan view. Go easy at the bow, and leave extra wood there for that misplaced swipe of a plane that would dub the end over when instead you want her plank ends to fit sharply at the stem.

You don't have to constantly redraw the station marks on the hull as you cut them away, but they must be kept at the sheer and keel rabbet. If you lose them, they're easily replaced using the appropriate templates.

At the last stage of fairing the hull, cut a thin batten about ¹⁄₁₆ inch × 1 inch by about 15 or 16 inches long. Give it a blast of spray glue and stick some 60-grit sandpaper on it. Glue blocks at each end for handholds, and go to it. After carving a number of hulls, I found that wood was generally left high between stations since I was aiming for exact shape on the stations themselves. There's nothing wrong with that, because this excess wood can be easily taken off. In the sanding process these areas will show up as high spots. Powdered chalk sprinkled on the hull shows any hollows quickly. Glue the backbone on at the very last finishing stage, and fair the hull to it. Draw a centerline on the outer face of the stem, and fair the stem as you see fit. The stem is wider at the stem head and decreases in width down to the waterline, then widens again as it flows into the keel. For the waterline (LWL), see Sheet 1. It runs straight through

Clockwise, from upper left: Trace deck line around hull and trim sides of deck to line. . . . Put support in hull and start carving, checking with body template; backbone is shown on at this stage, but I found out later it's better left off until last. . . . Loose holes are bored in lifts to let in ends of deck beams; lay deck template on and mark deck openings. . . . Bulwark sits on deck and is scribed to deck sheer. . . . Scribe lower edge of bulwark template or use ready-made expanded template with plans.

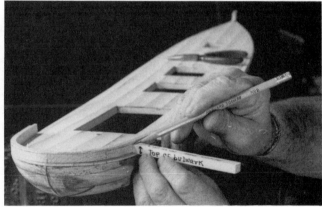

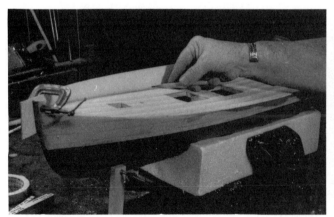

the hull where she would settle when loaded. All you have to do is mask it off for painting after the hull is carved.

Deck and Bulwark

We'll make the deck much differently for *Pauline* than we did for the *Laura B.* First, make a crowning board (see Sheet 6 and deck beam pattern) out of 3/4-inch pine and glue a piece of 60-grit sandpaper to its camber. Take the 2 × 4 support out of the hull (you can whack it out with hammer and chisel). Put the hull in the cradle you made for it, and put the hull back in the vise. Lightly sand the deck sheer area fore and aft with the crowning board.

This model has deck framing much like that on the real boat, but fewer, with only 22 deck beams running athwartships. At 3/8-inch scale, the deck beams—8 inches wide in the full-size boat—are 1/4 inch wide. I crowned their tops, but made the bottoms straight, since they're hidden. I spaced the deck beams about as shown; they're much farther apart than they would be in the real boat. (In the real *Pauline* the frames were doubled and spaced 8 inches apart.) The ends of the deck beams are let into the sides of the hull in loose-fitting bored holes after centering (you've marked centers on the deck beams). Each is set into the hull in stiff glue and checked for height using the crowning board spanned across the hull as a gauge. Locate the carlins for hatches, the pilot-house, doghouse, and forward ventilation hatch openings by laying the deck template on the deck beams and marking. The carlins don't need to be let into the deck beams; just butt them.

For decking, you'll need to saw strips to scale that represent the real boat's deck planks, which are 3 or 4 inches wide by 1 1/2 inches thick. The decking goes on full length and gets cut for the openings as the decking progresses. Use strips of pine, cedar, basswood, or most anything that has good, close grain. You can easily saw these out on your table saw using a tiptop-sharp hollow-ground planer blade. The wood you start with should be 32 inches × 2 inches square, straight-grained and clear of knots. It's hard to say exactly how much you'll need, but in doing something of this sort it's always far better to saw more than enough to avoid setting up the whole sawing process again, risking the chance of mismatching sizes.

In sawing the decking, grain is the thing to watch for. Wood that has grain running vertically through the thickness of the plank will be more stable, resisting warping or twisting, and, being close grained, is beautiful finished clear. Saw the 32-inch x 2-inch deck stock into slabs that represent the plank width (3 or 4 scale inches), then set your rip fence for sawing their thickness (1 1/2 scale inches) and saw each individual plank. Caulking seams are easily put on by planing their edges with a small hobbyist's hand plane, or they can be sanded on. The deck is laid starting at the centerline with these individual strips.

It might seem easier to make the decking from wider strips and scribe in the caulking seams, but take it from me: *Don't do it.* I misguidedly followed this suggestion from a modeler's book, and learned my lesson. Scribing the seams was not only time-consuming but a disappointment, resulting in runoff and uneven seams that were deep and shallow from soft and hard spots in the wood. (Of course, if you want your deck to look 100 years old to start with, then follow this advice.)

Let the decking run out flush to the stern. At the bow, cut it off with a razor saw or razor blade so that the bulwark (also called the waist) can set in against it. Remember, the aft bulwark sits on top of the decking or covering board (see Sheets 5 and 6). For the waist bulwark, the decking rabbets out to accept it. The waist bulwark planking and hull planking on the real *Pauline* were the same thickness. It helps to make a marking gauge of wood with a lip on it that represents the bulwark thickness, which you can use to shape each plank. This same gauge idea also works for shaping the inside of the covering board (8 inches on the full-size boat, ¼ inch on the model), if you want to use one; also for the railcap. Since the outside of the hull is already cut to the line, the hull itself is the reference point you scribe from. In building these models you'll find it very useful and accurate, besides being a timesaver, to make a simple gauge for any repetitive measuring.

The waist bulwark flows along with the hull flare, with its bow end burying in the stem and its aft end notched into the aft bulwark. The bow end is the hardest place to hold the flare. Here you can bore through the deck and insert a few stanchions and clamp the bulwark to them, which is the best way, or use any bracing-off method you want to try. The bulwark, as you see it on the plans, is expanded—already shaped to follow the flare—and will fit when edge-set on the hull. The bulwark template shows deeper on the plan (see top of Sheet 6) than needed, so once it's in place, make a marking stick the same height as the aft bulwark (10½ inches in the real boat) and scribe its top shape from the deck. After it's glued in place, put in the beveled stanchions (4 inches × 4 inches in the real boat; there are 39 on each side, spaced 16 inches apart; ⅛ inch by ⅛ inch in the model, spaced ½ inch apart, with the first one ½ inch forward of the stern bulwark) and glue them to the deck and bulwarks. Make a gauge for their spacing (see the top plan view of the deck, Sheet 6) and leave them high for trimming. Trim the tops of the stanchions with a razor saw to the camber of the crowning board, and finish sanding to that shape.

Limber Holes

Now for the hard part. *Pauline* has plenty of limber holes, and the way they're located seems a bit strange, because some are uphill of the way water runs. Why would there be holes on the aft side uphill of these stanchions at the bow and their forward sides downhill at the stern? Even the dumbest of us knows water runs downhill. The answer came when I asked *Pauline's* designer/builder Roy Wallace. "Those small, square holes served as holds for the pry bars for forcing the covering board down"—and, as Roy said, "It twan't easy!" The smaller limber holes start at the first set of stanchions forward of the mast and end at the forward ends of the aft bulwark. There are 37 of the smaller holes and 13 of the longer limbers, the forwardmost one starting abreast of the forward side of the aft hatch.

So that I wouldn't bore into the edge of the decking, I drew a parallel line representing the thickness of the deck on the outside of the bulwark, and bored out the limbers with a very small bit in a Dremel drill, since I couldn't tell exactly where the drill was coming out. I then rebored with a little larger drill and finished the holes with a small square needle file, since the holes were square on the original.

This is a good time to paint between the stanchions, because you can get in the corners before the inwales go on. Seal and paint these now, along with the covering board area, which in this case is an 8-inch-wide area painted parallel to the bulwarks completely around the deck.

The inwales are 1¼ inch × 3 inches at full scale and let out by the stanchions a hair when notched into them and glued in place. A gauge works well here also. Make a gauge to mark the tops of the stanchions for letting in the inwales, and make another one to mark their heights from the deck. With a razor saw, notch each timber horizontally, then cut from the top with a razor blade. The inwales are left slightly high so their tops can be worked off to the deck crown after they are glued in. At their aft ends their sides flow in a line flush with the aft bulwarks.

If I seem to spend a lot of time talking about gauges, it's for a good reason. Gauges take all the guesswork out of arriving from point A to point B, and it makes the job so much easier and faster to know precisely where you are headed and going to end up. This part of making the model was especially interesting because here was a special challenge that called for accuracy in a number of different views and required some thought, especially thinking ahead—like how am I going to fit a paintbrush under that inwale and get into all those corners with the inwales and railcaps on? The answer was to build a while, then paint a while. Of course the next model will have all new challenges. That's what keeps me interested—that's where the fun is.

Railcap

On the full-size *Pauline*, the railcap is 2 inches × 8 inches and stands about an inch outside of the bulwarks everywhere. Its top is flat and its outside edge rounded. Its inside edge is cut square, has its corners slightly rounded, and stands out by the inwale about ½ inch. Use your scale rule to figure these dimensions at ⅜-inch scale.

The general idea with fitting the railcap calls for fitting its ends at the bow and the stern bulwark, then scribing it to the inwale and to the outside of the bulwark.

Fit the railcap on the aft bulwark first, and make it with the grain running opposite to the bulwarks. I made this in one piece to the shape of the aft bulwark, with tapered cuts on each rail to catch the long waist caps. For the longer caps, saw a piece wide enough to make the curve; if you saved the scrap pieces from Lifts 6 and 7, these will do fine. Notch their forward ends to fit to the stem, and swing their edges in against the splice cut you made in the aft railcap. Set your dividers to the overhang (1 inch on the real boat; ¹⁄₃₂ inch on the model, a little on the strong side) and scribe the outside shapes of the railcaps first—then sand down for fit before scribing inside shape. To aid in sanding the overhang without humps and hollows, and for following the exact shape parallel to the hull, cut a small stick, put sandpaper on it, glue a spacer on it the thickness of the overhang, and let the spacer be your guide. It's the same idea as trimming the edge of Formica close with one of these cutters that has a stop that holds the cutter away a set distance no matter what the shape. Glue the railcaps on, and finish sanding them on the boat, blending them in with the aft railcap.

Chainplates

I made the chainplates from .025-inch sheet brass bought at the local hobby shop. First, saw this into 4-inch strips on your bandsaw, using a *fine-toothed hardened cutting blade*. (A skip-tooth blade won't do it; it'll catch and grab instead. I tried a table saw, a scroll saw, tinsnips—nothing else worked.) Run a piece of wood into the blade so it covers the saw slot before attempting to saw; this supports the thin brass. Cut the chainplates long enough to stand 3 or 4 scale inches above the railcap. Let them into the rails so they lay flat against the bulwarks, and save the scrap of wood you cut out to receive them; replace it later with a dab of glue on the outside of the railcap.

Bore holes in the chainplates' tops to catch the wire shackles you'll make out of 24-gauge brass wire to catch the turnbuckles. The safe way to drill the right size hole, if you're in doubt, is first to drill a very small hole and enlarge it if need be. Buy yourself a selection of drill bits from size 61 to 80, and you'll have all the drills you need for everything you'll put on the model. (My drills come 20 to a case, numbered 61 to 80 in thousandths; 61 is the biggest, 80 is the smallest.) If you're going to do much modelmaking, I suggest buying a drill gauge from 61 to 80 and a micrometer; these two items saves a lot of time and guesswork.

Figure where the guardrail is going to go (the top of the guardrail sits flush with the bottom of the bulwark, see sectional view, Sheet 6), notch the guardrail out for the chainplate with a flat needle file, and bore a hole in each chainplate so the fastenings go behind it. I glued and fastened the chainplates with brass dressmaker's pins. Locate the forward chainplate to center on the mainmast and its sister just under 1 inch (31 inches on the real boat) aft of that. The jiggermast's chainplate centers on the jiggermast, and there is another chainplate at the centerline on the transom to catch the stay.

Guardrails and Buffalo Rails

The full-size *Pauline*'s guardrail is made from basswood or other fine-grained wood, sided 3 inches, 6 inches deep, and 2¾ inches on its outside face, beveled 5 degrees on its top and 40 degrees on its underside (see Sheet 6). It is made and put on in one piece, so when you cut this piece to scale, cut it long enough. You can saw the guardrails out on your table saw but you may have to practice a bit to get them right with the bevels and all.

Starting at the centerline at the stern, wrap it around and bring both ends past the bow. Here, measure the ends for length to fit in the stem rabbet, but don't cut them off until you've glued and fastened the guardrail all along its length. Bending the guardrail around the transom is where it will give you trouble, so soak this area in household ammonia until it's soft and pliable—about an hour—or use dry heat from your shop stovepipe or a soldering iron. It's nice to have a helper here. The aft end will want to curl up and away from the hull when it's bent around, so hold it in place as best as you can with brass dressmaker's pins while someone holds a gentle strain at the bow, pulling on the ends. Fit the

Clockwise, from upper left: Make plug for pilothouse and cover with waxed paper . . . then build the pilothouse right on plug. . . . *Pauline's* pilothouse was double-sheathed but can be single. . . . Plug is pulled clear and pilothouse finished; here hand grabrail goes on side of house. . . . Stem iron for inner and outer stays is made from sheet brass and soldered.

guardrail to the stem and fasten along its length with brass pins. When you're satisfied with the fit, drive all the pins in for good, and cut off some of their heads where they're not needed for holding strength. Apply thin superglue, letting it seep into the joint. This method of gluing is way ahead of applying white or yellow carpenter's glue, trying to get the rail on before it hardens. Using this thin-as-water superglue, you're not faced with cleaning off lumps of hardened glue.

The buffalo rails, 4 inches square × 20 feet 3 inches long in real life, are fitted to the railcap, their aft ends are rounded and their forward ends fitted to the stem. The breasthook is same thickness as the railcap and sits flush with the railcap. The buffalo rail sits on top of the breasthook (see Sheet 6 for its shape).

Next are the doghouse, the ventilation hatch forward of it, the pilothouse, and the hatches (see Sheet 7). What they all have in common is that their forward and aft faces are all plumb to the waterline.

For the doghouse, make a plug, wax it (car wax worked OK for me), put the sides on, and cross-plank its top as shown on Sheet 7. Make the paneled doors by gluing a backing strip of wood between the doghouse sides and laying the door over it. Don't forget to raise the bottom of the door up enough to show ventilation. Note on the plans that the aft sides of the doghouse overhang its base by 3 inches (3/32 inch at 3/8-inch scale). The coaming (7 3/4 inches in height full size, about 1/4 inch on the model) is put on and glued to the deck.

The forward ventilation hatch is made to the size shown on the plans and has a port for light. On the full-size *Pauline*, its forward section was hinged for ventilation.

For the pilothouse, I'd recommend that you make a plug from the drawing on Sheet 7, wax it, and sheathe over it. Compared with trying to hold the pieces squarely in place while you fit and glue them, this is the easy way to do it. What could be more accurate than your tablesaw to saw out this plug for a building form? Cut the top of the plug square; you'll simply sand the small amount of camber on top of the roof, which goes on after the house is all put together.

Build the house inside-out, using two layers of sheathing. I'd recommend you use 1/32-inch or 1/16-inch aircraft plywood. As with the doghouse, this two-layer system allows backing for the paneled doors, and provides a rabbet for the window glass by making the window openings slightly smaller in the first layer. Building the pilothouse was no easy job; it took me more than a week to build and tried my patience and skill plenty, so I wouldn't feel the least bit offended if you didn't feel up to that much work and just stuck a block of wood on her, painted the doors and windows on, and let it go at that. On the other hand, since the house detail is one of the focal points of the model, I thought it was worth a try. Of course, there are other ways to do it: you can use the pilothouse views for templates and build the house without using a plug. Note that the lower part (trunk) of the pilothouse projects out square (see plan view, Sheet 7).

The plug came in handy for holding the split-level floors. In the full-size *Pauline*, their difference in height is about 15 inches. Measure the forward floor's height from either the bottom or the top of the house, and slide the plug out to that height. Make the floor from the plan view, slip it inside the house, and glue it. Pull the plug out the same height for the aft level, and repeat. Be sure there is plenty of wax on the plug while doing this. Make each floor about 1/4 inch longer at the partition so they overlap for the riser to set in between.

Finishing off the inside of the pilothouse is a matter of choice, and since you can only dimly see what's inside, you may feel it's not worth putting in the captain's bunk, his chart table, etc. Or you can put it all in, and light the pilothouse with a small wheat light, which you can buy in a specialty model supply store that deals with dollhouses and the like; there's room under the floor to stick the batteries and switch. With the light turned on, the glow from the air ports and pilothouse windows makes it look like the real thing riding at anchor at night.

Build the aft entrance door and the two side doors. I made waxed jigs for these and built them frame and all, set them into the outer sheathing, and glued all in place. Put a floor in the muffler cavity, and put the finish trim around the lower part of the pilothouse. The real boat has $1^3/4$-inch-square trim and a lighter trim that's $2^1/2$ inches $\times$ $^1/2$ inch. At $^3/8$-inch scale, this size trim is no cinch to saw out on a table saw, so if you can't do it, find some that will come as close as you can. For instance, $^1/64$-inch birch plywood you can get from a model shop would be close. In fact, a small "miniature lumberyard" isn't all that expensive and comes in real handy. I built *Pauline*'s pilothouse from $^1/16$-inch cold-molding veneers, which worked fairly well, but needed a lot of tailoring I would have been spared had I used hobby-shop aircraft plywood.

In real life, glass for the pilothouse windows measures $15^1/2$ inches $\times$ $19^1/2$ inches; for the doors, it's 11 inches $\times$ 18 inches; and it's $4^1/2$ inches $\times$ $23^1/2$ inches for the aft horizontal window at the top of the house. Both sides of the pilothouse are identical. I used acrylic plastic, the kind found for glass replacement for doors and windows, which seemed heavy but much better than the thin acetate available by mail order. You can cut this stuff right on your table saw or score it and break it—either way. For the air ports (port holes—$^5/16$ inches at $^3/8$-inch scale) I cut a long length, then cut it in squares larger than the size needed. While holding the squares with pliers, I ground the corners off on a cutting wheel, making them 8-sided, then 16-sided, then finished sanding by hand until they just dropped into the ridges provided for them. Not as much of a job as you might think.

It pays to be careful in the selection of glue for acrylic plastic. I learned the hard way by not only sticking the windows in with superglue, but also poured a bit over the "glass" itself just before leaving the shop for the day, figuring it would flow over it like epoxy does, leaving a mirror-smooth finish. Next morning, the "glass" looked like it had been hit with a hammer—ruined, totally useless—and had to be taken out. I glued in my next attempt with quick-setting epoxy. Superglue (cyanoacrylate) most definitely has its place in modelmaking, but it has to be applied with extreme care. I found out later that a needle with the tip of its eye ground off acted the same as a soap-bubble pipe: I could place a tiny drop of superglue exactly where I wanted it.

Put a $^7/8$-inch, eight-spoke steering wheel on the pedestal in her pilothouse, then add a chart table, a flare box, and the captain's bunk, and you're ready to put on the roof. Put three carlins (ceiling beams) in each level and glue the roof to them and to the top of the house sides. The finish on *Pauline* is different than I've ever seen before on a boat. At full scale, a piece of $2^1/4$-inch $\times$ 3-inch trim is fastened to the house, a 4-inch piece to it, and a 3-inch piece last. This gives a fair amount of overhang. Just translate this to $^3/8$-inch scale and you've got it.

The visor for the pilothouse is one of the tougher parts to make. Nine inches wide on the full-size boat, it starts 2 feet aft of the door, wraps around the house, tucked up under the finish, and has four mitered corners; the six knees that hold it in place are 9 inches across the top and 12 inches tall where they brace against the house at the angle of 26 degrees. For the model, you can make a pattern for the knees and cut them out with a scroll saw; you'll find a small stick with a pin stuck in it comes in handy for spearing these little suckers to hold them for gluing. I'm not going to try to tell you how to build the visor step by step, but I'll bet you can do it if you're patient and willing to give it a shot.

Sometimes I wondered about doing all that detail, but it all seemed worth it when Roy Wallace, her builder, saw me coming into his home with it tucked under my arm and said, "My God, look at that!"

Pauline's muffler is 39 inches tall × 13½ inches in diameter. I made one for the model from a ³⁄₈-inch dowel, which is 12 inches at that scale but was close enough for me. I made the stack from a piece of ¹⁄₈-inch dowel, with its top swung to miss the jiggermast, to which it's very close.

This pretty well completes the detail on the pilothouse, except for a little trim around the windows, the horizontal grabrails on the side of the house, and the ones near the side doors. Don't glue the pilothouse in place—in fact, don't ever glue it on for good. You'll find any number of reasons why you want to take it off again.

Now we'll do something easy.

Hatches

The two hatches are 6 feet square at full scale and stand 1 foot high. An easy way to make them is to cut out square blocks of the appropriate size jammed down into the deck openings to build each hatch around. The coamings and headers sit on the deck; rabbet their tops for the hatch covers, and build them right around the blocks set in the deck openings, then knock the blocks down in the bilge and pick them out through the pilothouse opening. There are three hatch covers on each hatch, with two beams underneath for each cover and two ringbolts to each cover on opposite corners. Sand the coamings and covers all to the camber of the deck using your crowning board. Check the plan view, Sheet 6, and sectional view, Sheet 7; plank with leftover decking or just use wider strips.

Rigging and Finishing

The mainmast and jiggermast both rake no more than 2 degrees. This isn't much, but it's enough to allow the boom to swing back to the center of the hatches. (If they rake aft excessively, the boom doesn't want to swing out.) Since *Pauline's* masts were lying on the ground, I had no way of knowing how much rake they had. I was lucky—her twin, the *Jacob Pike*, built by the same builder, was still in service lugging sardines. One day, I was fortunate enough to catch the *Pike* lying alongside the Port Clyde Sardine Packing Co. in Rockland where she had just discharged a load. So, standing on the municipal pier opposite her, and exactly in profile, I steadied my level plumb against a piling, sighted it at the mast, then laid my bevel board against the level, swinging the bevel board until it lined up with the mast, and read the angle. I was surprised to find that the *Pike's* mast raked only 2 degrees. Good thing the *Pike* was around— Roy Wallace had long forgotten how much he raked the mast 40 years ago, and there was no one else to ask.

Since the small turnbuckles I bought from a model supply house didn't turn, I saw no better way of tightening the rigging than the way I did it—by boring a hole in the center of the foot of each mast and putting a pin in it. I adjusted the stays as best I could, then slipped a very shallow wedge under each mast, bringing the rigging taut. This is the reason for leaving the pilot- house unglued, so you can wedge up the jigger through the hatches. Without a

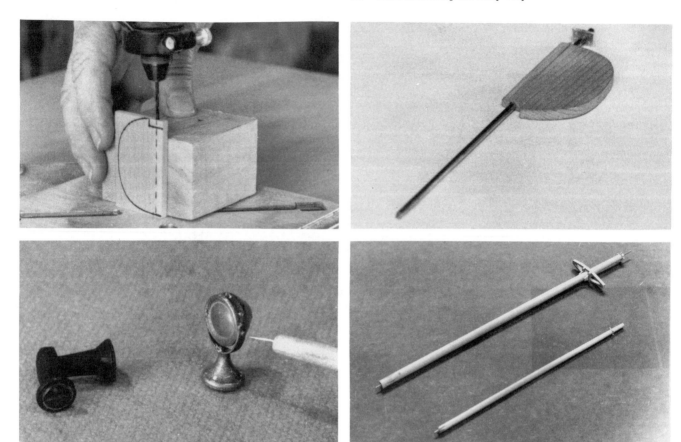

controlled environment, a model's rigging often tightens or goes slack, so it's good to have a way to adjust it. On *Pauline* I used ⅝-inch turnbuckles made from Britannia, which is too soft—they wouldn't stand the strain of taut rigging. I later found some ⅝-inch brass ones that were much better.

The standing rigging, shrouds, and stays were made from seven-strand tinned copper wire of the right diameter, which is very strong, soft, and easy to work with. This comes in 10-foot coils (item #1673) from BlueJacket Shipcrafters, at this writing costing all of 75 cents per coil). The drill size to use with it is #73. Buy at least two coils—this stuff has a way of not going as far as you think. I got the eyebands by mail order. I'm not against using mail-order parts if they're to scale—but stay away from white metal. The shrouds go on first: they loop over the mast, and are led through the crosstrees over the hounds to dummy turnbuckles at each chainplate.

The inner bowstay runs to the aft hole in a plate over the stemhead. Cut the stemhead iron from hobby-shop brass and bend it flat to shape, then cut its top to shape and bore and solder it on. Don't tighten any of this yet. Run the outer bowstay just as you see it, then rig the shrouds to the turnbuckles which are shackled to the chainplates. I bought some lovely shackles, just like the real thing, but outsmarted myself when I found that they couldn't be reeved through either turnbuckle or chainplate holes because of their large shoulders where the pin goes through. So I made mine from a spool of 24-gauge solid brass rod. You should have a few sizes of this stuff in your stockpile, and a spool of 28-gauge brass rod for seizings.

Clockwise, from upper left: Rudder is held against square-cut block for vertical alignment while boring rudderpost hole. . . . Rudder with post and bearing plate. . . . Mainmast and jigger; eyebands are on and pin is in mast heels. . . . Searchlight and horn turned on Dremel lathe.

For turning the small loops in the shackles for the pins, I cut a slot in the side of a fair-sized needle, drove the needle in a piece of wood for a handle, and turned these loops perfectly, with no problems; it was quick and easy after a few tries. Ratlines for going aloft measured 1¼ inches × 1¾ inches in real life—but for the model, use whatever you can saw out and looks reasonable. I found it was easiest to cut them all from one long strip. I painted the ratlines black, slotted their ends to slip over the shrouds, and spaced them ½ inch apart vertically at ⅜-inch scale. They are glued in place with a drop of superglue, not lashed like they usually are—my fingers and patience said "No way!" The bottom ratline (*sheerpole*) is a little longer and heavier and sits with the sheer, with three pins in it for belaying the ends of lines.

Running rigging is three-strand #4 nylon, made by Brownell Co., stained to look like manila from a soak in a cup of very strong instant coffee. I know cotton is short-lived soaked that way, but I'll gamble on nylon—we'll see. The blocks in real life were 6 inches; this means 3/16 inch at ⅜-inch scale. My fingers again said "No way," so I went to 7/32-inch blocks, which were just right for reeving this size nylon through the blocks. These blocks from BlueJacket are beautiful besides being functional. I'm told the famous modeler Erik A. R. Ronnberg, Jr. designed them. Every line works! And they're made from Britannia metal, an alloy that doesn't erode like white metal castings do when under glass for a time.

To get the three-strand nylon started in the sheave holes, I glued the end of the line, waited until the glue hardened, then cut the end at an angle so there was a pointy end; it worked great. Finding ways of doing things is the fun part of modeling. Sometimes I'd puzzle over how I was going to do something the next day, and the answer would wake me up in the middle of the night. This human brain of ours sure is something—but it can have a mind of its own! I found that if I didn't use the solution my brain came up with, it would shut down and not bother to give me any more information. The brain seems happiest when you use it.

For finishing off *Pauline,* mail-order model supply houses have a good bunch of stuff in a wide variety. I used pre-made items where I could, and made my own where I had to or where I thought I could do better. I couldn't resist the tiny ringbolts when I saw them in the Fisher catalog, so I bought a dozen; I learned later when building the *William A. Underwood* how easily and quickly I could make my own. Mail-order cleats, anchors, mushroom vents, air ports, chocks, life rings—all were good. The masthead light and running lights I ordered, however, came in brass and didn't look like much.

I called up my friend Jay Hanna, master modelmaker, and said, "Jay, what do you do with these things? They're nicely made, but this brass masthead light sitting way up there looks kinda blind."

"Paint it white, is all you can do," says Jay. "I make my own out of plexiglass—turn them out on my lathe."

As luck would have it, right after this bolt of inspiration, my friend Doug Alvord came into my shop one day and made me a present of a Dremel lathe, which I immediately put to use. I made all the lights, sawing square chunks off a discarded plastic tabletop given to me by another friend, including the running lights, which were made oversize, then quartered. I even went so far as making my own turning tools from cast-off screwdrivers. These are good because they come already hardened. The trick is, when grinding them to shape, don't heat them too much. Watch that they don't turn blue.

For making the lights, I ground a screwdriver into a chisel the shape of a

Fresnel lens, copied from the store-bought version, so now I can make them forever. I also ended up making the horn and searchlight the way I wanted them. With Floquil, I painted the searchlight silver, then put brass color over the silver so you could look into its depth. So, for me, buy some, make some, worked great.

Pauline has a 4-foot right-handed three-bladed propeller turning a 4-inch shaft, and her rudder is sided 5½ inches without taper. Cut her rudder to profile shape (see Sheet 3), and bore a hole for the rudder shaft up through the skeg. Then put the rudder in place and push the shaft up through the skeg into the rudder and into the horn timber that you bored earlier before the hulls were glued together. Don't forget to slip the collar on the shaft. The collar connection you see on the 4-inch rudderpost is so the rudder can be unshipped without taking the whole assembly apart. The deck plate directly above the post gave access for emergency hand steering with a big arm that fit down over the post.

Form the bail net by placing cheesecloth over a thimble-shaped piece of wood. . . . Stationary hoisting engine; wheels were turned on a Dremel lathe.

Bail Net

During her first years of lugging herring, *Pauline* didn't have pumping equipment for taking fish from herring weirs. Instead she carried a bail—or dip—net, which was dipped into the herring pursed up into the weir pocket. The net could lift a fair quantity of fish at a time, and with the help of a 3- or 4-h.p. engine sitting just aft of the mast, the net full of fish was swung inboard over one of the holds. A trip lever opened the bottom of the net, and the fish poured into the hold. The fish were quickly salted and soon on their way to the canneries, after their heads and tails were cut off, they were packed in cans, cooked, and sent on their way to market.

If you make a bail net for *Pauline* or *William Underwood* use cheesecloth for the net and make the bail hoop out of about 1-inch wire at ⅜ scale; the loom would be about 2 inches round. The net was carried triced up in the ratlines or some convenient place out of the way.

Herring weirs were common up and down the Maine coast from around the turn of the century up until the mid-1950s, when competition from seine fishermen gradually decreased the importance of the stationary weirs. Seine fishermen spotted schools of fish from the air long before the fish got anywhere near

Color Scheme:

Hull, flat white
Waterline, copper
Deck, flat light gray
Railcap and buffalo rails, light gray
Top of the house trunk, light gray
Grabrails on the house, light gray
Pilothouse, doghouse, forward ventilator, and hatches, white
Masts, light buff (white at tops)

Eighty-nine-year-old Roy Wallace, real life designer and builder said, "My God, look at that."

the weirs. Encircling the fish with a net, boats were able to catch thousands of bushels at a time. The sardine carriers would come alongside the pursed up fish, lower a big suction pump and pump the fish out in a hurry, and getting the bonus of bushels of scales that they could also sell for making such things as paint and jewelry.

The efficiency of the seine fisherman spelled the end of the herring weirs, and now the smaller herring that once were the mainstay of the packing houses have become scarcer, leaving mostly large herring used for lobster bait, fish meal, and some packing. There are only a few sardine packing plants left along the coast now instead of the many I remember in the 1940s and '50s.

So, that's about it; I see no point in clobbering you with endless detail. I'll gamble that with these instructions and a set of well-laid-out plans, you can build a model you can be proud of.

4

Mite
A Maine Harbor Tugboat

Materials Needed

- 16 running feet of 3″ × ³⁄₈″ basswood or pine
- one 4′ × 8′ sheet of ¹⁄₈″ tempered Masonite (smooth both sides)
- 2′ × 1′ × ¹⁄₁₆″ aircraft plywood
- ¹⁄₄″ dowel (6 inches, though stores may not sell sections this small)
- spray adhesive
- Weldwood plastic resin glue or epoxy, Franklin Titebond
- coil of seven-strand copper tinned wire
- assorted fittings: ⁷⁄₈″ steering wheel; 1¹⁄₂″ propeller; ¹⁄₈″ brass shaft; eight ⁵⁄₁₆″ brass ports; two ⁵⁄₁₆″ brass hawse lips; ¹⁄₂″ diameter cowl ventilator and assorted fittings; one ⁵⁄₈″ deck plate
- nylon line, three-strand (Brownel of Moodus, CT is a good brand)
- fine-laid nylon twine
- full-size plans

T here's something about steam power that appeals to almost everyone. When I was a kid growing up in the late 1930s and early '40s around the Rockland, Maine, waterfront, I was lucky enough to see and hear the last sounds of steam-powered locomotives and boats; even the sardine canneries ran on steam. At the time, coal was brought to Rockland by barge, and the harbor tugs would guide them to the wharves to be off-loaded, pushing and pulling with much whistle tooting. You'd often see tugs hauling strings of barges along the coast, heading to just about any port with some size.

Each day at noon, from a nearby hill overlooking the harbor, I'd hear a series of steam-whistle blasts signaling lunchtime—a joyful chorus to my seven-year-old ears, telling me all was well in the world.

Close by at Snow's Shipyard, I saw my first tug—the 140-horsepower *Sommers N. Smith*, built in 1887 in Philadelphia, serving then as the yard tug for Snow Marine Co. She's long gone now, but I found her again in Steve Lang and Peter Spectre's book *On the Hawser*—the most comprehensive gathering of tugboats I've ever seen. The book helped me tremendously in building this model. Somewhere I know I've heard said about her that "men may come and men may go, but the *Sommers N. Smith* goes on forever"—and indeed she does.

A few years back—some 100 years after the original boat was built—I ran across a model of the *Sommers N. Smith*, rough and not to scale, but done with loving care. Irving Gamage (relative of the famed Harvey Gamage) had built the model from scratch, without plans—"probably couldn't have built from plans if he had them," according to his grand-nephew Norman Gamage. Irving had worked as crew aboard the full-size tug, and in his model he set out to copy her as best he could. What impressed me most about Irving's model was his use of what he had at hand. For lettering her name he used Alphabet Soup macaroni letters, which are still on the hull today, looking as good as the day he put them on. The quality of a model, or its authenticity, has never mattered to me so much as the builder's thinking system—that's what I admire most.

Living here on the Maine coast all my life, I knew the Gamage family well, and I never saw a Gamage that couldn't build a boat. They also never had any illusions about making a living at it, so they all had other jobs as means of steadier incomes. But let a boat order come through, and Gamages appeared from everywhere, pooled all their talents, and pulled together to get the job done—and done beautifully. After the boat was built, they would all fade away back to their jobs again until the next boat. Master builder John Gamage, who was construction boss building wooden minesweepers for the U.S. Navy during World War II at Snow's Shipyard, would go back to selling insurance, the buyer quite likely unaware of this man's remarkable talents and family heritage.

Tugboat plans are hard to come by, especially plans ready to cut up for use as templates. Enter Phil Bolger and a model of a 45-foot harbor tug, *Mite*, drawn to a scale of 3/8 inch = 1 foot. Here's a sharp-looking tug guaranteed to delight the eye of any youngster or oldster. Phil designed this harbor tug from scratch, using many common tugboat characteristics but making it simple enough to be within the skills of the beginning modeler.

If there's one thing tugs have in common, it's that they're all different. The towing bitts (bollards) and their placement, though, have been pretty much the same all along, whether the tug was 1890 vintage or more modern. Generally you'll see tugs with a double bollard forward of the pilothouse and one bitt right up near the stem, but of course there are variations, like having bitts along the decks as well. The bitts were made square below decks, and round above.

The older harbor tugs like this, 40 to 50 or so feet in length, didn't have much filigree on them, compared to their modern oceangoing sisters. The front of their pilothouses didn't need a bridge deck around them because they didn't sit up that high. The sheer of the pilothouse roof and the aft portion of the pilothouse generally followed the hull sheer. The stack and masts raked with the front of the pilothouse. Windows and doors bisected whatever portion of the sheer they happened to line up with, thus giving an overall pleasing appearance. The newer oceangoing rescue-and-salvage tugs look too modern and fancy to me, so they lost their appeal for making a model.

Before we begin . . . did you ever wonder why tugs always look half sunk? This is because they carry considerable water ballast to get their sterns down; this way, the wheel gets a better bite in the deeper water for towing. In fact, tugboat skippers have to be aware of this low-freeboard vulnerability and avoid exceeding hull speed; otherwise, a tug could sink by burying herself in her own wake. Prudent tug skippers who pushed their craft for all they would go made sure all doors and hatches were closed tight.

Tools Needed

- table saw
- bandsaw, sabersaw
- vise
- clamps
- low-angle block plane
- spokeshave
- drill bits, sizes 61 to 80
- 10" mill file
- 7/8" gouge with inside bevel
- sanding fid
- sanding battens
- needle files
- combination square
- scissors
- #3 pencil
- sail needle
- narrow masking tape

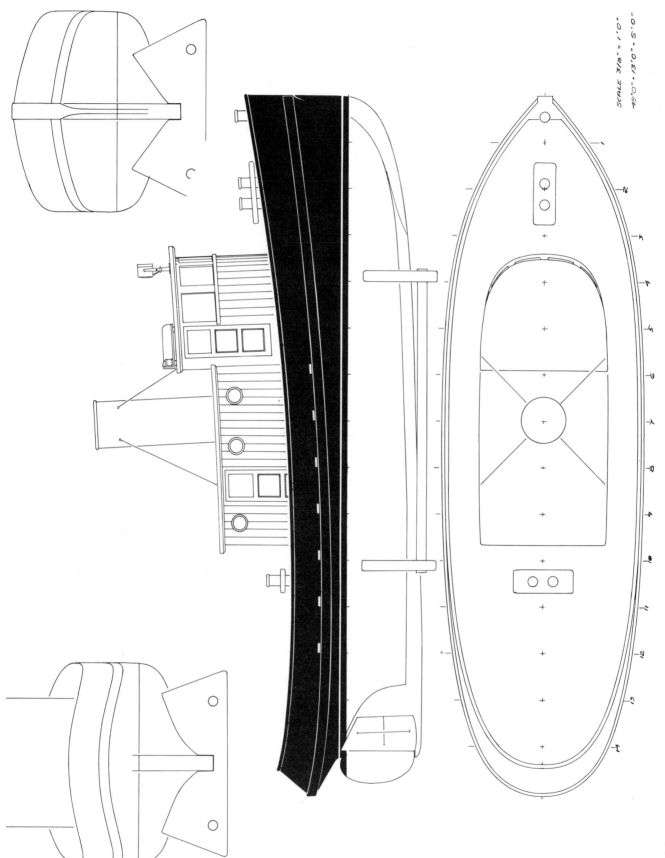

Sheet 1
Enlarge 230 percent for full-size plans

SCALE 3/8" = 1'0"
75'0", 13'0", 5'0"

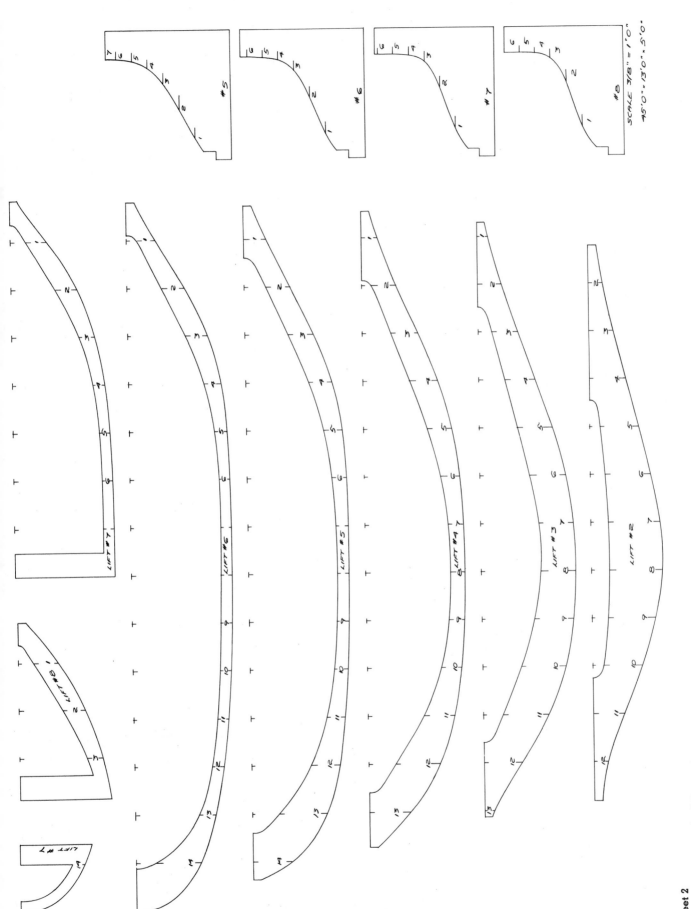

Sheet 2
Enlarge 227 percent for full-size plans

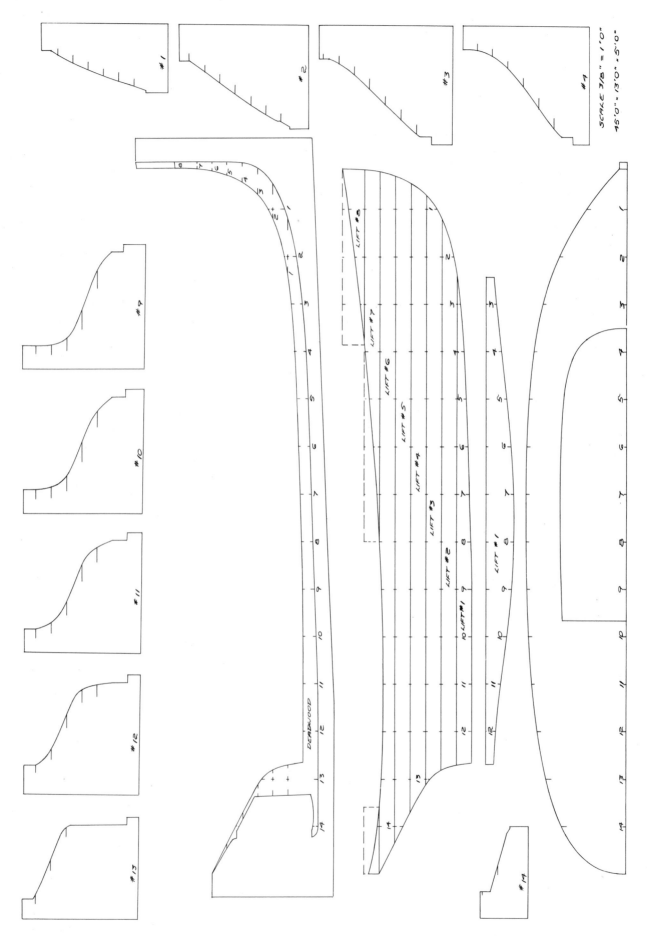

Sheet 3
Enlarge 230 percent for full-size plans

SCALE 3/8" = 1'0"
45'0" × 13'0" × 5'0"

#1 #2 #3 #4

#9 #10 #11 #12 #13 #14

DEADWOOD

LIFT #8 LIFT #7 LIFT #6 LIFT #5 LIFT #4 LIFT #3 LIFT #2 LIFT #1

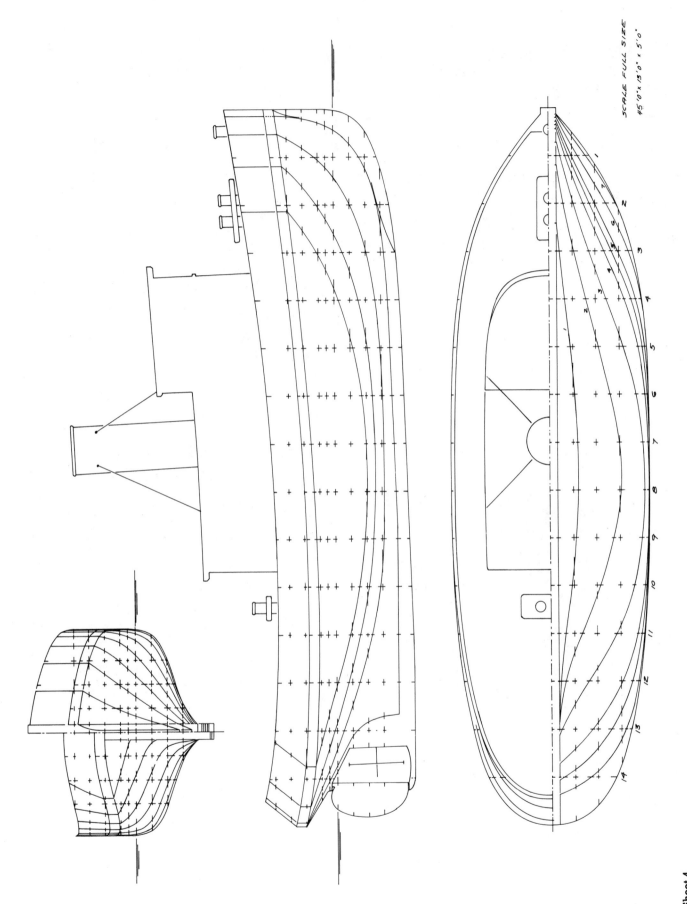

SCALE FULL SIZE
45'0" x 15'0" x 5'0"

Sheet 4
Enlarge 225 percent for full-size plans

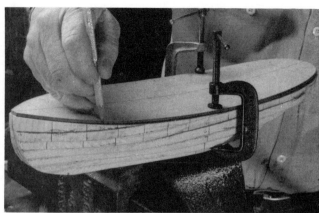

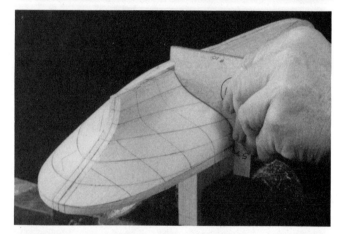

Clockwise, from upper left: *Mite's* two halves laid up. Don't forget to make mirror image. . . . Hull halves glued together and marking deck line. . . . Checking hull with station template. . . . Inner stem and deck beams are all in, deck planking has been started. . . . Deck is nearly planked; the inner sides are set back and the deck is rabbeted for the bulwark.

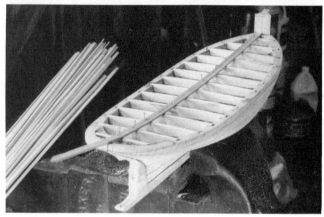

Building the Hull

First, cut out the templates from Sheets 2 and 3, using the same procedure for this and for cutting out the waterline lifts as already described for the *Laura B.* and *Pauline*, and start building *Mite*'s hull, being as fancy and as thorough as your patience and skill allow. I won't go into a lot of detail, since you're familiar with these steps by now.

Note that Lifts 1 through 7 are ³⁄₈ inch thick; Lift 8 should be made from ³⁄₄-inch wood. For this boat I built a jig long enough to lay up both hull halves at once, so things moved along pretty quickly. Once you've cut the sheer and glued the halves together, you can fair the sheer, mark the stations on top of the hull, then trace the deck template on the top and shape the hull to this line at the sheer using a block plane. (To keep things simple, we'll call this top edge of the hull the sheer for now; later we'll fair *Mite*'s actual sheerline on her bulwarks.) Redraw station marks on the outside of the hull at the sheer and on the keel area, if any are missing. Glue a stick in the hull for holding it in your vise, and you're ready to carve. Turn the hull upside down in your vise and mark the width of the keel (³⁄₈ inch; refer to Sheet 4). Before you begin carving the hull, mark a ¹⁄₄-inch line parallel to the sheer all around hull for the guardrail to follow (see Sheet 4). The body templates you'll use when carving the hull show the flat area around the hull sides at the sheer for the guardrail, which will appear when you're cutting the deck line flat to the sides.

When you've shaped the hull to your satisfaction, checking for fairness with the body templates, cut out the backbone in one piece and fit it to the hull as done in the previous chapters. Put in *Mite*'s 14 deckbeams, one at each station; you'll have to let them into the sides of the hull, as done for *Pauline*. Once the glue has hardened, you can camber them if you want, though it's not necessary. If you do camber them, make your own almost flat crowing board similar to *Pauline*'s or *Laura B.*'s, then fair the deck beams fore-and-aft with a fairing batten.

The inner stem, where the forward towing bitt will be mounted later, goes in next. See Sheets 1 and 4 for the plan view. The inner stem is cut so its sides are kept back enough to form the rabbet for the bulwark, the end of which is butted against the outer stem. Bevel the bottom of the inner stem 10 degrees to match the fore-and-aft slope of the deck, then glue and clamp it in place.

Deck, Bulwarks, Railcap, and Guardrails

Even out the deck with a spokeshave, getting the high spots off and finish with 100-grit sandpaper followed by 220 grit, then 320. You can sand by hand or with the sandpaper stuck to a crowning board if you prefer. As described for *Pauline*, lay the deck in individual planks, starting from the centerline and sanding the plank edges for caulking seams. I made the deck planking from white cedar, ¹⁄₁₆ inch thick by a strong ¹⁄₈ inch wide; in hindsight, I realize I could have made the strips from maple scrounged from a tabletop. To allow for the waist bulwarks (the midships and forward sections of the bulwarks), you'll need to recess the deck about ⅛ inch in from the outside of the hull—or whatever thickness you are going to make the waist bulwarks. Bear in mind there'll be a transition where the waist bulwarks notch into the stern bulwark. For the builders of full-size wooden tugs, this was a common practice for joining pieces that bent into pieces that didn't. Lapping the joint allowed one bulwark to flow into the other in a nice, smooth bend that was amply supported.

To make the stern bulwark, lay the plan view of the bulwarks (see Sheet 1) on a piece of wood 1¼ inch thick by 6 inches square. Cut to the bulwarks' outboard shapes, right on the line; cut the inner shape much wider than the finished look you see on Sheet 1 for now. Lay the stern bulwark in place on the deck and, using dividers, scribe it to fit the deck's slight camber. Mark the sheer height at each station on the bulwark and fair them with a batten; you'll cut to this line later, after dry-fitting both the stern and waist bulwarks in place. Cut the ends of the stern bulwark to length at Station 10. Now trace the top inboard and outboard shape of the bulwarks from the plan view on Sheet 1. Notch the ends of the stern bulwark ⅛ inch deep, ¾ inch aft from Station 10, to catch the ends of the waist bulwarks.

Cut the rake of the stern bulwark and spring a piece of cardboard in the deck edge rabbet for a waist bulwark template. Mark each station and its height. To help the job along, cut the waist bulwark pattern out of the plans and tick each station's height from it, then fair all from the bow through to the centerline of the stern bulwark with a batten. You may have to do more fiddling with the rake of the stern bulwark, so take your time here, cut and fair a little at a time. Cut the guardrail to the shape shown in profile on Sheet 1. Use basswood and make the guardrail long enough to go on in one piece, same as *Pauline*'s. Heat-bend it or soak it in ammonia and, starting at the stern, wrap it around the hull. Fasten the guardrail with pins then glue it with instant glue.

There are two ways to make the railcap: either by springing two narrow strips around the bulwark, one inside and one outside; or by fitting the railcap in one piece to the top of the bulwarks, marking its shape from underneath around the hull, same as *Pauline*'s. If you use the first method (I did), the sheer is going to look lower because the rails come to the top of the bulwark. If you set the rail on top, you'll increase the height of the sheer by that amount; round the railcap to suit.

Now is the time to cut the five limber holes in the waist bulwarks using a Dremel tool. This is a little tricky; you'll need to be careful not to mar the deck in the process, since the bottoms of the limber holes sit level with the deck. I wouldn't recommend cutting them in the bulwarks beforehand—not only would you have to be expert at getting them right, but you'd run the risk of breaking the bulwarks while bending them, as a result of some unseen poor grain.

Pilothouse

You can make *Mite*'s pilothouse in one piece out of a block of wood, or use the plan view and profile templates to make a hollow one. Both ways are shown in the photos. If you decide to build a solid pilothouse, use the templates as they are. If a hollow, planked-up house is your choice, you'll need to take off the template the thickness of the wood you're going to use. Either way, you'll want to start with a solid plug first.

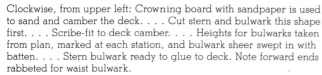

Clockwise, from upper left: Crowning board with sandpaper is used to sand and camber the deck. . . . Cut stern and bulwark this shape first. . . . Scribe-fit to deck camber. . . . Heights for bulwarks taken from plan, marked at each station, and bulwark sheer swept in with batten. . . . Stern bulwark ready to glue to deck. Note forward ends rabbeted for waist bulwark.

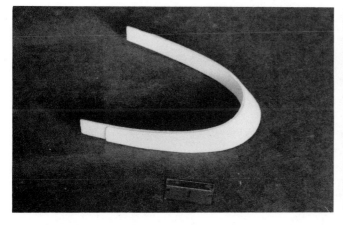

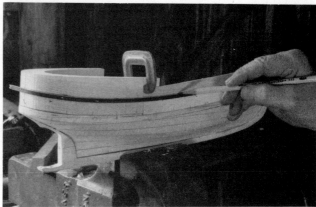

Start by making templates of the plan and profile views of the pilothouse minus the roof. Measure the overall height of the house from the deck and its width and length, and cut a square block a little larger than these total dimensions. Draw centerlines on the block vertically and horizontally for locating the two views of the pilothouse. Cut the profile shape out first, then the plan view. Cut and sand the plug carefully so as to keep the ends and edges crisp. Fit the plug to the cambered deck by hollowing underneath the plug slightly.

Most of the old wooden tugs had horizontal planking on the aft portion of the house and vertical planking for the forward portion, so it would easily accommodate the round shape. I chose vertical planking (staves) for the whole job since it was easier and looks better to my eye; besides, I'd just as soon avoid running the planks in two directions, because making a clean transition might produce a hard spot instead of a nice, even bend.

If you've decided on a planked pilothouse, first you'll need to draw the outlines of all the windows and doors and ports right on the plug. *Mite's* house has four doors with windows, six windows in the pilothouse, and eight ports. Assembling the doors from scratch is a bit of work, but it's this kind of stuff that makes the model come alive. Make a jig for the doors, cut all their pieces out, assemble them, pin them to the plug right where they're drawn, and plank around them.

For your planking, saw out a bunch of ³/₃₂-inch × ¹/₄-inch (real measure) staves of various lengths of basswood, cedar, or pine, and go for it. Start planking at the aft end of the crew's quarters. I used superglue for gluing the doors and for planking the house, because you can work real clean with it, avoiding any buildup that would take time to scrape off.

Experience will tell you what kind of glue to use and where and when to use it. Also, you'll learn a thing or two about how much to use after you've spent an hour removing built-up glue from a fitting in a very conspicuous but hard-to-reach spot.

As for the six windows, you can either cut them in roughly, smaller than you want, as you plank up the pilothouse, then neaten them up after the glue has dried, or you can plank the whole front and cut the windows in later. Don't waste your time trying to line up the staves for each window precisely. Here's how I did it: I sanded the ends of the staves flush to the top of the plug; then, with a combination square set for the top and bottom heights of the windows, I scribed their locations from the top of the plug. After the glue has set, pull the pilothouse out from the plug enough to clear the windows and rough out their openings with a woodhog stuck in a Dremel tool; this works fast and smooth without chatter. Then finish them square with needle files. Use acetate in the windows and airports, glued with a carefully applied dite of instant glue from off the head of a ground-down needle.

Now you can doll her up in grand style—as simple or elaborate as you have skill and patience for.

Should you wish to put a raised floor inside the pilothouse, you can use the top of the plug for the floor pattern. Scribe its height on the inside of the house. I use a sliding-clip depth gauge for this (see "Tools" in the Introduction), and it works great. The floor of the crew's quarters is the deck itself.

Since the pilothouse has so many windows and ports, it's well lighted by natural light. This makes it worthwhile to finish off its interior somewhat. You can make a stanchion for the steering wheel and a shelf for the helmsman's compass, and put in throttle and shift controls, if you want. These and anything else need to go in before you glue the pilothouse roof on—including the helmsman, captain, mate, or what have you. I happen to think having somebody aboard helps liven a model up, but this is a matter of choice. I put a captain in *Mite's* pilothouse, but some purist might say I've ruined the model for sure.

Little people of the right scale, that resemble sailors, are hard to come by. But you can find small space men, baseball players, and other varieties, and—

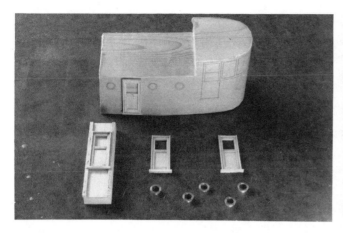

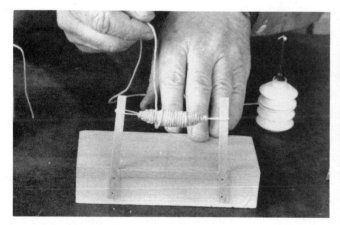

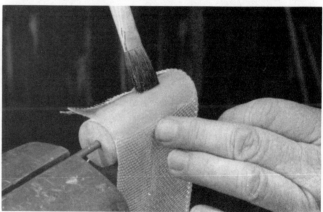

Clockwise, from upper left: Pilothouse plug covered with waxed paper. Doors pinned in place waiting to be planked around. . . . Pull assembly partway off plug and round portholes, file window openings, etc. . . . Pull house assembly from plug and glue to hull. . . . Making the stack: Wrap waxed paper around dowel and layup stack with 3-inch glass tape. . . . Temporary frame to hold bow pudding layup.

with a Dremel tool and a little ingenuity—make them over into salty sailors. I cut a piece of paper that represented a 6-foot-tall captain at ³/₈-inch scale, and went hunting in the kids' toy section of our local department stores. Much to my delight I found "Attack Leader Sgt. Borek of Star Com." Not only was he just the right height—about 2¼ inches—but his arms moved and his hands came already perfectly curved to fit naturally and precisely around the spokes of the ⁷/₈-inch-diameter wheel in the pilothouse.

The first kid into my shop got Sgt. Borek's miniature pistol. Using my Dremel tool, I gave Sgt. Borek himself a pretty complete remodeling job, removing his air pack, helmet, and all his square pockets. He ended up with an English-style cap, a beard, a yellow slicker, and I managed to turn his space boots into fisherman's boots by cutting his legs off with a synthetic rope-cutting heat gun. Put a shelf in the pilothouse to mount the 7/8-inch wheel, stick Sgt. Borek in, then put on the roof of the pilothouse, as shown or to suit. Sgt. Borek looks quite proper now in my pilothouse with both hands curled around the spokes; and, with his feet glued firmly to the floor, I expect he'll stay at his post.

It pays to think about everything you're going to add on, and in, the house before you put the roof on and seal it up. And don't glue the pilothouse to the deck until you're sure you're done adding stuff. I learned my lesson when building *Pauline*: After putting the floor in and the roof on her pilothouse, I sealed it up. Then I decided to put on a cowl ventilator. Without thinking, I drilled a hole for it (with power at that) and spewed wood dust all over the inside of the pilothouse, that was no longer reachable, and that I had so carefully cleaned before sealing it. Fortunately, the cowl ventilator on the tug is no problem because the crew's quarters has no floor until the house is glued to the deck.

Stack, Rudder, and Towing Bitts

Mite's stack finishes 1 1/8 inch in diameter by 3 inches, and rakes with the front of the pilothouse. You can make this from a dowel or lay it up out of fiberglass around a dowel—or anything else that's the right size. I wrapped waxed paper around a 1-inch dowel (I drove a nail in the end of the dowel to hold it in the vise), then wrapped a couple of layers of 3-inch fiberglass tape around it, then glued a plug in the bottom of the stack so I could glue it to the roof. Before the resin set up I wrapped another layer of waxed paper around the glass tape, and let it stay there until the resin cured. This gives a smooth, finished look to the outside of the stack, requiring little sanding. Leave the stack on the dowel while you work on it, as this comes in handy for holding it in the vise. Use 3M autobody glazing putty for minor dings or air pockets.

While waiting for the stack layup to cure, you can make the rudder and fit the propeller. The propeller's diameter, 1 1/2 inches at 3/8-inch scale, translates to 3 feet 6 inches in real life. I didn't like the pointy end on the propeller I bought from BlueJacket Shipcrafters, so I filed a "hexagon nut" on it. For an outboard motor a prop with a faired end is OK, but you seldom see one on a workboat.

Next cut out the rudder template and make the rudder. At full size it'd be 5 inches thick, so make it 5/32 inch thick to scale, without taper. For a rudderpost, you'll need to fit a piece of brazing rod or brass about 3/32 inch into a hole that you drill in the rudder. You can see about where to drill the hole from the way the rudder sits on the skeg and horn timber; there's nothing critical in its location. You'll need a Dremel drill press or some kind of accurate drilling equipment for this job (see the rudder profile on Sheet 1). To hold the rudder perfectly vertical for boring, saw out (on your table saw) a couple of blocks 2 inches or so square, set the blocks on the drill stand table so they're offset to form a right angle, and press the rudder in the corner. Bore about halfway through, then turn the rudder and bore halfway from the opposite end.

Now for the towing bitts, or bollards—five of them, including the short one at the stem. From a 1/4-inch dowel, cut four 1 5/16-inch lengths and a shorter one, 5/16 inch, to sit on top of the inner stem. Then cut 1/16-inch slices off a 5/16-inch dowel to glue on top of the bits to cap them. I cut these on my table saw using a sharp planer blade. Cut them almost through, then finish the cut with a razor saw. You can't cut them clear through with power, because they'll go flying, never to be seen again—at least in my shop. Glue these "lips" on the bits with epoxy; while you're at it, pour a little epoxy on top of them to fill their end grain and harden them for filing.

To make bases for the bits that sit on deck, bore two 1/4-inch holes, 9/16 inch apart on centers, in a block of wood about 7/8 inch × 2 1/2 inches × 1 inch or more deep; then cut off two 1/8-inch slices. Trim the sides of the block equally so it now measures 5/8 inch × 1 7/8 inches, and cut two more 1/8-inch slices for the top plates. Taper the bases from their centers out to their edges. Glue the bits at their bases and insert them into the holes. The forward bit on the inner stem sits at a 90-degree angle so you'll have to bevel its bottom before gluing. Finish them off by filing the lips with a flat needle file.

For an authentic look, you can show how the tow lines (hawsers) would wear the edges of the top plates. I copied the wear patterns from the photos in the book *On the Hawser*. The reason these top plates sit in profile well above the bulwarks is so the tow line clears the bulwarks to avoid chafing them. In case you're wondering, the aft bollards are up next to the crew's quarters so the tug's stern is free to turn when towing. (If the bollards were at the extreme end of the stern, the tug couldn't be steered.)

Pudding

Anytime you're waiting for glue to harden or paint to dry is a good time for making *Mite's* bow fender. Why it's called "pudding," I have no idea—other than the fact that it's made to cushion the bow. Some of the old tugs had worn-out tires for fenders, while others, perhaps because their crews were more ambitious and talented, had elaborate rope fenders and bow "puddings" made up out of rope. With a sail needle and fine laid nylon, I spent an evening making a scale pudding for *Mite*, the simplest way I could. It's nothing but a continuous round of half hitches stitched together, but looks great.

While beachcombing as a kid, I once found a tug fender made like that, and I was so intrigued, I decided I'd learn how to do it. I didn't get around to it until years later, when I kept dropping my thermos bottle while lobstering. After breaking its glass liner enough times, I finally buckled down to learning how to make a fender-style covering for the thermos. This did the trick, offering enough padding that I never broke another liner.

Mind you, this was more than 20 years ago. When it came time to do it again for *Mite's* bow, I was totally lost—I'd completely forgotten, and none of the local sea dogs could help either. Fortunately *Ashley's Book of Knots* came to the rescue—although Mr. Ashley sort of rubbed it in, I thought, when he said, "Hitching is the simplest form of sailor's decoration."

To get your fender started, wrap a paper pattern around the bow to measure how far aft you want the beckets (rope loops) of the fender to land on the bulwarks, then eyeball the length you want for the fender itself. Lay out a continuous loop of fine nylon line for the beckets and tie it off with a knot around the middle. It helps to stretch the loop on a simple frame, as you can see in the photo. Then, starting at the loop's center, wrap it with cheap twine to whatever shape appeals to your eye. I used a kind of fuzzy, soft, tan string and wound it heavier in the middle, tapering to the ends. I glued this with Franklin Titebond, then wrapped it around the bow to let it harden to this shape before covering it with the ropework.

Like everything else, it sure is simple when you know how. Here's how to work the half hitches: First, starting with one long single line, tie a single loop—snugly, not too loose—around the middle of the fender. Then simply stitch half hitches completely around this loop. This first bunch of hitches will need to be spaced just right for going around again. If they're too close together, you won't have enough room to go through them to make the next row and the next. If you don't start with enough hitches, the twine—or whatever you're covering—isn't going to look well covered, but full of holes. Working the hitches is a matter of eye and touch. Drop or add hitches as needed to provide an even covering; you'll find you need to decrease gradually as you work toward the tapered end. After working from the middle of the fender and finishing at the end of the taper, tie the line and cut it off, then go back to the middle and pick up the loop you first started with. Start hitching from here, and work your way to the other end.

The hitching itself goes slowly, but it's easy. Somehow it all flows together in a simple, beautiful pattern that any old sea dog will admire. It took me all evening to stitch this small fender . . . but stepping back in time to recover something I'd lost was a real pleasure.

To make this lily-white nylon look like the real thing, mix up some strong (mud, almost) instant coffee and paint the whole pudding with a small brush.

The other kind of bow fender or pudding, which looks like a lion's mane or a buffalo's head with all the fag ends hanging out, is made differently. You're on your own if you want to make this style of fender. I was quite content to learn the one way.

Painting and Finishing

With all the major woodwork finished, all that's left for trim is to put finish trim around the roof if it wasn't done before.

Running lights, a searchlight, and a cowl ventilator complete the outfitting for this model. I made the running lights and searchlight myself from Plexiglas by turning them on my Dremel lathe, just as I did for *Pauline*. I bought a cowl ventilator from BlueJacket, and painted its outside flat black with a touch of gray in it—the same as the hull—and its inside red. Make and paint all these parts and fittings separately before mounting them on the house.

Before rigging guys, you'll need to finish the stack. First plug the bottom of the stack with a piece of wood. Then make a lip for the very top of the stack. Starting with a strip of basswood about 1/16 inch × 1/32 inch, you can wet it with your tongue, wrap it around a dowel smaller than the stack, and let it dry slightly; then uncurl it, spring it around the top of the stack, and glue it in place. Then paint the stack—I used the same flat black for this as for the cowl vent and the topsides—and glue it to the house.

I guyed off the stack with seven-strand rigging wire fastened to 1/2-inch

Mite on the beach. Pleasingly powerful.

brass eyes, bought from BlueJacket. The problem here is, how do you tighten the wires without turnbuckles? I found that using a combination of undersize holes, wire that stretched a bit, and a spot of glue did the trick. First I bored undersize holes for the eyes that go in the stack. Rather than boring holes for the eyes that go in the house, I made a shallow prick with an awl, cut the eyes short enough so they wouldn't go through the roof, and stuck them in with a drop of hot glue aligning them in the direction of the stack. I cut the eyes for the stack about 3/16 inch long, shoved their shanks through their undersized holes, then pulled them back out so they just barely hung in the stack. I wound wires in the eyes as taut as I could get them by hand, then pushed the stack eyes in with their heads flush to the stack, thus tightening the wires almost as taut as a fiddlestring. A drop of superglue applied on their shanks inside the stack held them there.

Now you're ready to paint the hull. Seal it first with a 50-50 mix of shellac and alcohol or B-I-N, or your own concoction. Before the bottom paint goes on, you'll need to strike the waterline. Note that the waterline shown on the plans isn't the one to paint to, even though it's a lift line and would be handy. Instead, mark the waterline 3/16 inch above it for the top of the bottom paint. This is easy to do with a block of wood and a pencil. Finding a level spot isn't so easy; a good place might be your table saw, if you have one. Set the model so it's level fore-and-aft and athwartships, and mark the waterline lightly with a pencil. You'll need narrow masking tape (about 1/8 inch wide) to follow the waterline around the stern in a nice, fair curve, and wider tape (about 1/4 inch) for along the straighter parts of the hull from the bow back to Station 10 or so. Auto supply stores sell "racing" tape that does the job nicely.

This color scheme is just a suggestion; vary it to suit yourself. I mixed in a touch of gray to soften the dense black a bit, making it more the color of metal. Also, I used a touch of gray with white to avoid a brilliant white, and mixed a tad of black with the red to darken it for the pilothouse.

While waiting for the paint to set up is a good time to make the cradle. I made the cradle from Masonite, using the body templates for Stations 4 and 10,

Color Scheme:

Hull bottom, copper
Hull sides and bulwarks, flat black
Inside of bulwarks, gray
Deck, gray paint or clear stain
Pilothouse, red or maroon
House roof, gray, with white trim
Bitts, flat black
Lettering, white

and glued a couple of dowels lengthwise to hold the support pieces the right distance apart.

Paint the propeller the color of brass, and she's done, except for her name and port of hail. I used 18-point Clarendon Bold as a lettering style, and bent a strip of paper around the bulwark for a guide for spacing. (See the Introduction, "Lettering Transom Names," for tips on using transfer lettering on a model.)

5

William Underwood
A 1940s State-of-the-Art Sardine Carrier

A 1941 copy of *Atlantic Fisherman* blares the headline, *"William Underwood Joins Sardine Fleet"*—and goes on to record her construction, launching, and some of her history. I'll let the article speak for itself:

A noteworthy addition to the Maine sardine fleet, the William Underwood *slipped gracefully off the ways at Simms Bros. Yard, Dorchester, Massachusetts, on April 12.*

She was christened by Miss Helen Underwood, great-great-granddaughter of the founder of the William Underwood Company, for whom the vessel was named.

Practically the entire personnel of the Underwood headquarters office in Watertown, Massachusetts, were present, including the following officials: William J. Underwood, F. A. Harding, general manager; W. B. Durant, production manager; and Harry Wells, sales manager.

The new craft, usually known as a sardine carrier or smack, is outstanding in design, construction, and equipment. She incorporates many desirable features which should make her well adapted to sardine carrying service.

The William Underwood *was designed by Eldredge-McInnis, Inc. and has an overall length of 70 feet 7 inches, waterline length of 63 feet 3 inches, beam of 15 feet 6 inches, and draft of 5 feet 11 inches. She has a 'double-ender'-type hull, is framed with oak and planked with yellow pine.*

Materials Needed

- 22 running feet of 3″ × ³/₄″ basswood or pine
- one-half 4′ × 8′ sheet of ¹/₈″ tempered Masonite (smooth both sides)
- 2′ × 1′ × ¹/₁₆″ aircraft plywood
- spray adhesive
- Weldwood plastic resin glue
- superglue
- ³/₈″ #6 brass ribbon pins
- assorted rigging supplies: eight single blocks and one double, all ⁷/₃₂″; two eyebands; 10′ of seven-strand wire rigging; 10′ of three-strand nylon string; one spool of 23-gauge brass wire
- assorted fittings: one ⁵/₈″ deck plate; one ⁵/₁₆″ air port; one ¹/₂″ and two ¹/₄″ cowl ventilators; one length of ¹/₈″ aluminum tubing for Cape Anne stovepipe; one 1¹/₂″ kedge anchor; one 1¹/₄″ right-handed propeller; two ⁷/₈″ liferings; one ⁷/₈″ steering wheel; one ¹/₁₆″ aluminum tubing for overflow pipe for deck pumps; four ¹/₄″ hawse lips
- full-size plans

Tools Needed

- table saw
- bandsaw
- vise
- clamps
- ⁷/₈″ or 1″ gouge with inside bevel
- low-angle block plane
- spokeshave
- sanding fid with 60- and 100-grit sandpaper
- sanding battens
- rasps
- Dremel tool with drills
- needle and riffler files
- rattail files
- 10″ mill file
- combination square (small if possible)
- #3 pencil
- scissors

The fish hold, located amidships and divided into two tanks, each with a hatch, has a capacity of 1,000 bushels or 80,000 pounds. It has a concrete floor, portable fore and aft pen boards, two gurry troughs, and a pump-well.

The fo'c's'le has the usual galley equipment and bunks for four, while the pilothouse has one bunk. The lazarette has access through a deck hatch and from a door in the engineroom. The underside of the main deck and engineroom trunk are soundproofed. The mainmast is 39 feet from heel to truck and the gaff 16 feet from jaws to end. Auxiliary sails are provided.

Power is furnished by a model MRD-6 Superior Diesel, 5¹/₂ × 7, developing 150 hp, at 1,500 rpm with a 3:1 Twin Disc reverse and reduction gear. Pilothouse clutch and throttle control is provided. Fuel capacity is 500 gallons, with two tanks located port and starboard in the engineroom.

There is a specially designed 32-volt Exide starting battery for cranking the engine, in addition to a 32-volt Exide Ironclad battery for general lighting. These two batteries can be inter-connected by means of a switch so that in an emergency either battery can be used for service.

The Diesel generating set is of United States Motors make and consists of a 1-cylinder, 3-KW unit. The engineroom has a CO_2 fire protection system. Steering gear comprises an Edson bronze reduction gear type steerer connected to the quadrant with 5/8 flexible tiller ropes, running under deck, and an Edson 36-inch-diameter, combination AC heavy-duty wheel.

A 42-inch × 34-inch, three-blade Hyde propeller turns on a 3-inch Tobin-bronze shaft, with Hathaway flax-packed stern bearing. There are two Edson No. 2 non-chokable deck-style hand bilge pumps, arranged to pump bilge from each fish tank and from the manifold.Ferdico Seamseal seam filler was used for all seams throughout the boat, while New Jersey paint was used on the bottom and Dulux white on the topsides. Among other items of equipment on the boat are Shipmate range, Kelvin-White spherical compass, Tapatco life preservers, and Sands pump-type water closet.

The William Underwood *will hail from Jonesport, Maine, and will be in command of Captain Ernest Wolfe. She will join the company's fleet of five other boats, namely:* Kingfisher, Roamer, FishHawk, Alice, *and* Mooseabec.

This year the William Underwood Company is celebrating its 120th anniversary. It was a pioneer in the packing of seafood products, having started canning lobsters in 1844, oysters in 1850, and sardines in the late '80s. The company's seafood line now includes sardines, clam chowder, fish chowder, quahog chowder, clams, clam juice, and fish cakes.

Plants for the processing of seafood products are located at Jonesport and McKinley [now Bass Harbor], Maine, the former managed by Vernon McFadden and the latter by Vernon H. Latty.

For the information on the *William Underwood's* launching as well as her plans for public use, I thank Alan McInnis for his kindness and generosity. And we can thank Arthur R. Herrick, Jr., of Westmoreland, New Hampshire, for his skill and patience in redrawing these exquisitely detailed plans at 3/8 inch = 1 foot scale for modeling.

Building the *William Underwood* is basically the same as building *Pauline*, but with enough differences to keep it interesting. You'll note that the *Underwood* is much more yachty-looking. Her pilothouse rakes back, and the top is crowned in two directions. She has buffalo rails on her railcap at both ends (*Pauline* has one set of buffalo rails forward). All in all, the *Underwood* is more finely finished.

Building the Hull

The *Underwood's* hull is made of six waterline lifts: five of them are 3/4 inch thick, and the top, bow lift (Lift 6) is 1 inch (see Sheet 3). Since the waterline lifts are fewer and wider, compared to most of the other models in this book, it would be easy to flatten hard, curved areas—around the turn of the bilge, for example—by carving away too much. To help you control the hull shape, there are 21 body section templates to use as guides. Look at these carefully before starting to carve.

Note also, on Sheet 1 of the plans , the mean low waterline and the load waterline (LWL). The mean low waterline runs through the hull parallel to the other waterlines, but you can see on the plans that the top of the bottom paint on the full-size boat is 10 inches higher than the mean low waterline at the bow and 6½ inches higher at the stern. The idea is that when the sardine carrier is loaded down with her haul, she'll "float to her lines," with the top of the bottom

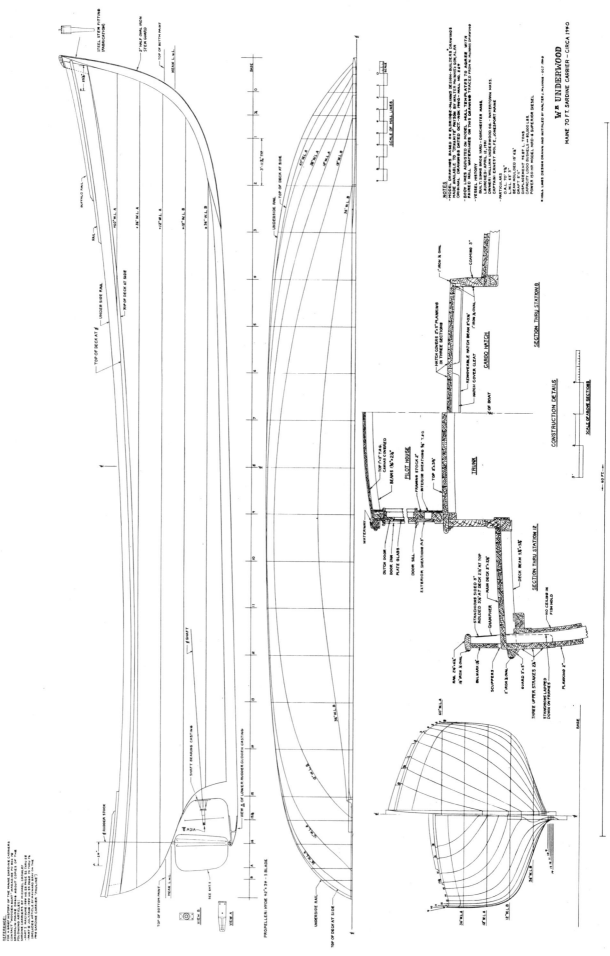

Sheet 1

Enlarge plan 300 percent for full-size plans.

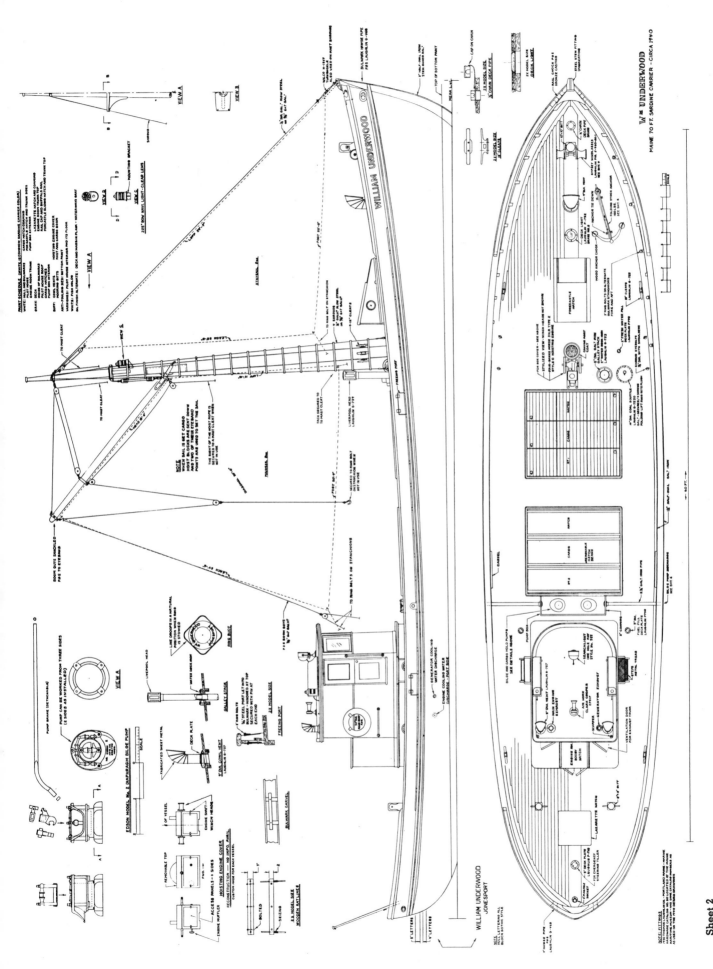

Sheet 2

Enlarge plan 300 percent for full-size plans.

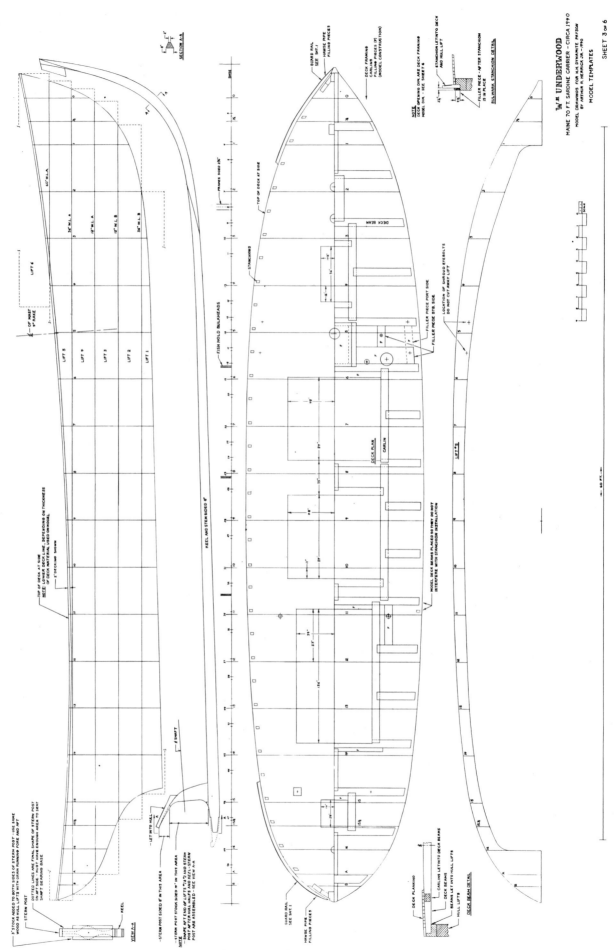

Sheet 3

Enlarge plan 300 percent for full-size plans.

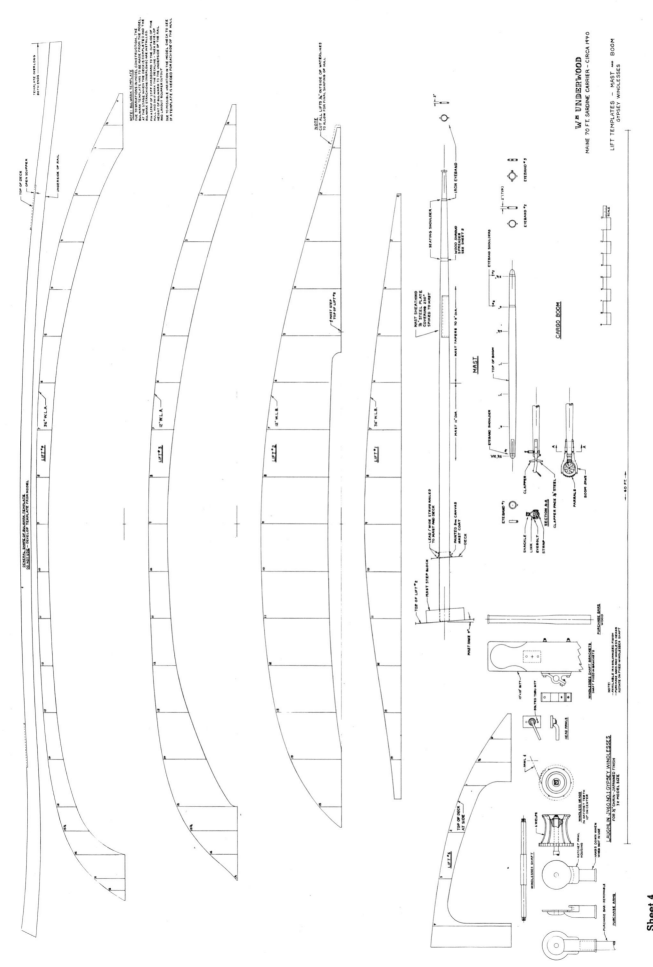

Sheet 4

Enlarge plan 300 percent for full-size plans.

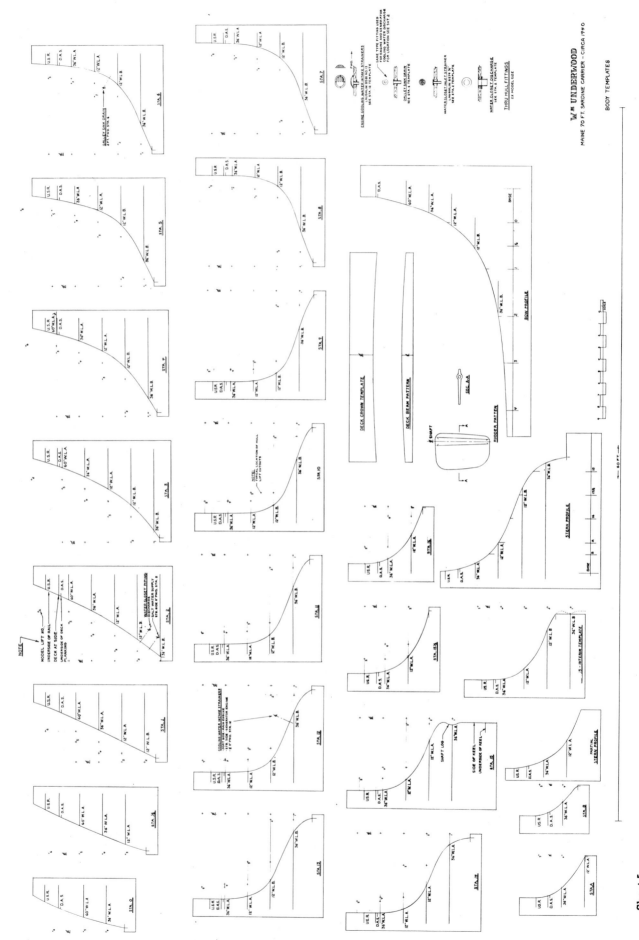

Sheet 5
Enlarge plan 300 percent for full-size plans.

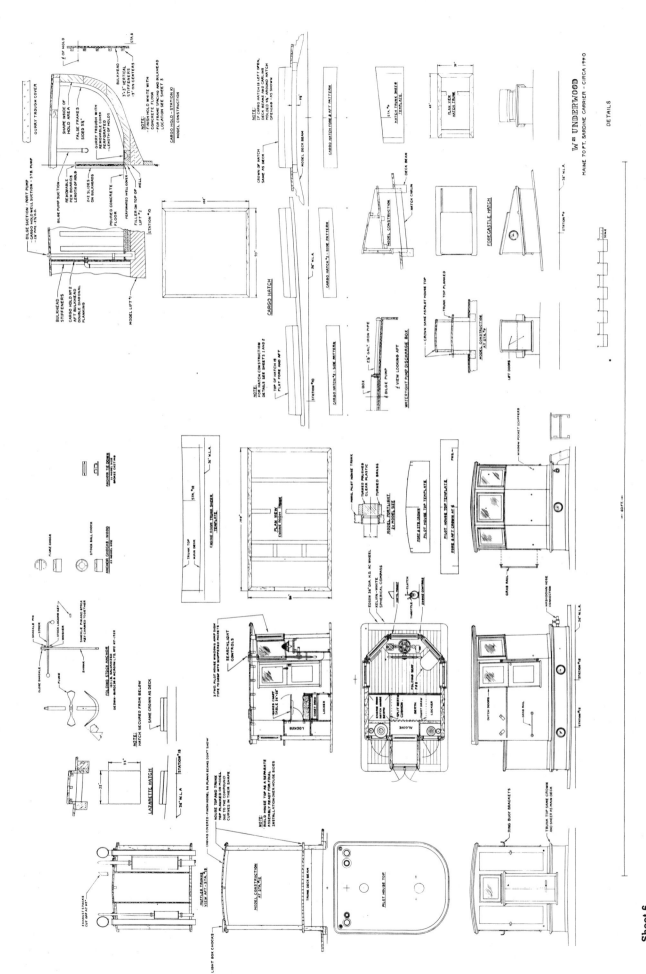

Sheet 6
Enlarge plan 300 percent for full-size plans.

paint at the level of the water. Mark the load waterline on the ends of the hull as soon as you can for later reference; just a slight cut with a razor saw will do it.

Following the steps described in the previous chapters, cut out the templates and lay up the mirror-image hull halves. Glue the *Underwood*'s waterline lifts on the jig, aligning Station 9 with the jig's plumb line. After the glue has hardened, lay the hull profile on the stack, matching waterline to waterline and Station 9 with Station 9. Mark the hull profile all around and spot the sheer on the inside of the hull with a combination square. If you're confident, cut the profile free-hand on the bandsaw, making sure the outside cut is higher; as I've mentioned earlier, tipping your saw table 2 or 3 degrees will take care of this. If the idea of free-handing on the bandsaw makes you nervous, cut the sheer by hand.

Work the sheer down on each half hull and the rest of the profile down close to the line. Measure the keel (backbone) width from the plans and scribe it, one-half of the rabbet to scale, on each half from the stemhead back to the aft end of the hull to the sternpost. Glue the two halves together and finish working the sheer down to the line of dots. When you're satisfied that the sheer is fair, lay on the deck template and match its forward stations with the ones on the model; then trace the deck shape back to Station 9. Move the template aft to match the aft stations, and trace the template forward to Station 9. Cut the hull sides to this shape, right to the line.

With the sheer faired, the deck shape established, and the keel width marked on the hull, you can begin carving the hull. First, to hold her in your vise, glue a stick of wood (about 3/4 inch thick and of suitable width and length) into her bilge. Checking carefully as you go with the body section templates, carve away the excess wood at each station between the keel rabbet and the sheer. Be sure you've marked each station clearly on the hull, so you'll know exactly where to hold the body templates, square to the centerline of the hull, to check for fairness and accuracy.

A spokeshave, a rasp, a block plane, and a gouge with an inside bevel are all handy for carving the hull. You'll also need a tapered sanding fid for sanding the tuck (the area near the sternpost) and long, flexible battens with sandpaper of various grits for final fairing of the hull (see the Introduction, "Tools"). After the hull is sanded smooth to her lines, cut out the backbone—keel and stem—in one piece and glue it to the hull.

Now you're ready to scribe the load waterline (LWL), which you've already marked on the ends of the hull. First mount a good, sharp pencil with strips of masking tape to a squared-off block of wood. Set the model right-side up on the upturned jig or a suitable level surface, and use wedges and shims as needed to trim the boat fore-and-aft so the pencil touches the LWL marks at each end. Level the boat athwartships (across her beam) and gently scribe the waterline. Immediately after doing this, seal the hull with a coat of varnish—right out of the can is fine. (You can do it the other way around if you want, putting the varnish sealer on first. If you do, sand the varnish down first, or your pencil point will dull in one short pass, making a wide, inaccurate waterline.)

Taper the stem from the body view on Sheet 1 if you haven't done it already.

Next comes the cradle, so you can hold the model in the vise while you install the deck beams. Using the body templates for Stations 5 and 12 as patterns, set up from the baseline to the height of the keel as shown on Sheet 1, cut the cradle arms out of 3/4-inch scrap and glue them to the base the proper distance apart as shown in profile. Put felt or masking tape on the cradle where the hull bears, for cushioning, so you won't mar the hull while working on it.

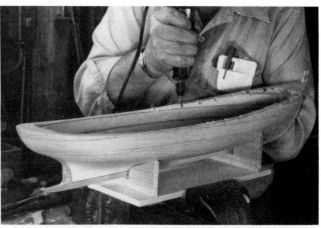

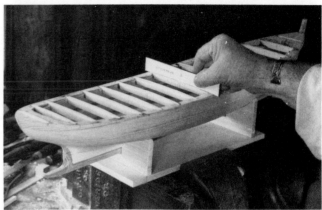

Clockwise, from upper left: Hull leveled athwartships; marking waterline. . . . Cutting loose pockets for ends of deckbeams. . . . Pull each deck beam up flush to crowning board. . . . Beveling edges of deck planking. . . . Fitting decking to covering board all in one pass.

Deck beams are next, but before putting them in, locate the center for the maststep, shown on the hull profile template (Sheet 3). Unless you're a purist, you don't need to make an elaborate maststep; simply bore a 5/64-inch hole in the centerline of Lift 2 for the brass pin or nail, which you'll later slip in the foot of the mast.

Deck Beams

Deck beam locations are shown on Sheet 3, along with the openings for the hatches, the pilothouse, etc. You'll install the deck beams all in one piece, then cut out sections later for the deck openings when you fit the fore-and-aft carlins.

First cut the deck beam template and deck crown template (crowning board) from Sheet 5. Make 17 deck beams and number them. With a Dremel tool, bore loose cavities in the hull sides, as shown, to bury their ends. Then mix some Weldwood glue to a stiff consistency and plop the deck beams in place. As the glue starts to harden, place the crowning board across the hull with its centerline aligned with the centerline of the hull, and adjust the beams as needed to bring the top of each deck beam flush to the underside of the crowning board. Keep checking to see that the deck beams stay in place while the glue hardens. The important thing is to center the deck beams and bring their ends even with the sheer. It doesn't matter if they're a dite askew sideways, so don't panic if you later spot one glued in that way, hard as a rock. Sand their tops fore and aft with a fairing batten to equalize them before laying the deck.

The easiest and most accurate way to make the deck openings for the pilothouse, hatches, etc., is to use the deck template (Sheet 3). Cut out the openings in the template, then trace them on top of the deck beams. Doing this locates the exact cuts you need to make in the deck beams for the carlins. Extend the lines of the openings across the hull and mark them on the lifts. Use these marks to square the fore-and-aft sides of the openings. Make the carlins about ¼ inch thick and cut the ends of the deck beams back for them accordingly; this is far easier and a whole lot faster than boxing the ends of the beams into the carlins, as shown on the plans (this is how the full-size boat was built). Just butt the carlins to the deck beams; use glue and pins to "nail" them into the ends of the deck beams. Once you've laid the deck, nothing will be going anywhere. Of course, if you want to take the trouble of boxing the beams into the carlins, go ahead.

The Deck

Cut the decking a scant ⅛ inch wide × ¹⁄₁₆ inch thick (see Sheet 2)—all except for the kingplank, which runs the length of the centerline from stem to stern; cut it a strong ⁷⁄₁₆ inch in width (at ⅜-inch scale, this corresponds to 14½ inches on the full-size boat). This is the kind of situation in modeling where you're free to take liberties: you can do without the kingplank if you wish, with planks all the same width; nobody would fault you for it unless you were building the model for a museum.

To saw out these 40 or so strips (saw extra), first cut ⅛-inch slices (the width of the planks) a couple of inches longer than the hull and an inch or two wide. Lay the slices on the table saw, and saw off the ¹⁄₁₆-inch-thick planks one by one. With a good, sharp planer blade, this is no job at all, and sawing the planks one at a time works better than stacking a bunch of slices and trying to saw a whole bunch of decking in one pass.

I started out with sugar pine but decided I didn't like the grain, so I threw

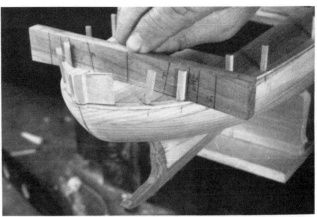

Clockwise, from upper left: Marking inboard location of stanchions. . . . Crowning board with stanchion angles marked. . . . Making your own bulwark template. . . . Putting on starboard bulwark. Note ends are pre-bent. . . . Fitting railcap.

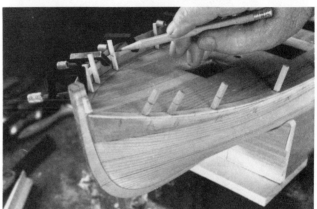

away the planks I'd cut and cut a new batch out of basswood, which gave me much crisper edges, smoother cuts, and, best of all, beautiful, fine-grained decking that when finished looks as nice as maple.

With a modeler's miniature block plane, bevel the edges of each deck plank. This isn't hard to do if you use a piece of scrap the same length and thickness (hold it in place with masking tape) to back the deck strip while planing. Give each edge a swipe or whatever it takes to make a clean bevel, and you're all set to lay the deck.

Note on the plans that the decking is nibbed into the inner side of the covering board. This amount of detail is more work than I have patience for, so I did it the easy way by fitting the decking to the covering board, and let it go at that. Even this may seem like a big job, but it isn't. To make the covering board, trace its shape from the deck template onto a piece of wood wide enough to reach the centerline at the hull's greatest beam and thick enough so you can saw out two mirror-image halves just under $1/4$ inch thick (this translates to $7^{1}/_{2}$ inches at full scale). You can fit the two halves of the covering board to the model just like on the plans, or ignore the nibbing as I did and lay the decking as done on *Pauline*. Here's how: Pin the two halves of the covering board in place so they're flush to the outside of the hull. Lay the kingplank first, with its centerline matched to that of the hull. As you fit the kingplank, trim its forward end so it lies flush to the back of the stem. With the covering board still in place, pry it up high enough so you can slip each plank underneath it, and, starting with the first one against the kingplank, lay the planks on one side. Let the ends run out by the bow and stern, and pin them to the deck beams. Use $3/8$-inch brass pins for nailing the decking and covering board; you'll pull them out later, when the glue has set, or cut off their heads and drive them in. The easiest way to deal with the deck openings is to let all the decking run straight over them for now; you can cut the openings in the deck later. If you wish, though, you can cut the decking flush to the openings as the deck planking continues.

When you've laid the decking on one half of the hull, press the covering board down on the decking and mark the planks to the covering board's inner shape. Then carefully remove the covering board, leaving the planks pinned in place, and trim all the decking to this shape. A razor blade does this perfectly; you can cut these ends all at one crack in a matter of minutes. This sure beats fitting the deck planks one at a time, and eliminates all measuring!

Slip the covering board back in place, using the same pin holes. If there's not much in the way of a caulking seam left showing between the decking and the covering board, take the covering board off again and sand the edge of the decking until you get the desired effect of a caulking seam. Glue the plank edges to one another with superglue, brushing the joints fore-and-aft with a throwaway paintbrush. (Keep cutting off the bristles as they fill with glue, thickening the brush and stiffening the bristles.)

After the glue dries, sand down any unevenness of the deck, and locate the hole for the mast. (It's on the deck template.) You can bore for it now or later.

Stanchions and Bulwarks

Like anything else, building models is ever a learning process. After struggling to get *Pauline's* forward stanchions (frame tops) at the right rake to allow her bulwarks to lie at the right flare, I hit upon a much better and easier way to install the *Underwood*'s stanchions.

There are 33 stanchions to a side; you can see their size and locations on the deck plan (Sheet 3). These hold the bulwarks out at the proper flare, so you need to put them in as accurately as you can. Note that they stand plumb (perpendicular) to the waterline, looking at the hull in profile, and that their inboard and outboard faces are beveled to follow the curve of the hull.

Cut the stanchions out of 2-foot strips, a strong ⅛ inch by about ³⁄₃₂ inch thick to scale. Bevel their inboard and outboard faces to match the curve of the hull, especially at the bow and stern where the curve is greatest. It's easier to saw and bevel far more pieces than you need and throw some away than to fuss with fitting each stanchion individually.

It would be too much work to peg in all the stanchions and then put on the bulwarks, but you do need to peg in some of them to hold the bulwarks in place while you put the rest in, simply gluing these to the deck and to the bulwarks. (Of course, pegging them in is stronger, so bury as many as you have patience for.) First, to allow room for the thickness of the bulwarks, scribe a line from the outboard edge of the covering board. Locate the stanchions inboard of this line, using the deck template to locate them exactly. The stanchions you'll definitely need to peg in are those at Stations ½, 1, and 2 at the bow; Stations A, 16, and 15 at the stern; and, in between, Stations 4, 6, 8, 12, and 14. You'll peg them through the covering board and into the hull.

To get each stanchion's individual flare, look at the body plan (the fore-and-aft view of the hull), copy the angle of flare with a bevel square, and mark it on the crowning board on both sides of the centerline, numbering each flare to avoid confusion. Stanchions 6 to 14 stand about plumb to the deck, so you'll have no problem with these, but the rest at the bow and stern need individual attention—these are the stanchions that take the strain of bending the bulwarks around and determine the bulwarks' flare, which is very crucial to the model's looks.

To peg the stanchions, first bore for them with a Dremel drill big enough to accommodate roughly the size of the stanchions. Then lay the crowning board on the deck, fill the holes with glue (five-minute epoxy is good for this), plop the stanchions into their holes and swing them to the marked flare on the crowning board, eyeball them to see that they're plumb to the waterline, let them set up—and you've done it.

Looking at Sheets 2 and 3 in plan view, you'll note at the extreme end of the stern a short section of sternpost that is notched (rabbeted), with wings on each side, to receive the ends of the bulwarks. You'll make this in one piece, wings and all, and glue it to the top of the deck. It's not easy to make, so plan on taking your time with it. The outside shape of this section has to curve with the hull, and its aft end is raked to the profile shown. You can get the rake from the hull plan profile (Sheet 3) and saw its outboard shape, but your bandsaw will make only one rabbet cut for the bulwark at that angle, so you'll need to shape the other end and part of the inner face pretty much by hand. Make it a bit oversize in height and keep working it to the shape you want. Eventually the railcap sits on it, so its height and shape must flow into the shape of the bulwarks, as seen from any point. Hollow the underside slightly to fit the deck camber. Once you're satisfied with the shape, glue this piece in place. Finally, mark the bulwark height on its aft end, and on each of the pegged stanchions.

You can get the height of the bulwark at each station from the body templates; Mr. Herrick kindly gives it as "deck at side—to U.S.R., underside of rail."

Rabbet the stem for the ends of the bulwarks with a very fine chisel, stick the end of a light (1/16-inch × 1/4-inch) batten in the rabbet, and let the batten flow around the stanchions, pinning it to each stanchion at the bulwark height, aligning the top of the batten to the marks you drew. Let the aft end of the batten into the sternpost rabbet. This will allow you to see if there are any hard spots before you bend the expanded bulwark around. Stand or sit back a ways from your model, and take a hard look at the batten—her sheerline. Does the batten show a smooth, even, graceful sheer, with no quick humps or hollows? Pretty, huh? Pleased with yourself? You bet!

The bulwarks are next. The bulwark template is shown upside-down on Sheet 4, with its bow end at the left of the sheet. The shape is expanded, meaning that it's preshaped to fit the flare of the hull when it's sprung around the hull. The shape also accommodates the flare of the bow forward and is long enough so the ends will bury in the notched sternpost bulwark. You can use the template provided or make your own, which is extra work but good experience. It's extremely easy to make your own template, now that you've done the hard part—pegging in the stanchions and establishing the sheer. Cut a piece of thin cardboard about 2 inches wide and long enough to do the job. Bend it around the hull, making sure it flows around flush against the sheer batten and twists to the flare forward. Mark along the top of the batten and the deck; these lines will give you a template that fits. Cut the top of the template first to get the sheer, then trace it on a piece of wood, Masonite, or stiff cardboard. Cut the top of the template to shape, then lay the template back on the wood or Masonite and trace its bottom. (The reason for doing it this way is to avoid edge-set and distortion, which you might get if you cut out the narrow shape of this template all at once.)

After marking the bulwark's shape on a more stable surface, like Masonite, cut the bulwarks out; then mark the long, continuous waterway on each piece and cut it out. You'll have to cut the top of each bulwark slightly with a small block plane and sanding batten, perhaps, to conform to your batten's version of the *Underwood*'s sheer. (When you realize that a pencil mark drawn around the template translates about 2 inches in height at full scale, you can see why model scale has to be continuously watched. Leave the line for sawing, and there's another 2 inches.) Of course the battens have to be taken off before the bulwarks go on.

Pre-bend both ends of the bulwarks with either wet or dry heat, pin them in place, and stick spacers between the waterway and deck so the bulwarks won't edge-set while you're gluing them to the stanchions. Use five-minute epoxy for this—it's strong and sets quickly, so you can glue in the rest of the stanchions. Simply glue them to the deck and the bulwarks, after you've eyeballed their bottoms and given them a swipe of sandpaper to fit against the deck. When you're sure the glue has set, cut off the tops of the stanchions flush with the tops of the bulwarks.

At this stage, you can leave the bulwarks and work on the hatches, the pilothouse, or whatever pleases you. Or you can put on the railcap, as I did— but first, be sure to paint the inside faces of the stanchions and bulwarks; otherwise, you'll have a hard time painting into corners up under the railcap.

Railcaps, Buffalo
Rails, and Guardrails

The reason for installing the railcap now is that there's nothing in the way on the deck to interfere as there would be later when the pilothouse, hatches, etc., are installed. This is also a good time to saw out the guardrails and glue them on. But first, let's put on the railcap and buffalo rails (the rails that sit on the forward and aft ends of the railcap).

Make the railcap from the template shown on the plans, or make your own custom template, using pretty much the same method as described above for a bulwark template. Make sure you saw the railcap wide enough for scribing to the bulwarks. The railcap's shape is shown on Sheet 2 in plan view and on Sheet 1 in body section. Note that it sits out over the bulwark by a bit and the same inboard. The easiest way to fasten it is to hold it in place with the tiny brass pins. Check for good fit, and round its edges first before gluing. You can make a simple tool to accomplish this by filing a groove in a block of wood and gluing in some sandpaper. When you're satisfied with the fit, squeeze superglue along the outside seam. Cut the heads off the pins you don't need for pulling strength, and tap the pins into the railcap, flush with the top.

The buffalo rails taper in profile and taper with the flare of the hull. Note that their forward ends line up with the stem rabbet line. You can copy their shape from the installed railcap or use the pattern shown on the plans. Note that

Clockwise, from upper left: Planking hatch covers. Note rabbet. . . . Jig for making cove molding for fo'c'sle and pilothouse. . . . Underside of pilothouse roof. Note center carlin to hold fore-and-aft camber. . . . Woodwork all done; forward cowl ventilator installed.

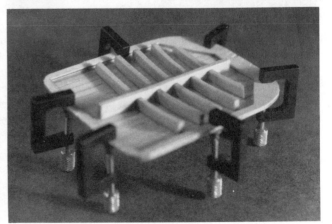

the after buffalo rail also tapers in profile and is wider at the centerline. I made this in one piece like a horseshoe because it's easier to install that way. The trick is to not break it while you're working on it. Your best bet is to cut the outside first, then cut the inside about ¾ inches wide to give it strength while you plane the taper. When the outside is shaped to the right flare and rake, cut the inside and very carefully work it to shape. Glue it on the railcap before you break it, and do any final finishing when it's firmly anchored.

The guardrails are shown on Sheet 2 in profile and on Sheet 1 in section. Make them from basswood or some fine-grained wood, soft or hard. Their full-size dimensions are 5 inches deep by 3 inches thick (molded 5 inches and sided 3 inches, in boatbuilders' language). The top is beveled 9 degrees and the bottom 38 degrees. Saw the guardrails out of stock that is about ½ inch or so wide, cut the 3-inch thickness next (at ⅜-inch scale), bevel the top, then set your saw at 38 degrees and rip the guardrail out to 5 inches depth. This is all very easy to do with a sharp planer blade. Be sure to put the guardrails on with their tops flush with the *bottom* of the deck planking (see Sheet 1). I managed to get them on flush to the *top* of the deck, all glued and pinned, before realizing my mistake. I can attest that superglue is plenty strong—especially when allowed to run into a joint like this, between the guardrails and the hull. I tried prying them off with a razor blade, but I eventually resorted to using a chisel. I ruined them, of course, and had to replace them.

You'll need to bend the guardrails at their ends, with steam or dry heat, but you'll find they go on quite easily. Pin them in place, then squirt superglue in the seam. This is much easier than applying regular glue and hurrying to fit everything before the glue dries.

Hatches

I chose to build the two hatches first because they're relatively easy compared to building the pilothouse. Note their coamings marked on Sheet 6; Sheets 1 and 2 show more detail. Cut out the coamings to the shape of the templates. You'll need to miter their corners and rabbet their tops to take the ends of the hatch planking. The easiest way to build the hatch covers is to cut a rectangular block from the deck template, oil or wax it so the coamings won't stick to it, and fit the coamings around this. No nails, just glue the coamings at the corners. Note that Sheet 2, looking at the hatch covers in plan view, shows three removable covers per hatch. Rather than make the six removable covers, you can simply plank the covers fore-and-aft as shown in the photos and fake the sections by scoring with a razor saw.

I won't cover every detail of building the *Underwood* right through to the finish; time and space don't permit. But let's take a look at the cove molding around the fo'c's'le hatch. Of all the modeling tools I have, it's the Dremel tool I wouldn't want to be without. This smart little device mounted in its drill stand makes it possible to do some fabulous modeling work, even for a beginner. You can make this miniature molding with about a dentist's-size drill (so it seems) placed in the jaws of this tool. Just make a right-angle jig by rabbeting a board that is about 18 inches long. Cut wide strips of wood for easy handling and to the thickness of the molding. Adjust the drill height and run the strips past the drill (it works like a shaper), then cut the molding to the tiny widths needed on your table saw. Using a sharp blade, you should have no trouble in cutting strips 1/16 inch and less.

The plans give ample views of the pilothouse and doghouse, so you should be able to build them by either cutting the different views out of the plans and using them for templates or copying them on drafting paper. Building the *Underwood*'s pilothouse was easier than building *Pauline*'s, so I didn't make a plug to build it around. I used 1/16-inch aircraft plywood for the walls. As for the fancy fore-and-aft cambered roof, I planked it as shown and held the fore-and-aft camber with a longitudinal carlin on the roof's centerline. I made the small portholes from cut-off slices of copper tubing, with hand-tailored acetate for glass.

Finishing

There's still a lot of detail left to do: running lights, searchlight, horn, exhaust pipes, deck fittings such as coal scuttle, water and oil deck filler caps, deck cleats, bitts, stovepipe (Cape Ann or Liverpool), and all those ring-bolts—12 on every other stanchion port and starboard, plus another 12 for the hatch covers, and the tiny eye-bolts for the rings. Making that many dreaded ring-bolts turned out to be no job at all. I just measured their size on the plans and made them from 23-gauge brass wire, continuously wrapped tightly around a dowel of suitable size, cutting each one off with a pair of nippers while still wrapped on the dowel so they'd all be alike. I made the eye-bolts by driving three "nails" or pins of fine wire (the same gauge) into wood close together, with their heads cut off, in the shape of a triangle, then stuck the wire in and bent it around the nails. This actually turned out to be a fun job, and the ring-bolts look great— just like they should. I made the searchlight from plastic, turning it on a lathe like I did for *Pauline* (see Chapter 3). I made it look like its lens was polished by a jeweler, simply by letting a drop of epoxy harden on it.

The *William Underwood*'s rigging (see Sheet 2) is easier than *Pauline*'s. Instead of being held by chainplates, her shrouds anchor to heavy eye-bolts (with shoulders) running through the deck.

She carried her boom high because it served as the gaff for her mainsail; her auxiliary power was a mainsail and staysail.

The mast is made from squared basswood, which you can round by cutting eight sides, then sixteen, then sanding (you can make a mast taper gauge or just eyeball it). Like *Pauline*, the *William Underwood* had a hoisting (stationary) engine just aft of the mast and carried a bail net. Both *Pauline* and *William Underwood* used the same hand bailing method of removing herring in their early years, before moving on to motor-driven suction equipment.

Follow the rigging sequence shown on Sheet 2 and using the fitting called for at the beginning of the chapter.

Building the *William Underwood* right down to every detail would certainly bring many pleasure-filled hours. If you've come this far, I'll trust you can do the rest. As far as I can tell, nothing got past the eye of expert modeler Arthur Herrick, for these are the most detailed model plans I've seen—enough to fill the requirements of any modeler interested in detailed workboats.

Later on, Walter McInnis designed the very yachty-looking square-sterned *Henry O. Underwood.* Her length was 70 feet 9 inches, beam 15 feet 6 inches.

Color Scheme

Hull, pilothouse sides, cargo hatch, outside bulwarks, engineroom trunk, fish holds, white
Pilothouse roof, inside bulwarks, lazarette hatch and coaming, engineroom trunk top, waterways, gray
Decking, oil finish
Bottom paint, antifouling red

She was built at Snow's Shipyard in Rockland 1945 and, like the *William Underwood*, hailed from Jonesport, Maine. I have plans for these, as well as an Eldredge-McInnis design redrawn by my friend, draftsman Tom Bernardi for modeling.

So, there you have it—three of the prettiest working sardine carriers ever designed. Desperation, determination, and luck brought me the plans of *Pauline*, then led me to the lines of the *William Underwood* and the *Henry O. Underwood*, making this perhaps the only collection of sardine carrier plans in existence for detailed modeling.

As for designer Walter McInnis, *WoodenBoat* magazine ran a three-part article about him in issues 52, 53, and 54, written by Llewellyn Howland III. Howland asks Drayton Cochran, owner of perhaps the most celebrated of all Walter's yachts, the 100-foot schooner *Westward*, to epitomize Walter in 10 words or less. Cochran, who chooses his words carefully and uses them sparingly, did the job in seven: "Thoroughly knowledgeable, thoroughly practical, and no bullshit." Of how many other naval architects can the same be said?

As for the *William Underwood*, 50 years after her launching she was spotted by Tom Bernardi, lying alongside the Stinson Canning Company's wharf at Rockland—still a proud old lady, but looking much the worse for wear. Her name had been changed to *Marion H*. Her two hatches had been made into one, and she was spending her last days hauling dogfish.

The finished *William Underwood* . . . and the real boat, now the *Marion H.*, 51 years later at Stinson's Canning Company in Rockland, Maine.

6

Lisa
A Pretty Friendship Sloop

O ver the years, much has been written on this beautiful native Maine craft, the Friendship sloop. Howard Chapelle gives his version of its development in his book *American Small Sailing Craft* (W. W. Norton and Company, 1951):

No one can pin its definite origin, but from all historical evidence the Friendship sloop evolved from the old 1850s Muscongus Bay centerboarders. The local fishermen, wanting a more seaworthy boat, were constantly changing the lines, looking now for a deeper-keel boat in place of the old centerboarder.

In 1914, Chapelle tells us, *Pemaquid* was built at Bremen by A.K. Carter, "a builder of sloops of local renown."

But it was Wilbur Morse of Friendship who is credited with turning out the most Friendship sloops, as described in the book *It's a Friendship*, published by the Friendship Sloop Society of Friendship, Maine.

Wilbur, when asked the question "What is a Friendship sloop?", is said to have replied, "A Friendship sloop is a sloop built in Friendship by Wilbur Morse." Wilbur was apparently never one to hide his light under a bait bucket, but in a certain sense his statement will stand up: If he had not come to Friendship to build his sloops, they most surely would have been known as "Bremen sloops" instead of Friendship sloops.

Materials Needed

- one 4' × 8' sheet of 1/8" tempered Masonite (smooth both sides)
- 20 running feet 4" × 3/8" basswood or pine
- 6 running feet 4" × 3/4" basswood or pine
- 2' × 1' × 1/16" aircraft plywood
- spray adhesive
- Weldwood plastic resin glue
- superglue
- one sheet of 1/32" (or thinner) flat brass
- 5/32" solid round brass rod
- 3/16" hollow brass tubing
- assorted rigging supplies: fifteen 7/16" single blocks and one 7/16" double block; two 1/4" deadeyes with chainplates; two 3/8" eyebands and two 5/16" eyebands
- 3/8" #6 brass ribbon pins
- full-size plans

To further clear up the origin of the Friendship sloop, the Friendship Sloop Society goes on to say,

We do not claim that Wilbur Morse originated the Friendship sloop as we know it today; Wilbur was too smart a man to think that the boat he dreamed up in his bunk on that trawler on the Grand Banks could not be improved upon. As he watched his boats perform, that keen mind of his analyzed their good points and bad points, and made change after change.

The Friendship sloop lives today because it's a splendid combination of sailability, seaworthiness, and yachting beauty, and all of the old-time builders can share in the honor of its development. Changes still go on today, reflecting their owners' wishes, so it's unlikely you'll ever see two Friendship sloops exactly alike, and that's as it should be.

And so in the spirit of Wilbur Morse I've left some choices up to you, as you build your model—such as how to plank the deck, what size cockpit area to put in her, how you're going to rig her, whether you'll steer her with a wheel or a tiller, etc. Whatever you choose, you can hardly go wrong, since you'd be hard put to find two Friendship sloops alike. All these things reflected the personal choices of their owners, also the period in which they were built and whether they were used as yachts or fishing boats. In many cases there were combinations of yacht and fisherman rigs, so you're free to choose your own style—it's mostly a case of just making up your mind.

By the way, if you plan to sail this model, it's unlikely you can get enough ballast inside her low enough to keep her from flipping over. You can scale the model, but you can't scale the elements. Anything that will make her move is likely a gale to this little craft, so you may have to resort to hanging outside ballast from the keel; remove this when she's ashore, plus any inside ballast.

When I asked Phil Bolger to draw up his version of a Friendship sloop solely for modelmaking, he patterned this one basically after A. K. Carter's *Pemaquid*. Phil also said he took the liberty of making changes where it pleased him. What pleased him also pleased me; to my eye, this version of the Friendship sloop is the prettiest yet. The plans for her, drawn at ³/₄ inch = 1 foot, are adequate for building a half model or a full model. Making the half model should take you about three days to a week, working fairly steadily. (You can follow pretty much the same procedure we went through in Chapter 1, for building the half model of the lobsterboat *Laura B.*) The full model might take you a month or more, and you'll need skill and patience for such things as cutting and fitting deck beams, bending the cockpit coaming, making the cuddy.

Tools Needed

- table saw
- bandsaw
- vise
- clamps
- ⁷/₈" gouge
- block plane, spokeshave
- sanding fid
- sanding battens
- needle and riffler files
- rattail files
- 10" mill file with handle
- combination square
- #3 pencil
- scissors
- narrow masking tape

Building the Hull

Basswood is my choice for this model and can be used for most of Lisa's parts, mast and all.

As usual, your first step is to cut out the plans and glue them to Masonite to make the templates. Be sure to number the body sections (stations) before cutting them out from the plans. Carefully cut out the hull profile, leaving the line. Even though this means losing the line on the inside of the backbone template, when you trace it again to make the backbone and saw outside the line, the backbone will come out just the right size to slip over the hull. For this boat the

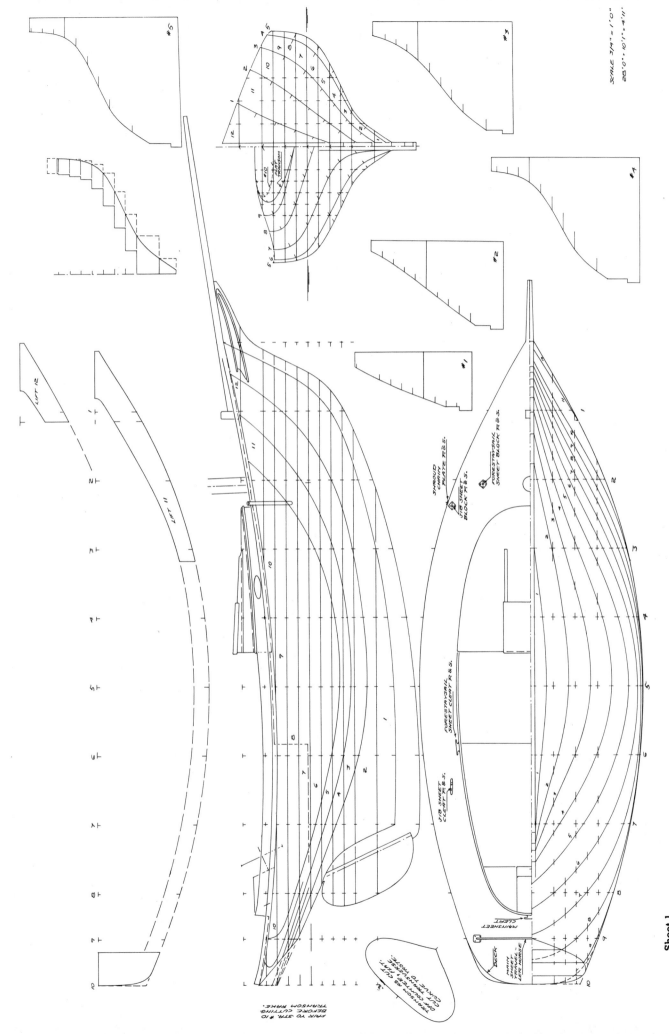

Sheet 1
Enlarge 312 percent for full-size plans.

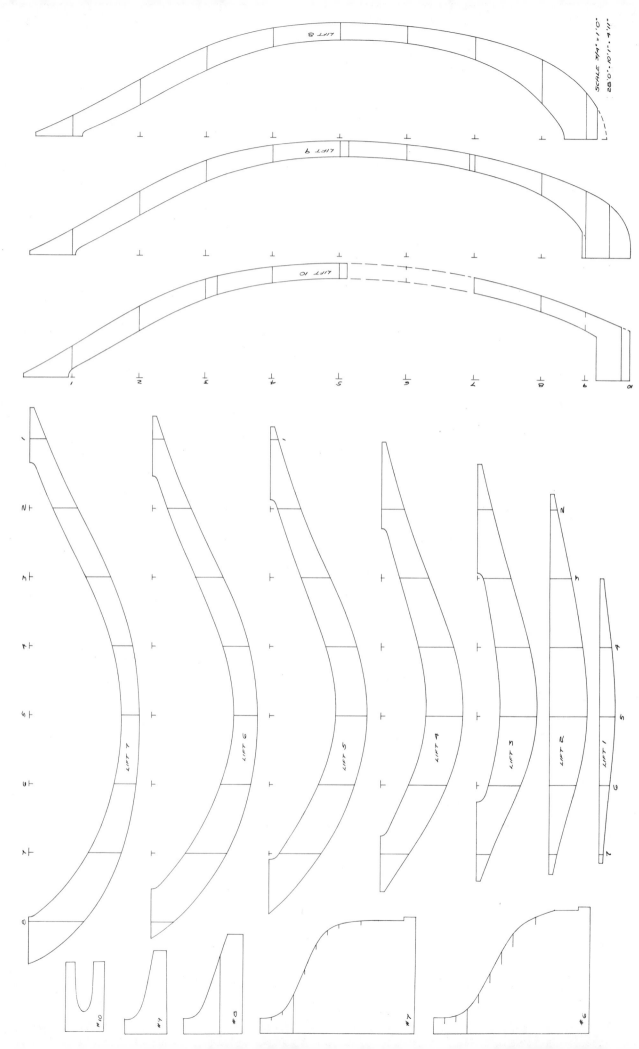

Sheet 2
Enlarge 312 percent for full-size plans.

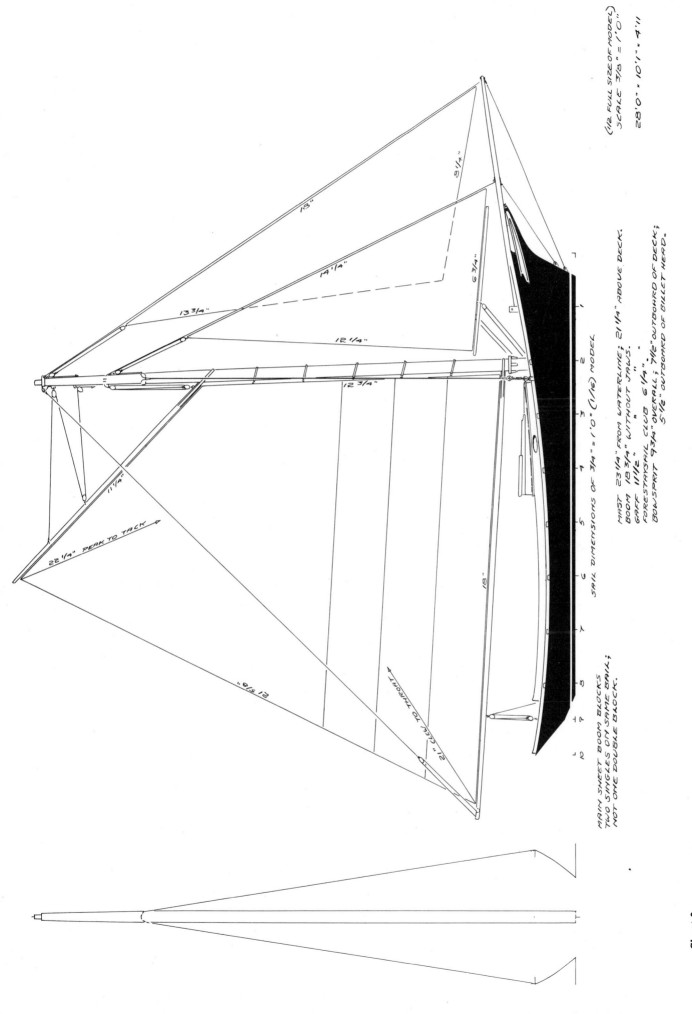

Sheet 3
Enlarge 365 percent for full-size plans.

(1/2 FULL SIZE OF MODEL)
SCALE 3/8" = 1'0"
28'0" × 10'1" × 4'11

MAST 23 1/4" FROM WATERLINE; 21 1/4" ABOVE DECK.
BOOM 18 3/4" WITHOUT JAWS;
GAFF 11 1/2" " "
FORESTAYSAIL CLUB 6 1/4".
BOWSPRIT 9 3/4" OVERALL; 7 1/2" OUTBOARD OF DECK;
5 1/2" OUTBOARD OF BILLET HEAD.

SAIL DIMENSIONS OF 3/4" = 1'0" (1/16) MODEL.

MAIN SHEET BOOM BLOCKS
TWO SINGLES ON SAME BAIL;
NOT ONE DOUBLE BLOCK.

13"
3 1/4"
14 1/4"
6 3/4"
13 3/4"
12 1/4"
12 3/4"
11 1/4"
22 1/4" PEEK TO TACK
18"
21 3/8"
21" CLEW TO THROAT
21"

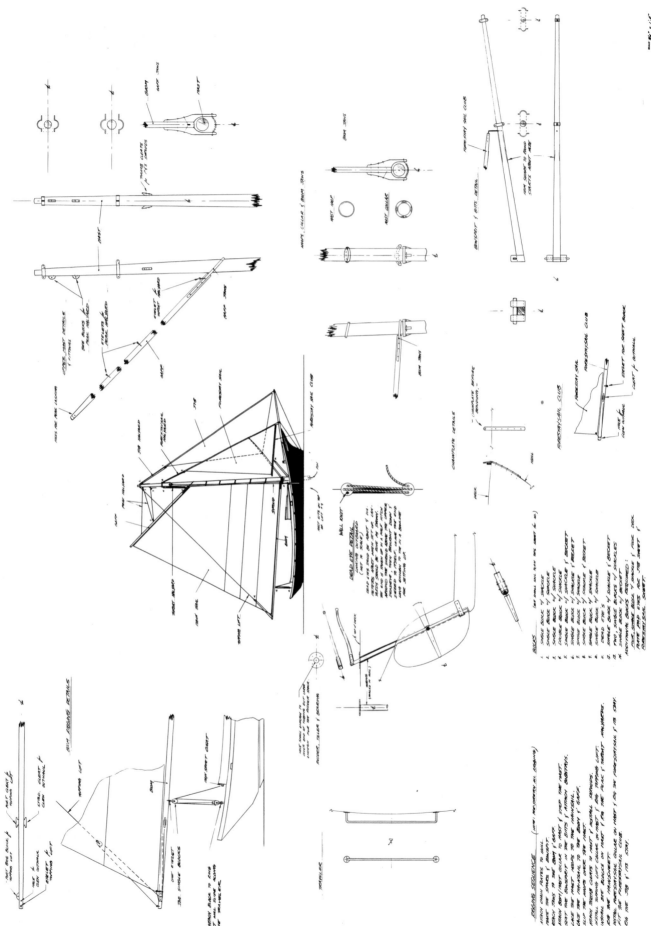

Sheet 4
Enlarge 312 percent for full-size plans.

transom pattern needs to flex, yet be strong, so I glued it to a piece of plastic milk carton rather than the usual Masonite.

Following the same procedure as described in Chapter 2 for the lobster-boat *Laura B.*, trace the waterline lift templates onto your lift stock, then cut them out on a bandsaw. Make Lifts 1, 2, 11, and 12 a full ³/₄ inch thick; the little dogleg on Lift 12 goes against the centerline of the jig to automatically position the outside of the lift the proper distance from the centerline. Make the rest of the lifts ³/₈ inch thick. Cut a test waterline lift into pieces, then lay them back on the profile to make sure your lift stock is thick enough.

One at a time, glue up the hull halves, making mirror images. If you're planning to paint her, you can probably just stack the lifts on the jig and weight them. If you're making a half model and will give it a natural finish, you'll want to wedge and clamp the lifts so the glue lines won't show.

If you notice some open places in the glue joints after taking the hull halves off the jig, you can fill these slack spots with fresh glue, using a putty knife made from part of a razor blade stuck on a wooden handle. When the glue has hardened, lay the hull profile template on each half with the load waterline (Lift 6) of the profile matching that of the hull, hold it in place with a clamp, and make sure you have enough thickness in the glued lifts for carving the hull. It doesn't matter if the lifts don't exactly line up with the profile, as long as they're thick enough to give enough overall shape of the hull. (The idea of running a test earlier for thickness is to avoid having to add on thickness at this stage.) With a sharp pencil, trace the profile on each half hull. Spot in the sheer as described in Chapter 1. Then cut the hull profile right to the line all around, or as close as you dare, and be sure the cut gains in height to the outside sheer—in other words, be sure you cut it higher on the outside of the hull than on the inside where marked. Tilt the bandsaw blade, look at the model, and think before you cut. Cut the transom nearly flat at this stage; you can give it some curve later if you like. Then clamp each half-hull in the vise and, with a small rattail file (about ¹/₈ inch), file in one-half of the rudderpost hole. While you're at it, take a few swipes across the lifts with 60-grit sandpaper—just enough to take off any glue buildup from laying up the lifts, fairing the centerline a bit. A sanding belt cut in half and stapled to a board does a good job. You can establish the keel rabbet now, or later after the hulls are glued together.

Mix up some glue, check to see that the profile shapes are cut right to the line, and glue and clamp the halves together. To give the clamps a sure grip at the bow and stern, saw wedge-shaped pieces of wood, fasten them to the hull with masking tape, and put the clamps on these; otherwise the clamps will slip off the bow's tapered surfaces.

When the glue has cured, put the hull in the vise and start working down the sheer with a spokeshave and a block plane. Wrap a piece of 80-grit sandpaper around a piece of closet pole and use this at the aft end to keep the hook in the sheer. Watch the sheer marks you spotted on the inside of the hull as you sand flat across the hull. When you're fairly close to the marks all along the hull, switch to an 80-grit sanding belt, 3 inches by 21 inches, stapled to a board 2⁷/₈ inches wide by 18 inches long. This long, wide sanding board flattens any humps and does a good job of fairing the rest of the sheer. Be especially careful in sanding the glued lifts where they feather out on the sheer. Constantly watch the sheer marks so that you sand and blend them evenly the length of the hull; this is how you get a nice, pleasing curve to the sheerline. Ignore the outside, all you see at this stage is a sort of flight of stairs with square corners, until you get them carved away.

Lay the deck template on the hull, aligned at Station 1, and clamp it in place. Trace around the deck from the bow to Station 5, and mark any missing station lines on top of the sheer. Unclamp the deck pattern and slide it back so the template and hull align at Station 9, trace from the stern back to Station 5, and again add any missing station lines. Make sure to align the centerlines of the deck template and hull.

Cut the hull sides to the just-traced deck pattern; a plumb cut all around is OK at this stage. Trim close to the line, and reestablish the station lines on hull sides; just a pencil dot right up under the deck line will do.

Next, to hold the hull upside-down in your vise, make a support from a 2 × 4, about 7 or 8 inches long. Jam it down between the lifts, and glue a couple of cross-supports to it and to Lift 4, using five-minute epoxy or Weldwood.

For shaping the hull, a block plane, a spokeshave, wood rasps, and a gouge with an inside bevel work well. Be cautious along the turn of the bilge; it's easy to take off too much here. At this stage, mark off the keel's width—the keel rabbet on the full-size sloop—along either side of the hull's centerline. Let the keel rabbet and the station marks guide you as you use the body templates. When you've carved as close as you dare to the keel rabbet, you'll fit the backbone to the hull, glue it on, and work very carefully shaping the hull to it.

But before we get to the backbone, let's consider the transom. Curved to suit, or to the plan view? Between Stations 9 and 10 there's plenty of wood left to do either. Having cut the rake of the transom flat across the lifts earlier, when cutting the hull profile, you can see even some semblance of the transom. Lay the transom template on the hull with its centerline matching that of the hull and with its top right to the sheerline, and you can see how its shape is going to flow into the hull lines. Trace around the transom template, and work all the waterline lifts back to its shape. It's easy to unintentionally dub (round) off the corners of the transom where it joins the hull's underbody because they're almost in the same plane, so use a mill file here across the transom to keep the edges crisp—and, for that matter, all around the transom where the hull lines flow into it.

Just forward of the top of the sternpost, at the tight turn of the tuck, is some of the trickiest sanding and shaping on the hull, and here is where the sanding fid really shines. For final smoothing of the hull, use homemade fairing battens in grits of 60, 80, 100, finishing with 220 to 320 grit. (For instructions on how to make the sanding fid and fairing battens, see the Introduction.)

Backbone

Why didn't we put the keel (backbone) on earlier? Not only would it have been in the way of carving, but it's all too easy to whack it unintentionally with a chisel, nicking or splitting it.

I cut the backbone in one piece from ³/₄-inch pine, sided ¹/₄ inch with no taper. If the resulting cross-grain of the stem and sternpost offends you, you can make it in pieces with grain running to suit. For me, this seems like too much trouble. Sure, the one-piece backbone is prone to splitting across the grain at the stem while you're handling it, but I'd rather risk this than take the time to make glued joints, with their potential of misalignment. When the backbone is glued to the hull it gets its strength back again, and at places like the stem and

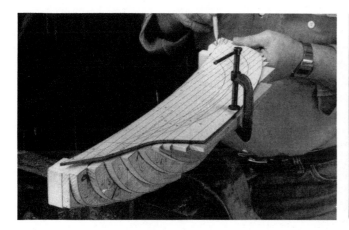

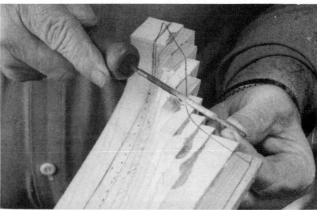

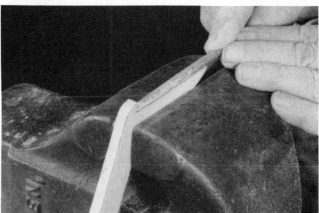

Clockwise, from upper left: Station to station, waterline to waterline, *Lisa*'s profile is traced. . . . Don't forget to file hole for rudder post before gluing hull halves together. . . Grooving the backbone for the sternpost. . . . With the deck template temporarily clamped, locate and bore hole for the mast; note the mast partner. . . . Trace deck and opening from the deck template.

billethead (the tapered piece that supports the bowsprit) the grain is perfect for shaping.

Try the backbone on the hull. It should just slip over it without being forced. If it doesn't, lay the backbone on the plan and see if it matches, then take a little off it or the hull. A shortcut that has worked for me is to saw the backbone template slightly smaller. By the time you trace and saw around it leaving the line, you're back to the right size again. When you're sure the backbone fits the hull, glue it in place. Groove the sternpost with a rattail file for the leading edge of the rudderpost. It's a good idea to make the rudderpost so you can make sure the groove will fit it.

You'll need a piece of 5/32-inch round brass rod for the rudderpost, and a shorter piece of 3/16-inch hollow brass tube for the sleeve bearing. You can buy solid and hollow brass rod in more sizes than you'd believe at your local hobby shop. Cut the rudderpost plenty long, and cut the 3/16-inch sleeve flush with the hull underbody, leaving its top high for the moment (see the plans for the lengths of the cuts).

When you put in the whole rudder assembly later (see "Tiller and Rudder"), after fitting the deck and cockpit sole, you'll slip the tube over the top of the rudderpost (the section between the seat and the tiller) to act as a watertight upper sleeve bearing, holding the rudder in alignment, with its top well above the cockpit sole. At that point you'll align and glue the sleeve in the hole with epoxy. For now, just put a drop of superglue or epoxy on the lip of the skeg—the notch on the backbone that juts out under where the rudder will go—to act as a rudderpost bearing.

Mast

Before we move on to the deck and cockpit, let's locate the hole for the maststep, because it's going to be inaccessible. It falls on Station 2, Lift 4 (see hull profile). You might have to remove a little wood from the lifts in that area to accommodate the maststep and the heel of the mast, which has a diameter of about 1/2 inch at 3/4-inch scale. The easiest way to step the mast is to drive a pin into the center of the heel of the mast which will set in a hole bored in the lift for it. You can shim the mast where it goes through the deck to get the proper rake.

Note that on the sail plan the height of the mast is given as 23 1/4 inches from Lift 6, which is her marked waterline, 21 1/4 inches above the deck. You'll need to take into consideration the extra length needed to step the mast on Lift 4, which brings the overall height to be 24 inches instead of 23 1/4 inches, since Lift 4 is two 3/8-inch waterline lifts below Lift 6.

Taper the top part of the mast, starting at the throat of the gaff, about 7 1/2 inches below the masthead. You can use a 1/2-inch dowel for the mast, and taper it to suit. This is easier than starting with a square stick, but it's also easier to screw up if you taper it by eye. For this reason I square the masthead end of the dowel and taper that end as I would if I were making the mast from a square stick. That's the way it was done in the time-honored way—cut square, then tapered, then 8- and 16-sided.

That's it for now—we'll tackle her bowsprit and other rigging details later.

Deck

Go back to your deck pattern and cut out the outline of the coaming and cuddy so you can use these for templates for the deck, cockpit opening, cockpit seats, etc.

The easiest and quickest way to deal with *Lisa's* deck is to cut the deck out of a sheet of 1/16-inch aircraft plywood and put it down in one whack, since it's going to be painted anyway. Cut it out right to the shape of the deck template, and set it aside for now.

On a full-size boat you'd have a hard time getting away with a one-piece deck, and you might not get away with it on a model if the deck had a lot of camber. *Lisa*'s plans call for the same deck crown as I used on *Pauline* and *Mite*; it's a bit flat, but the toerail goes on more easily later, and the aircraft plywood works out fine. It does very well bending in two directions, to the profile sheer fore-and-aft as well as the deck camber, yet it's stiff enough and lies fair enough so that you don't need carlins for gluing the coamings against.

If you like the look of an authentically planked deck and have the patience, you can plank *Lisa*'s deck the fancy way. We'll go into this in a bit.

As for the deck beams, we'll fit them all in one piece, then cut away the sections not needed in way of the cockpit. We'll put in nine crowned deck beams straight across, one for each station, let into the hull sides. Of course, this isn't even half of the number of deck beams there'd be in a real boat, but I can't see fiddling with something that's going to be covered up. Purists might cringe at the idea of "out of sight, out of mind," and I'll cheer them on. Some might want to build the model plank on frame, put all the deck beams in, and build the model exactly the way she was built full-size. I'd applaud it; I'm just not one of them.

A Dremel tool works great for boring (mortising) pockets in the sides of the hull to receive the ends of the deck beams. To make the deck beams, mark their profile on ³/₄-inch pine, saw them out to this shape on a bandsaw, then slice them to their ¹/₄-inch thickness on the table saw. I always saw out more than I need so I won't be caught short, and any deck beams left over can be used on the next model. Saw out a crowning board to the shape of the beams; this will help you position the deck beams exactly. Put Weldwood glue in the pockets, and slip each deck beam in place; then, with the crowning board spanning the hull from sheer to sheer, aligned on the centerline, adjust the deck beams as needed so their tops are flush to the underside of the crowning board. Check on them as the glue hardens to make sure they stay in place.

The next step is to fit the mast partner, which goes under the deck.

I intended to lay the deck with individual planks but changed my mind and opted for the plywood deck, which needs no backing except for where the mast passes through it.

If you decide on decking her the fancy way, the mast partner and stern will serve a dual purpose as backing for the kingplank, which your decking is nibbed into. Backing is also needed at the stern for the ends of the planks to rest on. It should be slightly wider than the kingplank and notched in flush to the deck beams. (Here again, boatbuilding is no different than house carpentering. How many first-time house carpenters have discovered, when they got ready to fasten their baseboards, that they had forgotten the backing, or went to nail sheetrock in a corner and found they had nothing to nail to because they hadn't framed the corner? And so it goes with houses and boats—much of it is common sense and thinking ahead enough to stay out of trouble.) The deck beams, put in properly, should hold the decking in alignment and produce graceful planking lines without humps and hollows. For cutting and fitting the individual planks, you can follow the instructions for planking the *William Underwood*.

With the mast partner installed, lay the deck template back on the hull, paying particular attention to alignment on the station marks, and clamp it in place. Bore a tiny ⁵/₆₄-inch (or so) hole right through the template to locate the

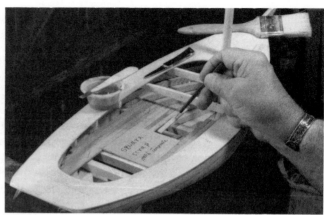

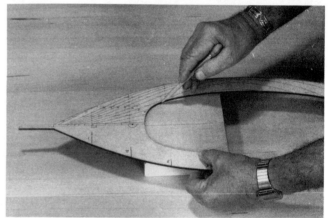

Clockwise, from upper left: Sawing deck beams for inboard edge of deck. . . . Planking cockpit area. . . . Marking shape of cuddy from deck template. . . . Sawing the cuddy to shape. . . . Checking cuddy roof camber with crowning board.

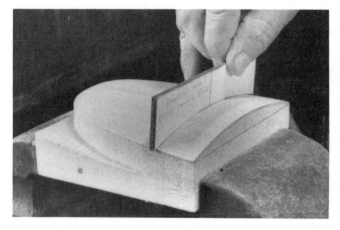

mast's center. This is also a good time to locate the center of the samson post, or you can wait till later.

Now for trimming off the deck beams for the cockpit area. Lay the cockpit/ cuddy section of the deck template on the deck beams, align it at stations and centerline, clamp it in place, and trace around it; this is the outline of the cockpit coaming. Then, using a razor saw, cut out the portions of the deck beams at Stations 5, 6, 7, and 8, where you'll put in the cockpit sole, coaming, and cuddy.

Cockpit Sole, Coaming, and Cuddy

Since the lifts are level and the cockpit sole runs with them, putting in the framing for the sole is easy. Cut some straight 3/8-inch-square beams for the sole to rest on; glue them on top of Lift 6. The sole planking covers these and flows out toward the hull's sides on Lift 7, underneath the plumb line of the coaming. I'll bring the coaming right down to the sole and fit seats around clear to the cuddy as a way of finishing off the cockpit, which makes a clean way of doing it. It's kind of yachty—it does away with the break and the fish well—but why not? What you end up with is a yachty version of the sloop with a fisherman rig. Or you can have it the other way around, if you want; you see plenty of Friendship sloops afloat rigged both ways, some even with roller-reefing. . . shades of Wilbur Morse.

If you're going to sail this model, then you'll want an access hatch for the bilge for putting in lead ballast, so plan on it before you plank the sole solid. Using the hatch template as a pattern, fit a carlin on each side of the hatch, fore-and-aft, and lay your planking flush to the hatch template. Of course, if you don't want to bother with planking here, you could put in the cockpit sole in one piece, using aircraft plywood.

With the cockpit coaming and cuddy, again the choice is yours. I like the looks of what Bolger drew for *Lisa*—the low profile suits my eye—so I made them as close as I could to his design. But you can make the cuddy shorter, longer, higher, with more or less camber, with ports in the sides or none at all. If you make a cuddy with higher sides, you can bring the coaming along with the deck sheer and swoop it up a little.

You can make the cuddy out of a solid piece of wood; cedar is my choice, because it's light and can lie right on the deck beams at Stations 3 and 4, which you left intact. Or you can cut those deck beams flush with the deck, spring a coaming around the whole cockpit area, and make the cuddy sides part of it. Some of the sloops have cuddy sides that run right with the deck sheer, only up higher, so all you'd have to do is make a coaming with a straight edge, rest it on the cockpit sole, and scribe the coaming's top to the deck; then, when you reach the cuddy, widen your dividers and keep going around for the cuddy. Then you'd put in framing and finish the cuddy top by planking it or covering it with aircraft plywood.

Let's look more closely at the cuddy as Bolger has drawn it. The top of the cuddy on these plans (shown by a dashed line) flattens out some; it doesn't run with the sheer but parallel with the waterline. The bottom dashed line shows the cuddy's depth at the top of the deck. Since the cuddy will sit on the deck beams, it needs to be made 1/16 inch deeper and cut to the deck sheer. The dashed line just above the window is the height of the cuddy side. Figure the height of the cuddy camber from this line and the top dashed line at its aft end. We have laid out the camber the easy way by measuring the height and width, doing it with sticks; here it is again in a drawing. The camber is 3/8 inches in 5 inches, measured on the plans.

To make *Lisa*'s cuddy, as drawn, out of a solid block, first cut a rectangular piece of wood to the width of the cuddy, and mark a centerline. Cut out the profile pattern for the cuddy, or make a tracing from the plans and cut it out. Lay the pattern on the wood, trace it, and with your bandsaw cut the cuddy's underneath curve to fit the deck.

Put the underneath part of the first cut back with the top of the block; then lay your cuddy plan-view template on top, trace around it, and cut this view. Don't throw away the side cuts—tack them back on, so you can hold the cuddy in the vise while crowning the top. Spring a batten around the cuddy sides as a guide. This line is straight, but your eye won't say so, so let your crowning board and your eye work together to develop this line for the final touch. Finally, shape the underside of the cuddy slightly to fit the deck camber. The cuddy's sides should fit snugly to the deck edges, so it won't rock athwartships or fore-and-aft.

The hatch cover and its slide supports are shown in profile and in plan view; make them to suit. You can leave the cuddy entrance open or closed.

When you're satisfied with the cuddy's fit all around, take it off and set it aside while fitting the cockpit coaming, which is next. When we're ready we'll glue the cuddy and coaming together, but for now it's best to leave the cuddy unglued.

To make the cockpit coaming, start with a piece of wood $1/16$ inch × $15/8$ inch × $211/4$ inches. It can be anything that will bend and is long enough so the ends can bury in the sides of the cuddy by about $1/2$ inch or $3/4$ inch. I used a piece of aircraft plywood. Whatever you use, you'll need to bend it to the aft curve of the cockpit. Water, ammonia, or dry heat will do the job on pine, cedar, or most anything. Dry heat from a big soldering iron did the trick for me in no time flat. (I tried using water, but it didn't help much because of the laminations in the aircraft plywood.) The cockpit sole template, cut out from the deck template, works well for bending the coaming around. Fiddle with it until the coaming fits like a glove, drop it in the hull, and pull it back against the stern where the hardest bend is. If you see a flat spot where the coaming doesn't mold itself against the edge of the deck, mark it, take it out, and hold that spot momentarily on the soldering iron until it takes more bend.

When satisfied with the fit, place the coaming in the hull and clamp it. Cut a block of wood $1/2$ inch thick, and use it (or dividers) to scribe the sheerline on the coaming, $1/2$ inch above and parallel to the deck. Set the cuddy on the hull and, using the same block or divider setting, scribe an extension of the sheerline on each side of the cuddy. This is where you'll make a notch or rabbet for each end of the coaming to bury into the cuddy. It won't work to simply butt the ends of the coamings against the cuddy, because there wouldn't be any holding strength for the glue; also, instead of having coamings that flow in a fair line with the cuddy, you might end up with a quick spot. Notch the sides of the cuddy for the ends of the coamings (about $3/4$ inch long, $1/16$ inch deep); this allows the ends of the coaming to blend into the cuddy and at the same time offers plenty of gluing area for a good joint.

With that done, cut the top of the coaming to the scribed sheer, and it and the cuddy are ready to go in the hull for good—that is, almost. Since the deck edge doesn't offer much in the way of surface area for gluing the coaming, it's a good idea to glue some pieces of scrap up under the deck between the deck beams for the coaming to bear against. Of course, the deck beams, cut off plumb in line with the edge of the deck, will help support the coaming. Now glue and clamp the cuddy in place.

Next comes the bridge deck, which is shown in plan and profile. You can make this from a solid block smaller or larger to suit, or leave it out if you want to. On the plan profile you can see that the top of the bridge deck runs with the sheer. Take the angle off with your sliding bevel gauge (or take my word for it that it's 3 degrees). Make the bridge as shown in the hull lines profile or smaller

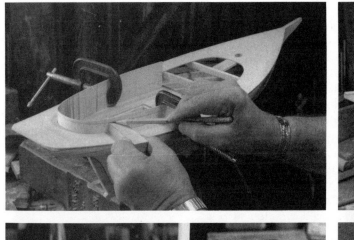

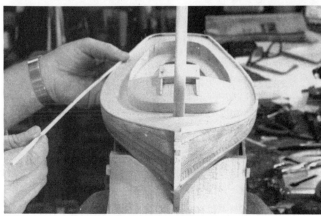

to suit. Use the plan-view coaming cutout as a template, and while you're at it you can use this same template for the wraparound seat.

You can make the seat from a solid piece cut on your bandsaw, fitting it as you did the coaming. Cut out a seat top from ¹/₁₆-inch aircraft plywood, and fit it over the seat, letting it overlap with a lip. Fit the seat to the bridge deck and the top of the seat, and glue all these pieces in together.

After the glue is dry, continue the rudderpost hole through the seat. Aligning the hole for the rudderpost through the seat down through the hull and boring it can be touchy, as it's easy to be off. That's why we made the rudderpost hole before we glued the hull halves together.

Clockwise, from upper left: Scribing coaming to deck sheer. . . . Insert blocking between coaming and deck beams. . . . Rudder assembly ready to slip in. . . . Toerail goes on in one piece.

Cradle

Now that we're going to be fiddling with more detail, turning the model this way and that, a working cradle will come in handy, so let's take a little break and make one. It can be as fancy or crude as you like.

The stations between Stations 3 and 6 on the hull profile are a good choice for patterns for the arms; they'll make the cradle the right length to support her. Measure down vertically from the top of Lift 5 at Stations 3 and 6—4¹/₂ inches—and draw a baseline. Measure back from the baseline to the bottom of the keel at these same stations; this gives the proper height so the model sits level. Use the station templates already drawn for the pattern, and lengthen their bottoms accordingly for the height of the keel. Make a 9-inch × 6-inch base, set the hull supports the proper distance apart, and brace them off. So as not to mar the model while working on it, stick masking tape or glue felt on the cradle where the hull bears.

I made the cradle from an old, weathered packing case, just because I took a notion to do it. As much as I like weathered wood, I seldom use it, because the minute you make a saw cut you expose bright wood, which spoils the whole effect if you want something to look naturally weathered. Since I had nothing to lose fooling with this working cradle, I thought I'd try to make the new-sawn cuts match the rest of the cradle. Somewhere out of the past I remembered an old antique-reproduction maker who specialized in making sea chests and making them look old. He would grab a handful of cobwebs, dust, and dirt, and apply it to the newly painted chest. This, along with a few well-directed swipes with chains and other techniques, made the chest quite convincingly into an instant antique.

Taking a page from his book, so to speak, I tried using dust and dirt from 30 years' accumulation here and there in my shop. But what worked best, surprisingly enough, was wood ashes right out of my shop stove applied to the newly cut end-grain with a paintbrush first wetted in water, then a little touch of dust. Beautiful! The match is nearly perfect—there's no question but the result would fool the eye of a casual observer.

The hard looker? Well, there's always one out there, like the ex-curator of an old car museum in Massachusetts, unbeknownst to me, who happened along one day when I was parked in my old 1930 Chevy sports roadster down at the wharf at Spruce Head Island. I'd spent all summer restoring it, even taking her paint down to bare metal. This was the first time out on the road, and I was real pleased with the job. The keen-eyed old gentleman gave the old car the once-over, then looked at me and said, "Fine old car you've got there; when are you going to restore it?"

Tiller and Rudder

Back to her rudder and steering arrangement again. You noted on the plans that *Lisa* steers with a wheel instead of a tiller. If you don't plan to sail her, you can buy a wheel, stick it in, and call it done. If you plan to sail her and still use a wheel, the hardware needed for steering linkage isn't that easy to come by or make, so I chose to steer her with a tiller. You can make the tiller yourself from a piece of maple or other fine-grained wood.

You've already cut the rudderpost and the sleeve bearing. For the rudder and tiller straps you'll need a strip of 1/32-inch or thinner sheet brass; in fact, it's a good idea to stock your hardware department with a few sheets of brass of different thicknesses. You'll also need some brass dressmaker's pins for fastening the straps—8- or 12-gauge will do.

It's best to make the whole rudder assembly, then install it. First, there's one last component you need to make, the rudder, which gets its profile from the lines sheet. Its thickness will be the same as the backbone, with a slight taper. With a small rattail file or a chainsaw file, hollow the leading edge of the rudder to receive the rudderpost. Bore the rudderpost for a couple of pins. It's up to you whether you'll want a rudder strap; none is needed since the rudderpost buries slightly in the end of the skeg. If you use one, make it out of a thin sheet (.020 inch) of brass. Cut a slot in the rudder, slip the strap through and fasten it to the sternpost with ³/₈-inch pins.

Make the strap for the tiller and bend it around the top of the rudderpost, more tightly than you did at the bottom of the rudder. Bore through strap and tiller and fasten; then, with a round file, shape the end of the tiller until it slides tightly against the post. Lay the whole rudder assembly on something flat, and bore the tiller strap for the pin. Remove the pin and insert the rudderpost, sleeve and all, up through the hull; fasten the rudder strap to the sternpost, and see that the rudderpost aligns right up through. Pack the sleeve with thickened epoxy so it stays where you want it (five-minute epoxy is great for this), and let it harden.

The final part of the assembly is to fasten a copper washer on top of the seat, to serve as a bearing for the rudderpost where the sleeve comes flush with the seat. Slip the washer over the rudderpost, slip the sleeve and tiller strap over it, and pin the whole assembly together. Cut the end off the burr and head it over, pin it to the deck (four pins should do the job), and gloat over a nice job. Of course, there are other ways of doing it, but this way is uncomplicated enough so you can do it yourself.

After I got her steering in, I was ready for a change from woodworking and metalsmithery, and decided to copper her bottom. This tells me she's nearing completion and cheers me on. The waterline is the top of Lift 6; use this or add a boottop if you like. I know her topsides are going to be white or green, so a red copper color is safe. I used an old batch of copper paint, mixed last year. The first coat didn't dry that well, but adding a few drops of Japan drier fixed it for the next couple of coats.

Toerail and Trim

With the steering system done, we can turn to finishing more of her topsides, beginning with the toerail.

The full-size sloop would have a toerail 1¹/₂ inch square; this dimension at ³/₄-inch scale is about right for the model. I like to put the toerail on in one piece; to do this, you'll need a 4-foot length of wood. I made *Lisa*'s toerail from a bolt of air-dried maple I'd stashed away a couple of years ago just for jobs like this. (If you don't have such a piece of maple, then an old table top will do.) Sawing the rail to size is easy: first, take off a slice the right thickness with an ordinary but sharp ripsaw blade; then switch to a hollow-ground planer blade and cut a strip.

The total length of the wraparound rail is the sum of both sides. Find the center of the rail's length, then make a template of the deck at the stern to bend it around and deduct the thickness of the rail from the template. This is because the rail sits on top of the deck; if you bent the rail around the outside of the template without deducting the rail thickness, the rail would be too big to fit on the deck. For bending the rail at the hard bends around the corners of the transom, I'd recommend you use dry heat. I tried ammonia first, but after an hour of soaking the rail cracked and I had to start over with a new one. Dry heat from a good-sized soldering iron worked perfectly, after I located the exact spot of the bend. Dry heat has the added benefit of eliminating any moisture, so the rail is ready to be glued on.

Gluing the rail on, as simple as it may sound, isn't quite that simple. What kind of glue and fastenings will best hold it in place for this one-shot deal? I use superglue, and apply it after the rail is pinned exactly in place. Prebore for the brass pins, then use them to fasten the rail; apply the glue to the joint between the rail and the deck, let it soak in, and wipe off any excess glue; then, cut off the heads of the pins and leave them in, grinding them off flush to the rail. This is the best way to do it. If you tried using a heavy glue like white glue or Weldwood and applied it first to the underside of the rail, you probably wouldn't get the rail on before the glue set, and would have problems like the rail sticking in the wrong places and excess glue hardening before you could remove it.

It might seem easier to cut the limber holes (also called scuppers or water-ways) before gluing the rail down, but this would be a risky way of doing it, since it would weaken the rail quite a bit. I cut them in afterwards by boring them out with a Dremel drill. This is risky, too, in that it's easy to wobble the holes, cutting too high into the rail, or mar the deck. It is a good idea to bore with a smaller drill first, then finish the holes with modeler's files. You can fill any tiny uglies by putting some filler on the file and applying it where needed, or by packing the hole with filler and refiling. This worked in getting the holes symmetrical.

With the toerail on, let's put a piece of half-round molding around the outside of the coaming and around the cuddy. Some Friendship sloops had this bit of trim, some didn't, but it really dolls up the looks of the boat, as does a piece of quarter-round molding around the cuddy and coaming along the deck.

It's not easy to put that little piece of quarter-round on, as innocent as it looks. The problem is in trying to bend wood that is both flat and round. If it were square, it would be quite easy to bend it around the coaming, but the top

Let's talk about hollow-ground saw blades. They're fragile at best, at least the ones that aren't carbide toothed. The teeth are without set and are meant only to saw through dry wood—not wet 2x4s. One thoughtless pass through a piece of wet plywood will ruin the cutting quality of the blade for cutting out fine molding from maple or any other wood. Even though the teeth still feel sharp to the touch, their cutting power is gone. So, I'd hide that blade, if you have other members of the family or "friends" who use your saw for casual sawing. Chances are, a saw blade is a saw blade to them, but you're the one stuck with a dull saw, and it's no fun to spend an hour refiling a saw that you used only once before someone used it to burn his way through a piece of wet, gritty wood.

So far, I haven't seen any carbide-toothed blades up to the job of sawing something 1/16-inch square; if there's just the slightest wobble or burr left on the teeth from filing, it won't do the job. So I stick to my ordinary hollow-ground planer blade that I file myself.

For extra-smooth jobs, Jay Hanna files his own blade, then puts it on his saw mandrel and turns it backwards by hand while holding a wetstone against the side of the teeth to get rid of burrs and even out the filing. I haven't done that on a planer blade because when filed sharp it has been adequate for my modelmaking, but I have used the method many times to even up the set of an ordinary ripsaw blade that was cutting roughly from too much set to the teeth.

Luckily, there's an easy way out for those who have neither the time nor talent for filing those finicky hollow-ground planer blades. Sears makes a "thin rim satin cut" veneer blade that is hollow-ground and loaded with 200 fine teeth. This cuts almost as well as my hollow-ground planer blade, and at seven or eight bucks the price is definitely right. Use it until it gets dull, then throw it away; with that many teeth, I doubt that you'd get anyone to sharpen it, even if they could.

inside edge, being round, wants to lift up and away from the coaming and turn itself wrong-side out, especially at the fore and aft ends, leaving a gap. You could try putting it on square (glue it) and then round it as best you can, but trying to round it after it's on isn't easy. As with the toerail, the best way is to fasten the molding on with pins, then saturate the glue line and wipe off the excess glue. Home-grown maple, again, was my choice for this, and so was using superglue to stick them on with.

Cutting the molding strips is delicate work, but with a tiptop-sharp hollow-ground planer blade you can do it (see sidebar). Cut the quarter-round molding square, same with the half-round coaming moldings, then round it by sanding. Wet it with your tongue and spring it around the coaming and cuddy in one piece; let the butt joint come midway along the coaming. Fasten it in place with pins, then put the superglue to it, and brush the excess off lengthwise with a small paintbrush. After the glue dries, you can fill any gaps with automotive glazing putty and brush again immediately with a small brush dipped in lacquer thinner; this evens out the putty and fills the seams nicely.

Bowsprit, Bitt, and Rigging

Now we get down to the rigging details—the bowsprit and bitts, a traveler for the mainsheet, and so on. You'll find the dimensions for the bowsprit and the rest of the spars on the sail plan. It's up to you to decide how far to go with rigging your model. I was happy to finish *Lisa's* bowsprit, bitts, and mast, and call her done for now.

Make the bowsprit first; this will help you glue the bitts the right height and distance apart for fitting the bowsprit tongue. Start with a piece of basswood $10\frac{1}{4}$ inches long. (Why $10\frac{1}{4}$ inches, when the plan says $9\frac{3}{4}$ inches overall? The extra $\frac{1}{2}$ inch allows for trimming and for the tongue that goes through the bitts.) A width of $\frac{3}{8}$ inch allows for the bowsprit's greatest width, which runs $\frac{5}{16}$ inch wide and $\frac{1}{4}$ inch deep for about one-third of the length, tapering to $\frac{3}{16}$ inch $\times$ $\frac{1}{4}$ inch at the tip. Note that the bowsprit is slightly hogged—that is, it has a convex curve fore-and-aft. Cut the underside straight and crown the top a little. Taper the bowsprit about as shown on the plans, and hog it by tightening the bobstays to suit when you rig her.

The aft end of the bowsprit (tongue), is notched to bury in a double bitt; this is what most of the Friendship sloops had, but you could use a single bitt and notch it to receive the end of the bowsprit, and you'd still be right.

Make the bitts $\frac{1}{4}$ inch square, spaced to accept the width of the tongue, and bore them for the crosspiece that holds the tongue, then cut them to length—$1\frac{1}{4}$ inches. Place them on your tablesaw with their ends resting against the fence and one side against a miter gauge to keep everything square. When done cutting, glue them in.

Note that the bitts sit plumb when mounted on deck; this means you'll have to cut them on a bevel. Take the bevel right off the profile view of the hull with your bevel gauge. Figure the depth they sit on the deck by the height of the tongue so the tongue just slides under the crosspiece; take a little off the top of the tongue if needed.

After you've located the bitts, bore holes in the deck for their legs, which

Lisa on the beach.

can be round—or any shape where they bury in the deck, out of sight. Don't fuss with fitting them; it's OK if they're a little loose. Mix some stiff epoxy and bed them in.

While waiting for the glue to set, you can make the traveler (see the rigging details). Use a piece of brazing rod or round brass of about 1/16 inch diameter, and bend it with roundnose pliers. Cut the pads from sheet brass on a bandsaw. Run a piece of wood into the bandsaw blade first to provide backing while you cut the square pads, then bore them for the traveler. Thanks to a tip from Arthur Herrick, a professional modeler, making the four false round-headed screws stand proud for each pad is easy: Just turn the pads upside down and with a sharp awl prick their four corners, then follow up by tapping lightly with a light hammer. Make the mast saddle as shown in the hull profile. The saddle is a doughnut-shaped piece of wood 3/16-inch thick that slips over the mast to hold belaying pins for sheets.

The model pros say that "Detail is what separates the men from the boys," but I'm going to call it quits right here, except for painting. Regardless of whether you stop at this point as I have or finish her completely, this lovely little craft will catch the eyes of admirers at any stage.

I painted *Lisa*'s hull with B-I-N; this is good stuff for covering wood that has a bit of pitch or oil or is stained. A few coats of it sanded down, with a last pass with 320-grit or finer, give a very satisfactory, satin-smooth final finish.

If you decide to go the whole nine yards, *Lisa*'s sail plan adequately shows how she's rigged, and you can buy the hardware from model suppliers, or have a crack at making it yourself. You can put on trailboards (see the description making them for the schooner *We're Here* in Chapter 9, "Finishing") and even knightheads if you want; these are vertical planks that were put up in the bows of some Friendship sloops for reinforcing the bow near the stem, which some builders must have considered a weak point.

Unless you plan to sail her, a model sailboat looks nice without sails, thus

Color Scheme:

Cockpit and hull, flat white
Toerail, Floquil "Rail Brown"
Deck, light buff
Bottom, copper red
Mast, light buff or varnished
Bowsprit, white or varnished

reducing the work by a whole lot. In fact, unless the sails are nearly perfect they can detract from the model, with their size overpowering the eye for finer details elsewhere.

I will eventually put on the trailboards and rigging and good stuff. In the meantime, sitting in my shop as is, her beautiful lines alone draw the eyes of admirers.

7

Foam
A Victorian English Cutter

My fellow boat modeler and buddy Peter Spectre built a half model of this boat and did a bit of history on her. This is what he told me about *Foam* and the English cutter type:

You must admit, the shape is rather weird in comparison to today's yachts. Yet in the latter half of the 19th century it was the dominant type in Great Britain and even had its advocates in America. This is a classical Victorian cutter in its purest form. It has both the cutter rig and the cutter hull, all tied together in a neat package.

The 19th-century cutter rig looks something like the sloop rig from that era, but with certain differences. Here's what yachting historian W. P. Stephens had to say about those: "The cutter rig as distinguished from the sloop had a much shorter mast stepped more nearly amidships; to this was added a long topmast so fitted as to be readily lowered, or housed, while under way; the ordinary topmast of the sloop could not be lowered through the caps. Similarly, the bowsprit was fitted to house, the fixed bobstay and bowsprit shrouds of the sloop being replaced by tackles by means of which it might be drawn in and fully secured." In addition, the cutter's topsails were much larger than on a sloop, and it carried a jib set flying; that is, it was not set on a stay.

That's the rig. Then there's the hull type, which confuses a lot of people because the word cutter *is used to refer to more than one type of craft. In the*

Materials Needed

- one board, 8½" × 8" × ¾", basswood or pine
- one 4' × 8' sheet of ⅛" tempered Masonite (smooth both sides)
- spray adhesive
- Weldwood plastic resin glue
- superglue
- ⅜" #6 brass ribbon pins
- rigging supplies: 1" of 3/32" brass rod: nine ¼" single blocks; 10' of #15 three-strand (Brownell); 10' of 0.040 stranded wire; two mastcaps; two eyebands, ten ¼" deadeyes
- full-size plans

U.S. Coast Guard, for example, all vessels that are not boats—in other words, all ships—are called cutters. Today's Coast Guard motor ships are called cutters, and yesterday's sailing ships, even those that were rigged as barks or schooners, also carried the name. (In Coast Guard parlance, the sail training bark Eagle is known as the U.S. Coast Guard Cutter Eagle.) To further confuse things, a certain class of ship's boat, carried on davits along the rail or on skids on the boat deck, has always been called a cutter.

Our craft, Foam, would be more easily identified if she were called a cutter-yacht to avoid confusion with the other types. She is extremely narrow and deep, with substantially more hull below the waterline than above. Her type is an outgrowth of working sailing craft of the British Isles that were popular as dispatch vessels for the fighting fleet, pilot boats, revenue cutters, small privateers, and smuggling craft—any purpose that required speed, quickness, handiness, and dash.

A craft with the latter qualities makes a good yacht, and yachtsmen of the 19th century readily adopted the cutter model. Over the years they modified the type—yachtified it, in essence—and made it more extreme. The rating rules of the time had much to do with this extremeness: in the mid-19th century, for example, shifting ballast was banned, causing fixed ballast, deep down, to become the rage. By the late 19th century, as much as 60 to 70 percent of a cutter's displacement was carried in ballast, which was necessary because the hulls had become so narrow and the sail area had become so large. To keep the boats upright, the greatest percentage of the ballast was in the keel.

The British cutters were defined in beams, as in beam-to-length ratio. A six-beam cutter, which was extreme but not uncommon, had a waterline length that was six times the beam. There were even seven-beam cutters. By contrast, the typical American centerboard sloop of the same period was only three or four beams.

As you can imagine, a boat shaped like a sharpened plank on edge, with a huge press of sail and heavy, concentrated ballast deep down, was fast and virtually uncapsizable, but extremely wet underway. What's more, in anything greater than a breeze, it sailed on its ear. A cruise or race in a cutter was a spectacular balancing act and required the agility of a monkey combined with the seamanship of a Banks fisherman in a gale.

Extreme cutters may have been popular in Britain, but they were scorned in America. Wags called them "lead mines" (for all that ballast), "planks on edge," "submarines," or "death traps" (once overcome in heavy weather, they could sink like a stone because of their heavy ballast). Yet there were in America, where in the 19th century the wide, shallow centerboarder was king, some Anglophiles who favored the cutter and promoted the type as superior. They were known as "cutter cranks" because of their argumentativeness. Because many of them contributed to the yachting press of the time and therefore commanded a platform, they fostered a great debate on the supposed superiority of the shallow centerboarders over the deep cutters. This debate didn't end with the victory of one type over another. Rather, it ended with compromise. American sloops took on some of the characteristics of the cutters, and the British cutters borrowed from the sloops. Thus was born the modern yacht, which has elements of both.

To me, the greatest advantage of the old-style cutter was its tremendous headroom because of its depth. You could stand up straight in all but the smallest of them. But which would you rather?—stand straight at the mooring and be soaking wet underway, or stoop and be dry?

The advantage of making models instead of building full-size craft is that you don't have to answer questions like the above.

Tools Needed

- table saw
- bandsaw
- vise
- clamps
- 7/8" or 1" gouge with inside bevel
- block plane
- spokeshave
- sanding fid with 60- and 100-grit sandpaper
- sanding battens
- rasps
- Dremel tool with drills
- needle and riffler files
- rattail files
- 10" mill file
- 6" combination square
- #3 pencil
- scissors
- narrow masking tape

Building the Half Model

Peter built his half model to Phil Bolger's plans of Claude Worth's original design of *Foam*, which appears in the book *Small Yachts* by C. P. Kunhardt. I'll let Peter continue with telling how he went about it:

Lacking space in the house for a full model, I decided to make it as a decorative half model so it could be displayed on a wall. I followed the plans for the hull itself, but modified the upper works a bit to satisfy my own tastes—but don't worry, I referred to the plans of other cutters from that period, so the result is authentic for the type.

I glued up the lifts with Titebond carpenter's glue, which worked fine. I made the lifts of number-two-grade white pine and laid them out to avoid knots. The stem, keel, and rudder could have been white pine, too, but I had some basswood of the appropriate thickness, so I used that instead.

I cut the deck line 1/16 inch lower than shown on the plans and then glued down (with contact cement) a piece of 1/16-inch Western red cedar for the deck. The red cedar was scrap from a cold-molding project in a nearby boatshop. It is rift sawn and has perfectly straight grain with contrasting light and dark striping. The effect is a laid deck.

The bulwarks and rails are white pine. I pinned them temporarily in place and then fastened them permanently with the thinnest superglue applied with the modified eye of a needle. (I picked up that trick from Jay Hanna. You cut off the end of the eye, dip the modified eye into the glue, and run it along the seam; the glue is wicked into the joint exactly where you want it. If you're careful, there's no oozing excess.)

The spars are clear white pine, rounded and tapered as indicated on the plans. As the mast and boom are right on the centerline—and this is a half model—I planed them in half and glued them directly to the backboard. The mast is actually a stub, cut off at an angle to indicate there's more that's not showing. The bowsprit, set off the centerline, can be housed, just as on the original boat.

I made the house separately, then glued it in place. I sliced a piece of solid cherry into veneers and glued them to a block of white pine that I'd carved to the proper shape. I got the cherry from a small block in Jay Hanna's scrap pile. I didn't want to mess around with glass for the skylight, so I painted the areas where the glass would be with flat black paint.

The tiller and rudderpost are light-colored applewood, to contrast with the darker cherry and the deep brown of the backboard. I used dark apple for the coaming; it was cut to a cardboard pattern, soaked in hot water, and then bent over a form to give it the proper shape. I made it curved rather than squared-off as in the plans. The coaming kept its shape perfectly after it dried; all that was necessary was to put it in position and do the superglue trick. I harvested the applewood myself—cut a dead limb off a tree in a nearby orchard. You know me: I hate to fiddle with tiny things, so I skipped the details on this model. No blocks, rigging, hardware, or fittings of any kind. I rationalize my choice by saying the result is the epitome of simple elegance.

I wanted this model to have the feel of something right out of the Victorian era, so I finished it with subdued colors and a satin sheen. The topsides look satin black, but the paint is actually flat black cut to the deepest brown with a little red pigment. Varnish was added to reduce the flatness of the paint. The effect is of black paint gone slightly to seed with age. The bottom paint is a similar concoction: eggshell green darkened with flat black and juiced up slightly with varnish. Then after the paint was thoroughly dry, I rubbed the surface with a soft cloth dipped in pure tung oil and powdered with rotten-stone. There's a shine to the finish, but not much; it is a deep shine, not a surface one, if you know what I mean.

The part of the model that is finished bright—in other words, the territory from the deck line up—was given a coat of thinned varnish to seal it, then sanded with 220-grit. After that it was given several rubdowns with tung oil with a little varnish added. The result is a deep sheen with no buildup.

You'll recognize the backboard. It's the center extension piece from an ancient, falling-apart dining-room table, the one you were about to cut up for the shop stove awhile back. I gave it the tung-oil-rottenstone treatment, and framed it with pine. I painted the frame with maroon made deeper with black pigment.

What should you watch out for when building this model? Pay special attention to the sheerline and the stern section. The sheer is long and not particularly deep, but it has a fine sweep that can be ruined by hard spots. I fooled around with it for a long, long time. Getting the stern right was also very difficult. The stern seems to be the toughest section to carve in most solid models, and this one took the cake. I made it as accurate as I could and then concentrated on making it fair. Right, wrong, or somewhere in between, I think the result is still rather handsome.

My model, which hangs in the living room, is neither wet nor dry; her skipper neither stands straight nor stoops. She just looks great. Thanks for the plans.

Building the Full Model

Note that Bolger's plans for *Foam* are drawn at a scale of ¾ inch = 1 foot, except for the sail plan (Sheet 1), which is at ⅜-inch scale. She has nine lifts, all ¾ inch thick. Sheet 2 has 14 station templates, two buttock templates (12 inches and 24 inches), plus sectional views of these and a sectional view at the centerline to help you visualize her shape in the stern area. Note that Lift 8 runs the length of her. The shape of her stern bulwark at the extreme end is shown in plan view, top of Sheet 3, and in profile on Sheet 2.

Following the usual procedure for making the templates (see the first two chapters), roughly cut out all the waterline lifts and station templates from the plans and glue them to Masonite; finish cutting them right to the line on a bandsaw, scroll saw, or sabersaw.

You can get all the waterline lifts out of a board ¾ inch × 8 inches × 8½ feet. Square the lift sections across the board and telescope the lifts as a way of saving wood; otherwise, if you use narrower boards, expect to use a lot more footage.

Lift 1 doesn't quite make it for depth to the keel at its aft end, so the plans say to fill this area with putty. I used a ¾-inch scrap of wood for this rather than putty, since wood is easier to shape. (You'll use the hull profile template later on for marking and cutting the hull shape at the stern.)

Mark all the stations across the lifts and number them. On Lift 8, which is the sheer lift, mark the stations on the edge of the lift as well. Mark Station 6 on the edge of every lift; you'll use this station as a reference point for alignment on the jig. Square this station across the edge of each lift when gluing the lifts together. You don't need to square every station. As described in the earlier

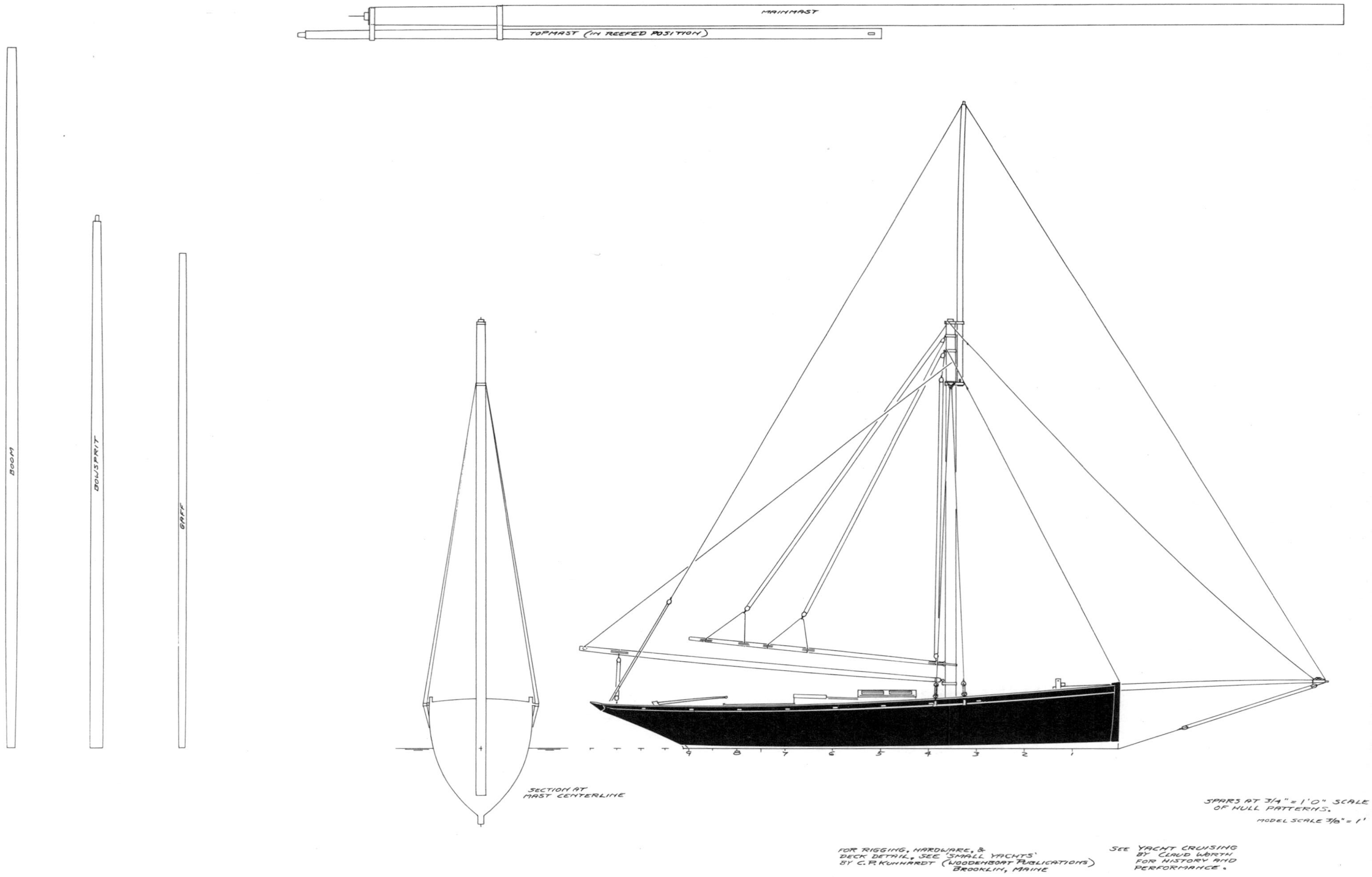

Sheet 1
Enlarge 624 percent for full-size plans.

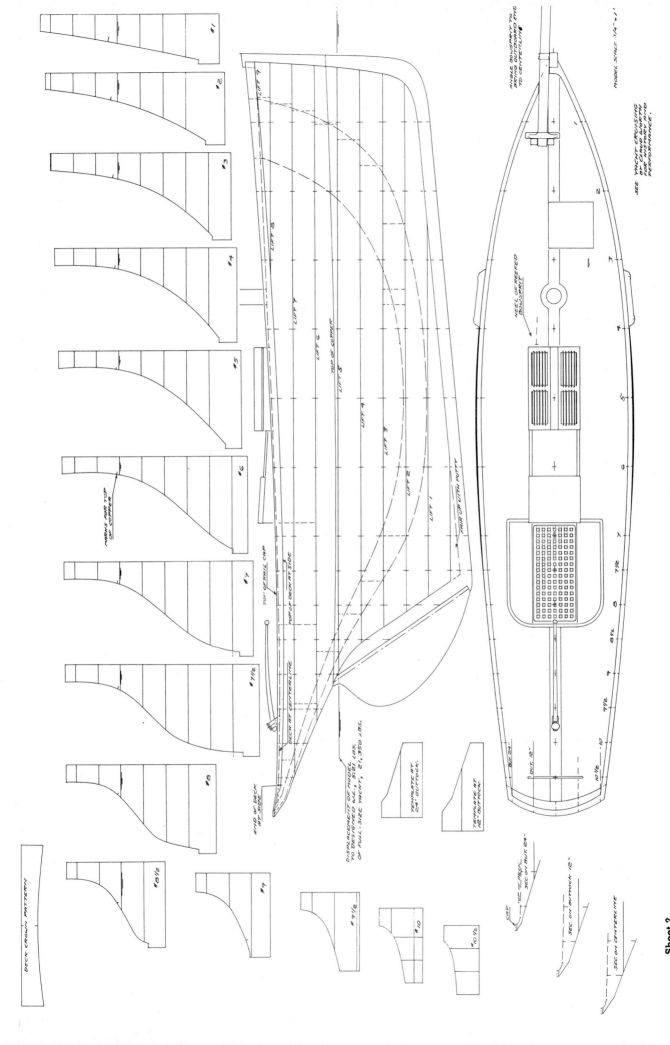

Sheet 2

Enlarge 312 percent for full-size plans.

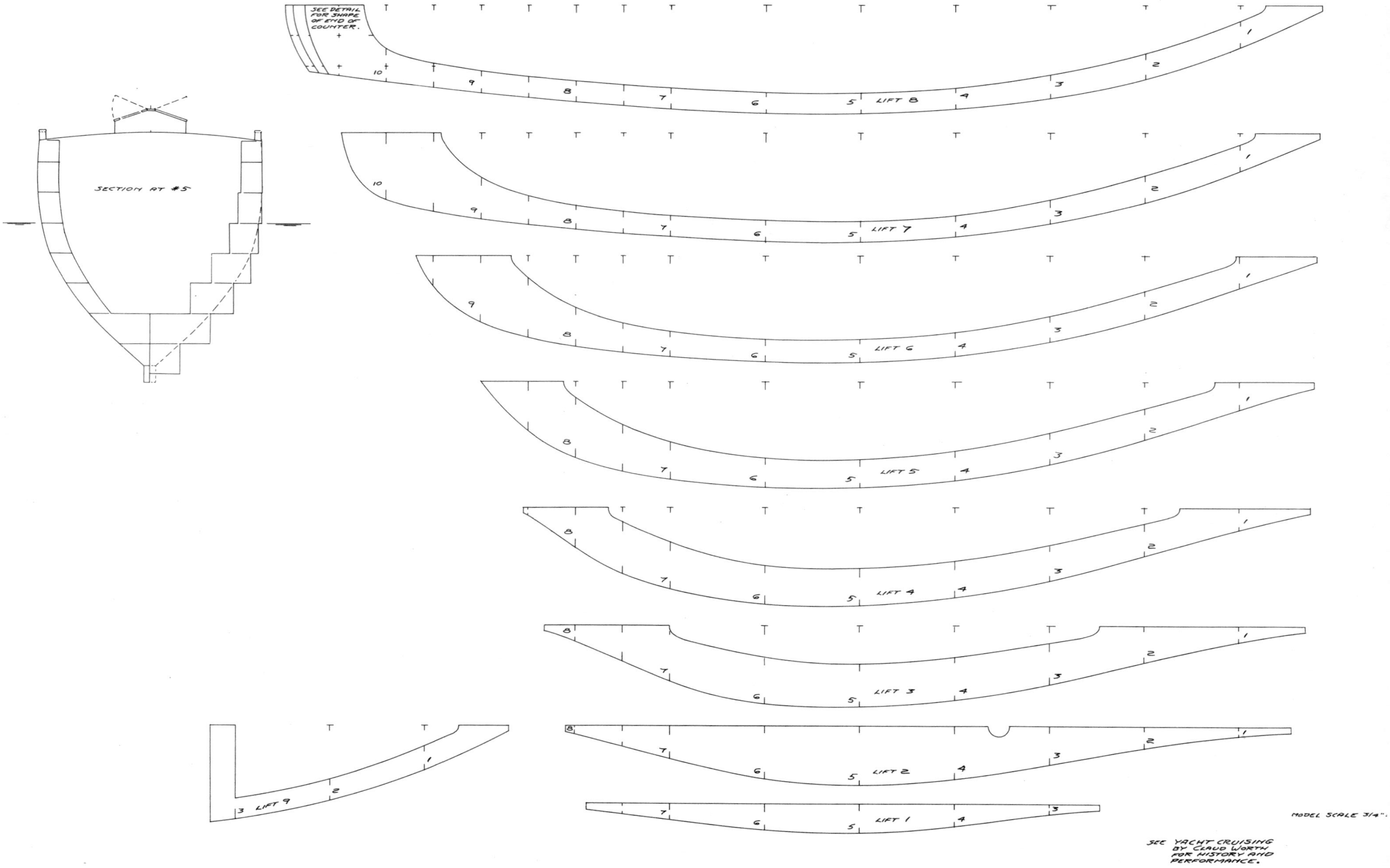

MODEL SCALE 3/4".

SEE YACHT CRUISING
BY CLAUD WORTH
FOR HISTORY AND
PERFORMANCE.

SEE DETAIL
FOR SHAPE
OF END OF
COUNTER.

LIFT 8

LIFT 7

LIFT 6

LIFT 5

LIFT 4

LIFT 3

LIFT 2

LIFT 1

LIFT 9

SECTION AT #5

Sheet 3
Enlarge 312 percent for full-size plans.

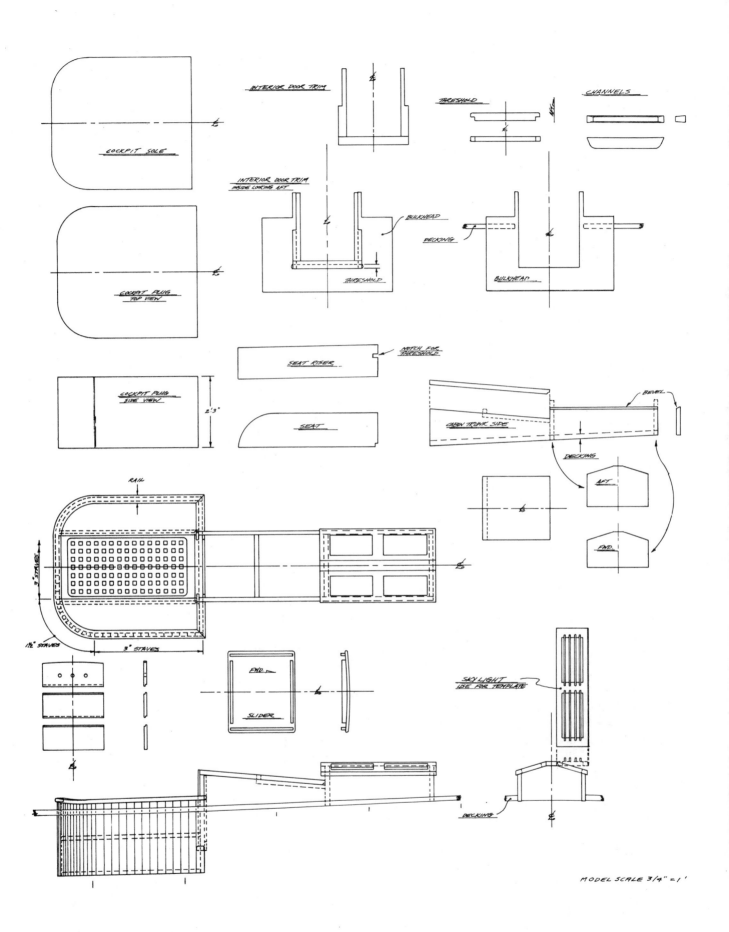

COCKPIT SOLE

INTERIOR DOOR TRIM

THRESHOLD

CHANNELS

INTERIOR DOOR TRIM
INSIDE LOOKING AFT

BULKHEAD

DECKING

THRESHOLD

BULKHEAD

COCKPIT PLUG
TOP VIEW

NOTCH FOR
THRESHOLD

SEAT RISER

COCKPIT PLUG
SIDE VIEW

2'3"

SEAT

CABIN TRUNK SIDE

BEVEL

DECKING

AFT

FWD.

RAIL

3" STAVES

1½" STAVES   3" STAVES

FWD.

SLIDER

SKY LIGHT
USE FOR TEMPLATE

DECKING

MODEL SCALE 3/4" = 1'

Sheet 4
Enlarge 312 percent for full-size plans.

chapters, trace the outline of each lift on the lift below to show you where to spread the glue. Mix up some Weldwood dry-powder glue, and "butter up" the lifts. *Foam*'s narrow lifts should lie together nicely without clamping, as long as you picked straight wood in the beginning. If clamping is needed, clamp a stick of wood at the top of the jig and slip a wedge under it, and against the lift. Use only finger pressure; you don't needed to press hard. Just see that each joint is filled with glue. If you spot some open joints later after you remove the half hull from the jig, mix up some more glue and squeeze it in. You can make a putty knife from a portion of a razor blade (as wide as you want) stuck in a wooden handle—this does a great job at working glue into the slack seams.

With both hull halves off the jig, you'll soon be ready to mark the hull profile on each half. But first, before you make the hull profile template, there are several important jobs to do.

Take a look at Sheet 2. Note that the rudderpost goes up through the deck at the centerline. Draw the hidden part of the rudderpost running through the hull on the hull profile—this establishes the hole for it—and mark it on each hull half. Now, before gluing the halves together, is the time to file out each half hole with a rattail file. This way, you can't miss—otherwise, you'd have to be sitting on the right-hand side of God to bore the hole freehand later, hoping for perfect alignment.

Before you cut the hull profile from the plans, it's a good idea to make a pattern of the rudder—post and all—by slipping a piece of drafting paper over the drawing and tracing its shape; the same goes for the tiller, since both will be gone when you've cut out the template. Note on Sheet 2 that the line "top of deck at side" is shown after the deck is laid; this means you must allow for the thickness of the deck when cutting out the hull profile template. Since this dimension is not given, I'll suggest an appropriate thickness: chances are that a boat of this length, about 33 feet 3 inches, would have decking no more than 1¼ inches or 1½ inches thick, so scale this down to suit, mark the thickness under the deck line, and sweep the line in with a batten. I use a 32-inch adjustable plastic curve for this. You can buy one at an artist's supply store if you plan on using it in the future; if not, a thin strip of wood will do.

There's no easy way I know of to describe the exact shape of this boat at her stern, so I'll simply say that I let the deck line run into the stern bulwark as shown "end of deck at side." There are a couple of ways to handle the aft end of the deck where it flows into the bulwark: you can either let the deck run out by the stern, leaving the bulwark to be put on top later, which is no easy matter; or you can leave the bulwark on as shown on the lower lift of Sheet 2 in profile and in plan view next to it, and butt the ends of the decking to it. I decided to use the latter method, since I hadn't done a deck this way before, and it preserves the shape of the top of the stern in profile and plan view.

Before making the hull profile template, you'll also need to make a pattern of the waist bulwark. Note that it tapers in depth from stem to stern. Make it 25¼ inches long, a little longer than shown in plan view. Cut a strip of drafting paper about 4 or 5 inches wide, lay it over the bulwark in profile view, and draw its shape, allowing for the thickness of the decking, which the bulwarks will lie against—not on top of. Give the pattern a shot of spray-glue and stick it to Masonite. The bulwarks on this boat sit plumb, so the pattern doesn't need to be expanded to fit. Note that most of the station templates are plumb at the deck line—in fact, at amidships her sides even tumble in a bit (see "section at #5," Sheet 3).

With the rudder and bulwark templates made, you can now cut the hull profile out of the plans, right to the line. Give it a shot of spray adhesive and stick it to Masonite. If you have a scroll saw or a very narrow-kerf bandsaw blade, cut out the keel (backbone) template and stick it in the position it has on the plan relative to the hull, then saw the hull and keel templates apart. The saw kerf is about right to allow enough slack when the hull and keel are to be married. In other words, a pencil line drawn around the hull profile template onto the lifts and around the keel template onto the keel would result in too tight a fit if both were cut to the line. Sawing a little from each template makes both hull and keel the right size for final fit.

If you have neither bandsaw nor scroll saw, cut out the keel template separately with a sabersaw. Number all the stations on the keel; this'll come in handy later, when you get to carving the hull—you can simply plunk the backbone over the hull to reestablish the station lines. With a razor saw, make tiny cuts at the ends of the hull profile at Waterline 5, and for the rockered waterline, and at Station 5 at the bottom of the template, and tiny cuts marking the hole through the hull for the rudderpost. These cuts are so that when you shift the hull profile template to the starboard half hull, using it back-side to, you'll be able to align the lift lines to those of the templates.

Before marking the lifts to the profile hull shape, put each half hull in your vise and sand the hull free of glue buildups, fairing the centerline a bit. A sanding belt cut in half and stapled to a board works great for this.

Now it's time to mark the hull profile shape on the lifts. Lay the hull profile template on the lifts, matching both at Station 5 and Waterline 5. I chose Waterline 5 because this divides the hull about in half; if there's any deviation in the layup of either half hull, you can use Waterline 5 to even it out when you trace the hull profile on the lifts. With the half hull in your vise, clamp the profile hull template to the hull after determining its exact location, waterline to waterline and station to station, and trace around the template with a sharp #3 pencil. Leaving the template clamped in place, spot in the sheer by squaring across the template; just dots about 1/2 inch or so apart will do it.

With the sheer and profile marked, next comes sawing the sheer. Tilt your bandsaw so the cut is slightly higher to the outside of the hull, to ensure that you won't be surprised by slack spots on the outside of the sheer after you've cut down the sheer and faired it in. If you have no bandsaw or don't feel confident about freehanding, you can cut down the sheer by making a series of handsaw cuts, fairly close together, across the sheer. Get rid of excess wood first with a chisel, then finish with a spokeshave, a block plane, and a sanding board. If you goof, cutting the sheer too deep, mix some five-minute epoxy with sawdust and fill the depression.

After the two hull halves are cut right to the line all around (except for the sheer), scribe the keel rabbet on each half. Sheet 3, in the upper left corner, shows the body section at Station 5 and the width of the keel, which is 4½ inches on the full-size boat.

With half a hole for the rudderpost already filed in each half hull, you're ready to glue the halves together. Since I used Weldwood dry-powder glue for the lifts, I mixed another batch for this job, mixing it quite thick to even out any irregularities. It doesn't take much clamping pressure—just a couple of small clamps at the bow, a couple at the stern, and a couple along her bottom, about amidships. You'll need to cut a couple of wedges, one for each side at the bow, to clamp to; it's impossible to clamp the bow together at the top, because a clamp will slide off the tapered surfaces.

After the glue is dry, let's proceed with that tricky stern. Sheet 2 shows the

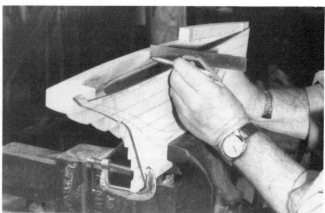

Clockwise, from upper left: Marking centerline of layup. . . .
Spotting the sheer. . . . Leave the wood higher on the outside. If
you've cut too much you'll have to fill the depression with epoxy and
sawdust. . . . Wedges tacked to stem will help clamps hold. . . .
Trying on one-piece backbone.

sectional views and the plan view. With your deck pattern mark the inner face
of the stern bulwark, and with the hull profile pattern mark the rake of the transom on the outside of the hull. This gives you two views to control your carving
of the inner face of the transom. Carve it with a sharp chisel to the depth of the
deck sheer, and sand it to a smooth surface.

With the transom's inner shape carved and sanded and the hull's sheer
planed and sanded, the next step is to mark the shape of the deck in plan view
along the hull sides. Match the template stations with those on the hull, and
trace her deck shape. Just line up the template's centerline with that of the hull,
and you can't miss.

Carving the Hull

With the hull upright in your vise, carve the outside of the hull sides to the deck line you just drew. With the deck line established and her keel rabbet drawn, you can start carving everything between these two points. Use the station templates as a guide to show you exactly where to carve and how much. The bow area is the easiest to carve because there isn't much shape there, so it's a good place to practice.

The carving gets much more difficult as you near the stern. For this you'll need to have the hull upside down in your vise, so jam a piece of 2 × 6 down into her, glue it with five-minute epoxy, and you're in business.

A gouge with an inside bevel and a spokeshave are all good for carving; even a drawknife is OK to start with, if you're careful. You can use a rasp early on, but not in the later stages of fairing the hull, where you'd risk leaving deep scratch marks in the hull. (Rasps have a tendency to cut much deeper than you expect.)

Note that the counter—the underside of the hull from the sternpost to the transom—is concave in profile, so don't make it straight. Besides using the two buttock templates provided, you might find it worthwhile to make a template of her underbody shape at the centerline. Looking at the stern area and especially the shape of the transom, you'd swear there's no way you can carve it to look like much. So, when you get to carving in this area, take your time. Draw the buttock lines on the hull, and use the buttock templates and the station templates together. Carve a little, checking both ways, and keep reestablishing the buttock lines and station lines as soon as they disappear. The best tool for doing this fussy work is a mill file; it'll allow you to get a reasonably sharp definition between her counter and her transom.

After you've carved this area reasonably close, go back to carving the rest of the hull, using the station templates as you go. Note that in the stern area, from Station 7 to 10½, where the carving gets fussy, Phil has doubled the number of station templates. Here you carve a little with the gouge, and sand a little with the sanding fid, checking constantly with the station templates. Note that Lifts 1 through 4 are hollowed in at both ends. The bow area's easy to carve, but at the stern you're apt to think something has gone wrong when you find yourself digging a hole. Stations 7, 7½, 8, and 8½ take a lot of careful carving, so take your time here.

Now's the time to trace the transom template and shape the aft face of the transom and the crown of the top.

Allow for the ⅛-inch thickness of the Masonite when holding the station templates against the hull. Pay attention to which side of the station line you're holding them; also, be sure to hold them as square as you can to the hull's centerline. There'll be high spots on the hull left between the stations as each station is carved close to its shape. For final sanding, stick some 60-grit sandpaper on a flexible batten and start sanding high on the hull close to the sheer; you know this line is right, since you marked and cut it from the deck plan. Work the batten back and forth, hitting the high spots. Shift to 80- or 100-grit paper on battens and sand some more, then shift to 220- and 320-grit sanding pads for final fairing, sanding freehand.

Backbone, Cradle, and Rudder

Making the keel (backbone) in one piece, using your keel template as a pattern, is the easy way. You'll need a scroll saw or bandsaw to saw it out. I made the keel from basswood, because of its close grain; it's pretty tough and will take quite a lot of mishandling without the cross-grain breaking at the stem and sternpost. If I didn't have a scroll saw or bandsaw, I'd use a coping saw and make the backbone in three pieces—stem, keel, and sternpost—and glue them together onto a piece of waxed paper placed on the keel template drawing.

Carefully fit the backbone to the hull so it slips on without distorting. When you're satisfied, glue and pin it in place, making certain the backbone fits precisely between the rabbet lines and is perfectly straight from stem to stern.

After shaping and sanding the hull to your satisfaction, knock the 2 × 6 support out of the hull. A few good whacks will do it.

Now's a good time to make a cradle for the model, using Stations 3 and 6 for the arms. The following is an easy way of making the cradle and takes the guesswork out of it. Stick the profile template into the keel template, lay them together on a piece of cardboard or paper, and trace around the whole works. Extend lines down from the sheer at Stations 3 and 6. Measure down from the top of the keel 1¾ inches at Station 3 and 1⅛ inches (both measurements are real measure) at Station 6, and draw a baseline. Plane a board 20 inches × 5½ inches wide × ⅜ inches thick. Saw the end square, draw a centerline, and square the 1¾ height across the board. Set the Station 3 template on top of the 1¾ mark and trace each half up to the waterline shown on the template, or to the top of Lift 4 if you want. Mark the keel depth from the rabbet line. Cut the board across the waterline, and cut out the hull shape of Station 3, including the keel area. Repeat this procedure for Station 6, using 1⅛ inches from the base. Lay the baseboard on edge on the drawing and mark it for the station locations. Square these across the baseboard, set the cradle stations on the baseboard, matching their centerlines, glue and nail them, and cross-brace them if you want. It's a good idea to pad their bearing surfaces with masking tape, so as not to mar the hull.

Cut out the rudder—post and all—in one piece; leave the post about ¾ inch higher for now. The rudder's the same thickness as the keel, but with some taper aft. Round the rudder's leading edge so it'll pivot in the groove you cut for it in the sternpost. With a small rattail file of about the rudderpost's diameter, file the hole in the hull and in the sternpost to ensure alignment.

Try the rudder and see that it turns freely in its hole, then stick a pin up through the bottom end of the skeg into it for it to pivot on.

Big morale booster, this rudder. It takes very little time to make and does a whole lot for the boat's looks. Leave the rudder in place while you're putting in the deck beams so you don't put one where the rudderpost comes through the deck.

Carlins are placed fore and aft between the deck beam section, where the rudderpost comes through to catch the decking. Nothing fussy, just be sure they don't interfere with the rudderpost turning.

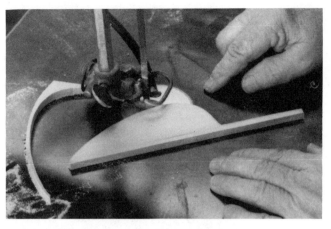

Clockwise, from upper left: Sawing out *Foam*'s rudder, post and all. . . . Checking height of deckbeams with crowning board. . . . Cutting out *Foam*'s bulwark. . . . Make sure you use a sharp chisel to notch bulwark ends. . . . Boring scupper holes. A piece of thin aluminum taped to the deck will prevent marring.

Deckbeams and Decking

The deck beams are next, and are made to the deck crown pattern (Sheet 2). One deck beam for each station is all you need, except for the stern area, where you'll need one each at Stations 7, 8, 9, 10, and 10½. The fastest way to make the deck beams to scale is to draw their shape on ¾-inch or thicker wood. Make

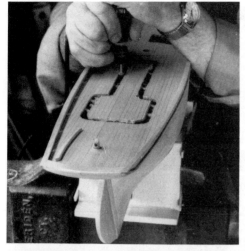

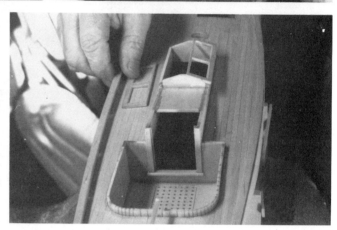

the deck beams 1/4 inch or so deep, and don't forget to draw their centerlines. Cut out their shape on your bandsaw and then saw them on your table saw into 1/8-inch or thicker slices; slice them carefully by sawing them over a piece of scrap wood put over the table slot to keep them from falling through, and use a push-stick and awl to save your fingers.

Next, bore pockets for the ends of the deck beams. Rough-cut the pockets first with an ordinary drill the width of the deck beams, and be sure to make them deep enough; then switch to a Dremel tool with a high-speed (Micro Mark's "I" or "J") cutter for finish-boring the pockets. Go as close as you dare to the side of the hull. Cut all the deck beams to length for the pockets, then mix a stiff batch of Weldwood glue and plop the beams into place. Lay the deck crown pattern across the hull and bring each deck beam up to it or push it down, whichever it takes, so that the ends of each beam lie flush to the sheer. Fit all the deck beams across in one piece; later, you'll cut out the deck beams fitting the cockpit and cuddy area.

For *Foam*'s decking, you'll need to cut 24 planks and a kingplank. Basswood is a good choice, and makes a handsome deck with a natural finish. It's a good idea to cut more decking than you need in case any of the planks are blemished or you happen to saw some thinner than others. First pre-saw some slices 26 inches (real measure) long by the plank width (3 real inches) to scale. Then run them through the table saw, cutting individual planks 1 1/2 scale

Clockwise, from upper left: Cutting out cockpit and cuddy area with ball cutter in Dremel tool. . . . Cutting round holes in cockpit sole grating using Dremel tool. . . . Companionway bulkhead and top, dropslide guides, and door sill. . . . Finished cockpit and cuddy; note the open sliding hatch.

inches thick or thicker, so they end up being about $1/16$ inch thick in real life—anything less would be too fragile. The kingplank is twice the width of a regular plank—6 scale inches. Bevel the planks one at a time, for the caulking seams; one swipe on each edge with a modeler's plane will do it. Even though all this may seem a lengthy task (about a day's work), the quality of the job beats making the decking out of wide strips of wood and trying to scribe in caulking seams later; because of hard and soft spots in wood, plus grain running off, my attempt at trying it that way (*Pauline*) was a disaster. *Laura B.* didn't show planking seams, the idea with her was a solid deck.

Before laying the deck, figure out the thickness of the bulwark (about 1 scale inch but make $1/8$ inch in real life), and make a gauge—a piece of wood with the bulwark's thickness sawed out of it in the form of a notch. All you'll have to do is roughly fit the ends of the decking to the hull sides, then place the gauge against the hull and pull it along while marking the decking for the thickness of the bulwark—in other words the bulwarks are let into the deck by their thickness. Lay the kingplank first with a mast partner under it fitted between Stations 3 and 4. The mast partner is glued with its top flush to the deck beams. Mark the kingplank for the rudderpost location and bore a hole before gluing it on for good. Cut the aft ends of decking at the angle they touch inside the transom bulwark. A razor blade works fine for cutting; also a cutting board made of some kind of self-healing plastic is a good investment in that it protects wooden surfaces from the sharp edges of razors (even razor saws won't damage it). Most mail-order hobby suppliers sell cutting boards, and will sometimes include one as a bonus with an order. When you've finished laying the deck, now's the time to sand it.

Bulwarks, Tiller, and Railcaps

Bulwarks are next. Trace them from the bulwark template, and notch the stem for their forward ends. Remove their thickness from the transom so that you can let them run by. It's a good idea to pre-bend the bulwarks to the general shape of the bow area. I prefer my shop stovepipe for this, since I can immediately put them on and glue them, bending them dry this way. (My wife's electric curling iron is my next choice; ammonia's the third choice.) To locate the limber holes on the bulwarks, see the sail plan, Sheet 4, drawn at $3/8$ inch = 1 foot. There are eight limber holes, from Station 3 through 10. Note that they're all located forward of the stations and measure about 1 inch high by 3 inches long and three feet apart on centers. Switch the scale to $3/4$ inch and you can locate them on the model.

You'd think cutting the limber holes in the bulwarks would be an easy matter, but it's not. The bottoms of the holes should be flush with the deck, while the tops should be at various heights from the tops of the tapered bulwarks. You can either cut the limber holes before gluing on the bulwarks, which makes the bulwarks a bit fragile when bending them, or you can put them in later after you've fitted the bulwarks, which calls for some fussy work but is my choice. Either way, mark each limber hole's precise shape and location, making sure the bottom of each hole is flush to the top of the deck. With an awl, prick-punch them prior to boring, putting three holes in each limber hole with a small drill (about a .61). Work the holes out with the drill and an X-ACTO modeler's knife, and finish the holes with a square modeler's file. Tape a scrap piece of aluminum plate (the kind used by newspapers as printing plates) on the deck to protect it from being marred while you bore and fit the holes.

Make the tiller to the shape shown in the profile and plan view on Sheet 2. The tiller mounts in the hole of the rudderpost and goes on after you cut the deck opening for the cuddy and cockpit.

After the limber holes are cut, you can put on the railcaps. Use the deck template to determine their shape and cut them from basswood, making them about 1 scale inch thick by whatever width suits you so that their edges protrude a bit on each side of the bulwarks. Fasten them with pins and superglue. There's a 1-inch-square molding running from stem to stern (see Sheet 1). Cut this out, glue it on, and this completes the bulwarks.

Cockpit and Cabin/Companionway

It's now time to cut the deck for the cockpit and cabin area, cutting away both decking and deck beams in one step. Lay the deck template on the deck's centerline, matching the station lines (still on the hull), and matching the mast holes for fore-and-aft alignment. Trace around the template for the cockpit area and forward to the bow end of the ventilation hatch. It's easier to cut out this area for the cabinsides to fit against than it is to fit them to the deck. A variable-speed Dremel tool with a "wood hog" cutter turning at 30,000 rpm makes easy and fast work of it. All you do is make a few starting holes at corners, simply by pressing down with the tool, and away you go—nothing to it, except to watch what you're doing. Come close to the line with power, but finish the final cutting with a sharp chisel and mill file. I like Japanese chisels; I haven't seen any other chisels that compare for quality steel and cutting ability.

In the book *Small Yachts*, by C. P. Kunhardt, Claude Worth's original profile drawing of *Foam* shows the sides of the cockpit built of staves about 3 inches wide and 1 inch thick by 2 feet 3 inches in length on the straight areas and about 1½ inches wide for the corner curves. The 3-inch staves edges are beveled on the outside to show seams; the corner staves need no beveling since putting them around the corners opens up their outside seams as a matter of course. For forming the model's cockpit, you'll need to cut the staves to scale and glue them around a plug made from the deck template, from which you've deducted the stave thickness (1 scale inch; see Sheet 4). Wax the plug and wrap waxed paper around it before gluing the staves in place. Use superglue, as it leaves no buildup. (White carpenter's glue or Franklin Titebond would not be a good choice, since you couldn't remove any glue buildup from the back of the staves against the plug.) You'll need to use a few brass pins to hold the staves against the plug.

Fitting the cockpit floor is about as easy as it gets. Pull the stave assembly vertically away a bit from the plug, then lay the exposed plug on the wood you're going to use and trace around it (can't miss this way). I made the floor of basswood about ³/₁₆ inch thick, all in one piece—grating and all. Put the deck template in place, and with a sharp awl prick the center for each hole in the grating. Bore the holes with a ⁵/₆₄-inch bit and finish them square if you want with a modeler's square file—that is, if you can face all 112 of them. I tried but they got out of square freehanding the filing job, so I left them round. Before you glue the floor in place, cut in the lines around the grating showing that it's supposed to be removable (in real life). Glue the floor to the cockpit with the cockpit on the plug, pull the plug out, and glue the assembly in place to whatever height you want the cockpit sides above the deck; a couple of scale inches looks about right (see Sheet 4). Note that on Sheet 1 the tiller clears the top of the cockpit, so keep the cockpit sides low. The cockpit railcap will add to the overall height, so take that into consideration. All the English cutters of *Foam's* era were different in this way, so you're free to fit the cockpit as suits your eye.

Building the companionway bulkhead is next. My friend Bob Steward's *Boatbuilding Manual*, 3rd Edition, (International Marine, 1987) was a great help for this job. Take the height of the bulkhead off the profile of Sheet 2 and its width and depth to the inside of the cockpit area. The width of the companionway opening is to the rough deck opening plus the inner slide guides; leave enough wood inboard for these. The inner slide guides are the same thickness as the cabin trunk sides, and their aft ends butt against them. Cut the bottom of the companionway opening about 4 scale inches higher than the floor; we'll add a doorsill along with drop slide guides, which are small vertical strips of wood (like door casings) that sit on the doorsill to catch the three drop slides we'll use in place of doors.

Cut out the trunk and skylight sides—one piece for each side—to the profile shape shown on Sheet 2, and glue these in. Cut the ends of the skylight, flatten them slightly on top for a filler piece (like a ridgepole), and glue them in. Cut out two sashes square across so they'll be exactly alike (in one piece, for now, for ease in working) and the filler piece. Make two skylight openings, 9 by 15 scale inches, in each of the two sashes; lay these out carefully with a square so they're identical. Then, with a modeler's drill and a #66 bit, which is .033 inch, bore four tiny holes at both ends of each glass opening (16 holes in all), for fitting the protective bars on the skylights. You'll need three 12-inch lengths of .033 brass rod to make the 16 bars; cut the pieces long enough for two right-angle bends. Make a wooden or metal jig to bend these over so they're exactly alike. Give the sashes and filler piece a coat of shellac, thinned varnish, tung oil—your choice. After they dry, cut some plastic for the glass; I use 3/32-inch hobby-shop acetate. Lay each sash over the acetate and scribe with a needle for a tight fit, then cut to the line with scissors or a razor blade. Fit the panes of glass in the sash and carefully spot-glue them in with superglue. Press the ends of the brass rods into their holes, and glue the sashes to the skylight, checking to see that there's overhang at their ends and sides, and glue in the filler piece.

The companionway top fits in between the trunk sides and butts against the end of the skylight. Line it out with the sliding hatch in mind, so that it'll be long enough for the sliding hatch to cover its aft end with the hatch closed. The slide logs are cut square, 1½ × 1½ scale inches, and extend from the extreme aft end of the companionway to the aft end of the skylight to which they're butted (don't forget the limber holes in their forward ends where they butt to the back of the skylight). A beam of the same dimensions fits between the logs at the aft end of the companionway top, and serves as a stop when the sliding hatch fetches up against it in its fully retracted position.

The slightly cambered sliding hatch has outside trim that serves as precise guides for tracking, as it slides back and forth on the slide logs. The ends of the hatch beams are kept back from the guides 1½ scale inches to form slots for the slide logs. The easiest way of closing the companionway is to use "drop boards,"

as Bob Steward calls them. These are three horizontal boards, shiplapped, that slide between the guides you installed earlier. The top board shows three ventilation holes of 1 scale inch or so diameter.

Cockpit seats (use the plug pattern for the seats) are fitted butted to the companionway bulkhead and around the sides and ends of the cockpit area. Leave a lip on their inboard edges.

The cockpit railcap goes on now. Use the cockpit plug as a template. Remember that the plug is to the inside of the staves, so the railcap sits about 3/4 scale inch inside and outside of the staves when you line it out for cutting. It should end up being 3 scale inches wide by 1 scale inch thick.

Make the forward ventilation hatch (shown on the deck plan, Sheet 2) 1 1/2 inches square by 3/8 inch deep (measurements are to scale), and scribe a line around it to show the cover. To get the hatch to sit properly so it's not cocked one way or the other, glue a couple of small pieces of wood under the deck for it to sit on.

Make the traveler from 3/32-inch brass rod. Sheet 2 shows its location aft of Station 10 1/2. The same sheet also shows the channels, protrusions on both sides of the hull between Stations 3 and 4. Why these are called channels I have no idea, but if you decide to go further with *Foam*'s fittings and rigging, you should fit them, because her deadeyes are supported by chainplates running outside of them and fastened to the hull. Channels were common practice on these narrow English cutters, and helped to widen the base of support for their masts.

At this point I'll stick a stubby, cut-off mast in her and leave the rest until later—or maybe I'll keep her as is. The natural color of the wood finished with only one coat of rubbed shellac looks quite nice; so do the lift lines, which show her construction. I'll wager if you can get her this far, you can do the rest.

8

Alice
A Low-Power Day Cruiser

Phil Bolger, *Alice's* designer, writes in *WoodenBoat* No. 97:

When I drew Alice (as in Wonderland) I made an attempt to recover some of the tranquility of the 1910 [motor] boats. . .[that] it might be possible to build something in keeping with a relaxed mood. . . . At six knots in a crowded waterway, with much to look at, a boat like this is where she belongs, doing what she does best. She looks it, and her well-being is infectious. The cockpit is deep, roomy, and clear. Perhaps some wicker armchairs can be found. . . . The white fabric awning glows overhead. No glass or plastic dims the view. . . .

Outside, the sides of the raised deck are bright-varnished. The cockpit is soled with laid teak, probably also varnished. . . . The skylight and wheelbox are, of course, bright mahogany, as is the spoke wheel itself. . . . She has a small signal mast, a straight round stick with decorative taper. She will show textbook-correct colors. . . .

This boat's inspiration was a modest craft for modest people, with no pretensions to style or status. She hovered on the outskirts of the occasions of the rich and famous, enjoying without much envy the spectacle of big-schooner racing, processions of steam yachts, and the vicissitudes of the primitive racing motorboats. . . .

Some such boats were much better than others, no consensus having been reached at the time about their shape. Alice *is harder bilged and wider than most of them, with what passed for moderate flare at the time. Her displacement is spread out forward and aft as is compatible with a bow that will slice cleanly through the wake of a modern boat without either bringing water on deck or throwing it wide with a noisy splash. She is not a bad seaboat, though bouncy in her motion compared with a 1980s boat slowed down to her speed. . . .*

The real virtue of this boat is that she will bolster everybody's self-satisfaction. Her owner will congratulate herself on her good taste as she admires the wood grain and the unaffected style, her good sense in taking an afternoon on the water without foolish excess of power and equipment, and her independence in choosing distinction without pretensions.

But at the neighboring landings, the owners of the 70-knot catamaran on one side and the four-story seagoing condominium on the other will feel just as contented, knowing that their boats are faster, more seaworthy, more comfortable, and much more expensive.

Building the Hull

Boats like this reflect a long-bygone era when we lived less hurried lives and had, and took, the time to enjoy the scenery. *Alice's* power is a mere 22 horsepower—ample for driving this kind of hull and easy on the pocketbook, too.

As you'll notice, this day cruiser is an uncomplicated waterline model, with only five lifts. You can make the model fairly ultra and mount it on a reflective surface, or you can take a more modest approach with it and give the cruiser to a kid to push around on a rug. The plans are drawn at a scale of 3/4 inch = 1 foot, and the lifts are all 3/4 inch thick except for the bottom (Lift 1), which is 3/8 inch thick, seen in profile at the top of the sheet of lift patterns.

This model is built like the others—upside-down on a jig, one half at a time and her raised deck is crowned. A 3/4-inch pine or basswood board 6 inches wide and 10 feet long is all the lumber you need to build the full model.

Cut all the lift patterns out of the plans—roughly at first, well outside of the lines, including the centerline. While you're at it, it's a good idea to cut out the plan view of the raised deck and cockpit area in case you lose the shape of her topsides. Give the plans a shot of artist's spray adhesive and stick them to tempered Masonite. Then cut out all the lift templates on your bandsaw, this time right to the line. Smooth them up, then cut out the cockpit areas of Lifts 3 and 4. Lift 5 is cut to Station 6, plus a small projection that is part of the coaming; this will be cut down later, after the profile of the hull is laid on each half hull and the coaming sheer is squared back from the centerline.

Note that on Lift 1 the bottom waterline is shown as a dashed line; this means it's on the underside of the lift. The easiest way to copy this line is to make another template, call it the bottom waterline, and mark its shape on the underside of Lift 1. The dashed lines on Lifts 4 and 5 show the raised-deck molding and the top of the guardrail.

You can use Weldwood dry-powder glue or epoxy or the glue of your choice to glue the lifts together. Pick one station (Station 6 was my choice) to

Materials Needed

- one-quarter 4' × 8' sheet of 1/8" tempered Masonite (smooth both sides)
- 10 running feet of 6" × 3/4" pine or basswood
- 1' of 3/32" brazing rod
- one .020" to .030" sheet of clear acetate
- spray adhesive
- Weldwood plastic resin glue or epoxy
- two 2" square pieces of 1/16" aircraft plywood
- one 2" × 12" sheet of thin brass (.020")
  1' length of 1/8" brass tubing
- two 1/4" running lights
- two 5/8" stern cleats
- full-size plans

line up the lifts, and go to it. Since these lifts are solid forward, any slight cupping of the wood will translate into open glue joints on the outside of the hull, so these lifts call for clamping. Since there's no easy way to clamp this stack of lifts after they're glued together on the jig, the best way is temporarily tack the lifts to each other while you lay them up. Small (#17 or #18 wire) 1¼-inch brass brads are good for this. Then, with the lifts tacked together, remove the layup from the jig, clamp it, and immediately clean up the oozed-out glue. It took me 10 hours to get to this point, with both hull halves laid up.

Now's a good time to cut out the body templates, while you wait for the glue to harden.

Let the glued halves sit overnight if the weather's cool; if the temperature's 75-80 degrees, four or five hours is long enough. Then clean any remaining glue from the centerline faces of the half hulls, and check to see that they're dead straight and flat. I've never laid up a model yet where there hasn't been some slight fluctuation along the centerline of the lifts, even though they were held securely at a right angle against the jig. To even things up, I test across the model half with a combination square, then smooth everything down flat with a farrier's (horseshoer's) rasp. Put the halves together and try the centerline joint for tightness. If the halves held together rock slightly and you can see a slight gap between them at each end, give the centerline face of each half a slight hollowing with a block plane. Check the half hulls to see that the station lines are marked at the crucial points—the top and bottom of each station—to guide you in carving the hull as you check for accuracy with the body templates. You don't need to put every station mark on every lift, except for Station 6 (the key aligning station) and Lifts 5 and 1 (the top and bottom lifts)—don't lose these marks.

After the two halves are exactly matched, lay the hull profile on each stack, matching its bottom waterline with that of the lifts. Clamp the profile template in place, mark around it, and use a combination square to square the sheer of the coaming back to the inside of each half hull. Hold the edge of the tongue against the coaming template with the end of the tongue touching the inside of the hull, and keep spotting the curve along with a series of dots about ¼ inch apart; this is close enough so that you don't have to sweep the curve of dots with a batten. Tip the saw table of your bandsaw 2 or 3 degrees, so the cut is higher on the outside of the hull than on the inside, then lay the half hull on the bandsaw and start sawing at the stern, sawing carefully to where the coaming butts up against the bulkhead. Trim both ends (stem and stern) of each half hull, then work the stern deck areas right down to their profiles and square across to the outside of the hull. You'll be delighted to see how easily the coaming and deck all fair in. (If you're a bit doubtful of your skill, cut each stern deck right to the profile of the centerline, but leave the outside of each deck a bit high, then work both down together after the two hulls are glued together.)

To glue the two hull halves together, spread Weldwood or epoxy on both hulls, and align them. Tack a couple of brads—one at each end—to keep the half hulls from slipping, clamp them, and wait for the glue to harden.

Next, we'll carve the sides of the hull. It makes sense to do this now, because with two flat surfaces—the raised deck and flat bottom—you can hold the model in your vise, with no need to make a holding device. (You'll crown the raised deck area later.) In carving, the idea is to flow all the lines in together. You can carve a bit with a block plane and a spokeshave, but don't risk flattening the hull between lifts as a result of taking off too much. Try the body templates early, just to train your hand and eye for what you're supposed to take off,

Tools Needed

- table saw
- bandsaw, sabersaw
- vise
- clamps
- spokeshave
- block plane
- small modeler's plane
- 10" mill file
- needle files
- farrier's rasp
- sanding battens
- needlenose pliers
- electric grindstone
- cutting wheel
- combination square
- soldering iron or small butane torch
- razor saw
- #3 pencil
- scissors
- narrow masking tape

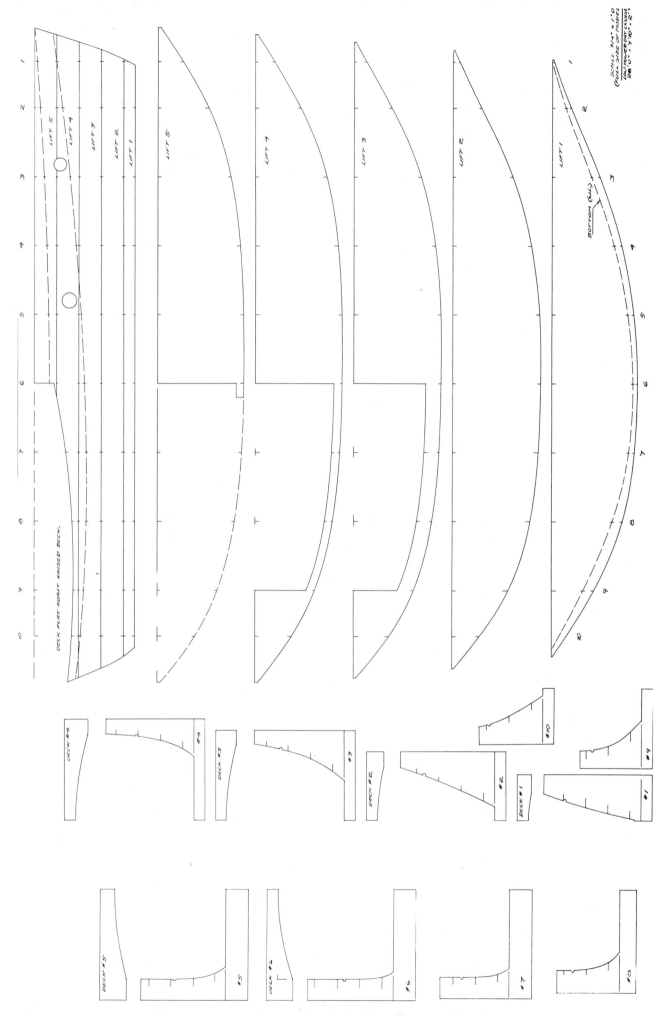

Sheet 1
Enlarge 327 percent for full-size plans.

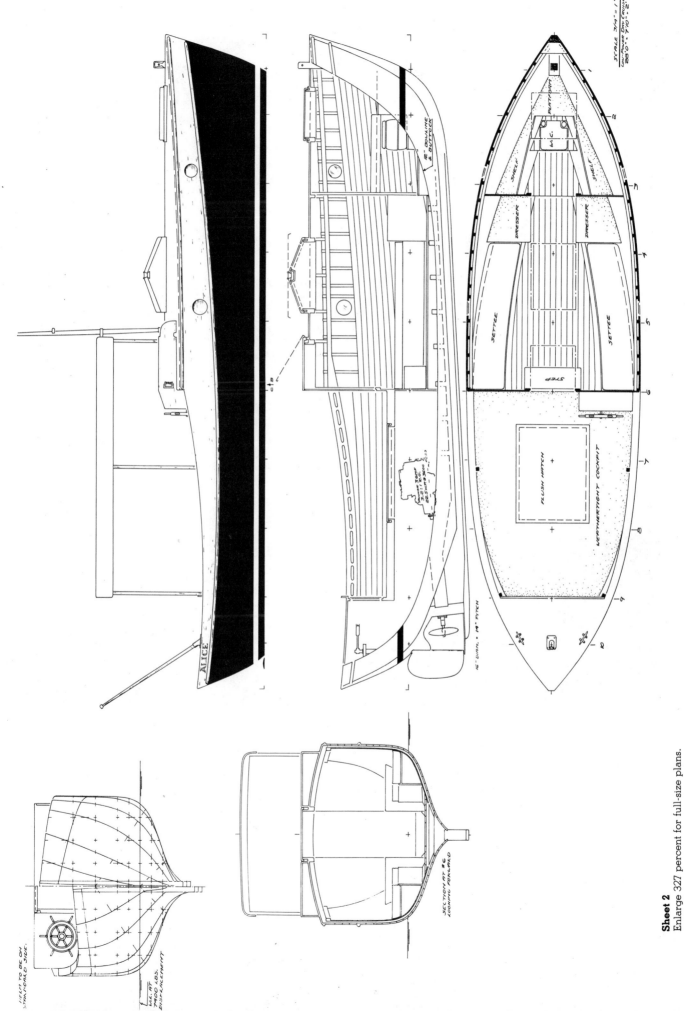

Sheet 2
Enlarge 327 percent for full-size plans.

Clockwise, from upper left: Marking the shape of the bottom from the template. . . . Squaring sheer to inside of hull. . . . Sawing sheer on bandsaw while keeping an eye on the dots. . . . Checking hull shape with station template. . . . Locating moldings using a template.

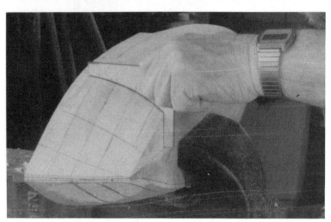

rather than just guessing at it and finding that you've overdone it. Look at the body section (end view) of the hull, and note the shape of the stem and stern-post and the way they're faired. Make a stick shaped about that way, put a centerline on it, and mark the ends of the hull so that you have lines to work to, instead of just guessing at it. When you're satisfied with the shape of the hull, give her a final fairing with sanding battens of various grits (see the Introduction, "Tools"; also see Chapter 1, "Carving the Hull").

Moldings, Companionway, Deck Furniture

Note that the raised-deck moldings sit below the dashed line in profile. After the hull is carved and sanded, measure from the edge of the raised deck (it's still flat) at each station down to the location of the half-round molding, spotting it in. Do the same for the guardrail as far back as Station 6—or spot it in using the body templates, which show the guardrail's location. In each case, run a batten along the marks, and eyeball the results; the curves should be fair.

There's still another way of marking the locations of the moldings and guardrails: Cut out the profile view of their location from the plans, making a template from stem to stern. For this kind of template, flexibility is a nice feature, so I used thin aluminum plate from my local newspaper. Bend the template around the hull, and mark the height of the molding from the top of the raised deck at each station. (As you can see in the photos, I went ahead and cut the crown for the raised deck before fitting the moldings and guardrails; see the plan body section at Station 6 for the shape of the crowning board. If you've done this too, you can cut the template along the sheer, and it'll still work.) Sure, the cut-out profile doesn't match the hull since it's shorter, having been drawn out flat on paper, but that's no problem. Just mark the heights of the profile at each station, and sweep the whole curve in with a batten. Of course, you can do it by measuring, but the template eliminates the chance of mismeasuring.

On the full-size boat, the half-round moldings and guardrails measure $1\frac{1}{2}$ inches × 1 inch. To make these at $\frac{3}{4}$-inch scale, you'll need to start with two strips 2 feet long to wrap around the hull sheer and two strips 13 inches long for the raised-deck area. Since they're going to be finished bright, hardwood of some sort would be nice. I used maple. You can start the rounding process by making a saw cut in a board, long enough to support their length. Cock each strip of molding in the slot at a 45-degree angle, and with a small modeler's plane knock off the corners. Then make a shallow groove in a scrap piece of wood, again on your table saw. Round the groove to the shape you want your molding, glue a piece of 100-grit sandpaper in it, and use this little sanding block to finish the rounding. Leave the moldings natural and varnish them, or you can stain them first. Put them on separately so you don't get stain on the hull if you intend to have it clear varnished.

Bolger calls for mahogany color for *Alice*'s woodwork and deck furniture, but stain darkens end-grain and leaves flat grain a lighter color. The sensible solution is, don't bother to try to stain pine or some light wood; use mahogany in the first place, or just paint it with something that would pass casual inspection. I used pine and simply gave the companionway and hatches a coat of red D-Rusto and Coast Guard orange mixed to suit. (Remember, this craft is no museum piece, but a way of showing a prospective customer the general characteristics of the boat. But, suit yourself.)

I made the companionway from a solid block $5\frac{3}{8}$ inches long by $1\frac{3}{4}$ inches × $\frac{5}{8}$ inch deep (real measure) cut to fit the camber of the deck. The wheelbox is $1\frac{3}{4}$ inches × $\frac{5}{8}$ inch; its bottom end sits on the cockpit sole—which is simply sanded and painted—and its top is angled flush to the top of the companionway. To get the effect of the riding light mounts, I cut the companionway's length

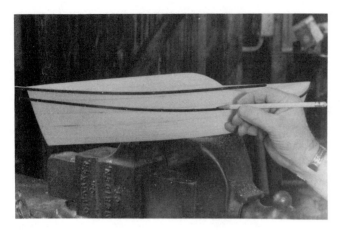

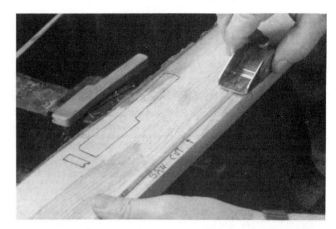

Clockwise, from upper left: Spotting-in molding and guardrail—batten marks the sweep of the curve. . . . Taking corners off gunwale guardrail. . . . Scribing waterline using a block as a gauge: level the hull, rest a pencil on block and slide it along the table to mark the waterline boottop. Saw 3/32 inch from the block, then go around again. . . . Dishing out portholes with ball cutter. . . . Use circle template and scribe port lights with sharp awl, then cut them out on bandsaw and grind edges to shape.

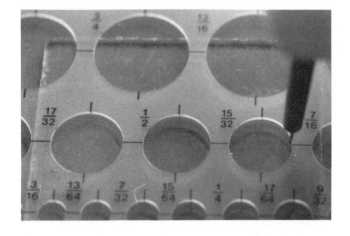

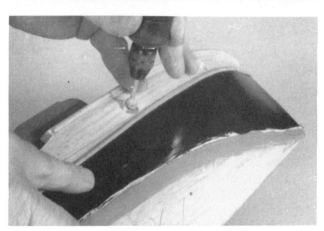

short enough to allow for them. Don't forget the limber holes (see the profile view on the plan, and note the limber holes forward of the running lights.

For the skylight, just forward of the companionway, use a chisel to cut a rabbet for glass. Paint black, or cover with a piece of aluminum foil, the area where the glass goes; then cut out a piece of glass from thin acetate (available at hobby shops) and recess it into the frame. The forward hatch is just a block cut square with a bit of trim around it. This completes the woodwork for the model except for the canopy, the steering wheel, and the forward mooring bitt—which you can make while waiting for the hull paint to dry.

Store-bought running lights and cleats; homemade wheel—not bad. . . . Flagstaff socket. . . . Sawing flag socket to length with razor saw.

Finishing

First you need to put a sealer coat on the areas that will be painted. This can be B-I-N for the hull and deck, or you can use shellac thinned about 50/50 with alcohol. After the hull is sealed, scribe the boottop, mask it off, and give the hull a coat of black undercoater up to the guardrails.

In painting the cockpit, stern deck, and raised deck white, this is where B-I-N works great for the primer and finish coats. Forget about trying to apply B-I-N with a brush, flowing it on in a nice, even coat; you aren't likely to succeed at this, because it dries so fast you can't get it on evenly. What does work is to put on two or three coats, pretty much one after the other. Make sure you get plenty on, and fill any uglies with "Pic and Patch" (a white water-based putty you can get from Model Expo and other mail-order hobby suppliers), then sand it down with 320-grit sandpaper. This leaves a somewhat flat, but very smooth finish that looks as good to my eye as if I were a professional modelmaker. Even Jay Hanna, who happens to be one, asked me how I did it. I told him I'd used his idea of using B-I-N as a primer; he sprays his paint over that, but I generally use a brush, and in resorting to sanding the mess I made with sandpaper, I stumbled on this great and simple way of achieving a great finish. Occasionally, and joyfully, something works out by accident better than you could possibly hope for. Modeling keeps me constantly on the borderline of elation and despair, but never bored. Win some, lose some, learn some—that's the way it goes.

The hull is painted semigloss black, the boottop white, and the bottom green.

While waiting for paint to dry is a good time to make the steering wheel. For this, three layers of $1/32$-inch aircraft plywood glued together with superglue is a good choice; or you can use two layers of $1/16$-inch plywood. Either way, you'll get six layers of paper-thin plywood, which makes one tough wheel. Copy the wheel's shape right from the plans with dividers, and lay out the six spokes for boring (like the Star of David). Cut the disk round, then bore a hole for the inside cut, and finish cutting on a scroll saw. The hub can be held in place with an awl while you cut it out roughly on a bandsaw and work its shape with sandpaper and needle files.

Brass belaying pins, if you can get them from a mail-order house, would make great spokes and grips, but of the three sizes I had on hand, all were too small for the job. Rather than paw through more catalogs and wait for shipment, I decided to make them from brass rods of about .040 inch diameter. The easiest way to bore the wheel hub for brass rod is with a Dremel tool held in a miniature drill press, something I wouldn't want to be without. For drawing the holes straight, place a square block of wood on the drill base, and hold the wheel hub vertically flat against it. My wheel looked OK and is very usable. But it would have looked nicer if the spokes had been spaced better—but spacing them and boring for them is tricky. They only need to be out of alignment a hair and it shows; even professionals have trouble with spoke alignment.

I made the canopy from a block of wood $8^{1}/_2$ inches $\times$ $5^{3}/_8$ inches $\times$ $^{9}/_{16}$ inches (real measure). This is a lot easier than making a frame and covering it with cloth to simulate canvas. Carefully locate the six supports, which show on the plans as square sticks. I found these easier to make from brass rod instead of wood, and to my eye they looked better; this way, you can easily bore for them, and they look very classy.

If you decide to make a signal mast, shown on the plans forward of the canopy, it's supposed to be 8 feet (6 inches, at $3/4$-inch scale) above the deck.

Now for the four portlights, two each side. Measure them on the plans, locate them on the hull, and swing their circles with dividers. Note that they're different in size: the aft ones are $1/2$ inch in diameter, and the forward ones $^{7}/_{16}$ inch. To add depth, bore for them with a wood hog placed in a Dremel tool. If you find you've wobbled the hole and it's out of round, wrap some waxed paper around a dowel, stick it in the hole, and fill back against the paper with natural wood dough. Let it harden, pull the dowel out, glue a piece of sandpaper tightly around a dowel of the right size, and sand the hole perfectly round.

Prime the portholes with shellac or varnish to seal the edge-grain, and paint them with flat black paint. For an even better effect, as if you were standing on a wharf trying to peer into the hull on a bright, sunny day, stick some glass in them. Of course, if you don't want to go to that much trouble, the portholes painted black look OK, too. If you choose glass. ordinary window-replacement acrylic plastic makes a neat, strong job; once the glass rounds are firmly embedded, kids aren't likely to jab them out.

For this and other finish work on models, I highly recommend buying a circle template with holes ranging 3 inches down to $1/16$ inch; you'll find it's very useful in modelmaking. For making your own portlights, just plop the template on the hull profile and match the hole sizes to those shown on the plans. Lay the template on the acetate or acrylic plastic sheet, and with a very fine-pointed awl scratch the shape of the holes, then cut them out roughly on a bandsaw. For grinding their edges round, you'll need something to hold them

Color Scheme

Sides, gloss black
Boottop, white
Bottom, flat green
Topsides, bright varnished (or mahogany color)
Companionway and wheelhouse, bright varnished (mahogany color)
Cockpit, white
Raised deck and stern deck, white

with. Needlenose pliers work well, but first put some masking tape on the jaw ends so you won't mar the portlights while grinding. Just an ordinary medium coarse (electric) grindstone is OK for rough shaping; then hold them against the side of a cutting wheel for smoother shaping, and finish them to size with sandpaper and needle files. Don't try cutting the glass with an electric scroll saw, because it won't work; it melts the plastic, and should you slow down the cutting or stop for a second, everything welds together—most frustrating. The plastic also melts slightly when grinding on my slow-turning grindstone, leaving a burred edge, but this can easily be picked off with a thumbnail, leaving a crisp, sharp edge again.

The two stern cleats are ⅝ inch in length and are available as Item 62 from BlueJacket Shipcrafters. They're made from Britannia metal, which is more durable than white metal, and, because Britannia holds details better, they look very nice indeed. At 35 cents apiece (at this writing), I very willingly bought them.

A socket for the flagstaff was another matter. It isn't likely that you'll get one the size you want, so I didn't even try. I like working with brass, so I made the socket from a piece of ⅛-inch (inside diameter) hollow brass rod, and made the pad from brass plate. I drilled the pad for the rod, and soldered both together while I held them in a wooden jig, which was nothing but a scrap of board with a slot sawed in it on my table saw to accept the diameter of the rod. The jig has two functions: it holds the flag socket for soldering, and aligns the pad horizontally so the flagstaff isn't off to port or starboard. Saw the socket to length with a razor saw.

If you don't want to deal with flags, this completes this model. If you do— yacht ensign at the stern, club burgee at the bow, private signal at the masthead, and about anything at the starboard spreader; nothing at the port spreader.

Alice needs no cradle, she sits here on my bench, on her flat bottom, seemingly waiting for some kid to come along and bring her to life.

That kid is me as I remember the unhurried times she reflects back in the '30s . . . Saturday nights in Rockland, 10-cent movies, hot dogs, ice cream parlors, and penny candy.

9

We're Here
A Gloucester Fishing Schooner

Materials Needed

- one 4' × 8' sheet of 1/8" tempered Masonite (smooth both sides)
- four pieces of 6' × 3" × 1/4" pine or basswood
- one sheet 2' × 12" × 1/64" aircraft plywood
- two 3' × 3/8" dowels for masts
- two 3' × 3/16" dowels for gaffs and jibboom
- two 3' 1/4" dowels for main and fore boom
- spray adhesive
- Weldwood plastic resin glue
- one .040" brazing rod
- 2" × 2" × 1/18" scrap of flat brass
- one yard, 4-ounce fiberglass cloth
- pink acetone or lacquer thinner
- 1/2" throwaway brush
- one 7/8" eight-spoke steering wheel
- seven-strand tin-plated copper wire
- 15' of #3 white nylon twine, three strand
- full size plans

When he was a small boy, Phil Bolger used to look up at the fishing schooner cradled in the arms of the Virgin Mary standing atop Our Lady of Good Voyage Church in Gloucester, Massachusetts. Much to his delight, his older brother Bill made a waterline model of the Gloucester fishing schooner, placing it in his younger brother's arms, which Phil still remembers vividly today. It's part of the inspiration for Phil's waterline version of the Gloucester fishing schooner *We're Here*, meant to be built as a kid's toy, to pull across a carpet. For this reason, Phil's design cuts her hull off a bit below the waterline so it's flat; there's no keel on the model. You can see the real schooner's body profile, stern view, on Sheet 2.

As Phil says, *We're Here* "reflects the construction of a conservative and somewhat more obsolete Essex–built fishing schooner as described in the book *Captains Courageous* by Rudyard Kipling—the action of which is set about 1895. One reason I wanted to do this model is to get people who have seen the movie to read the book, which is something else again." Phil goes on to say the movie is great for the sailing scenes, and for the cast; but the plot made no sense after James Connolly got through with it. "The *We're Here* in the film was no racing machine, and Captain Disko Troop's leading characteristic was portrayed as conservative prudence; he saw no sense in dares. The book, on the other hand, is an exact picture of how offshore fishing was really done in the late 1800s. The only criticism my great-uncle Sylvester Cunningham, who owned 26 schooners at one time, could make was that a mixed crew like that never happened; Portuguese shipped with Portuguese and Irishmen with Irishmen, and so on. I'm drawing the model with the sails they used through most of the book."

While building my model of *We're Here*, I found great pleasure and plenty of information in looking through several books, including the 1896 and 1937 editions of *Captains Courageous*. The famous modelmaker and historian Erik A. R. Ronnberg, Jr.'s *Gloucester Clipper Schooners* is about building a fully detailed model of the mackerel seiner *Smuggler* (available from BlueJacket Shipcrafters). Captain Douglas Lee of Rockland, Maine, has written *Modeling the Coasting Schooner* Heritage about building the model of his schooner *Heritage*. (Doug and his wife Linda sail the full-size *Heritage* out of Rockland each season, carrying passengers.) These two books provide the modeler with about everything he or she would want to know about fishing schooners. I'd also recommend *American Fishermen* by Albert Cook Church (published by W. W. Norton). All were helpful for understanding rigging and terminology.

Back in the heyday of the fishing schooners, as the function of the various parts that drove them became more perfected, so did the terminology. In fact, learning to name all the parts that made them go is like learning a new language—and a standard college dictionary is of little help. Most of these aren't labeled on *We're Here*'s plans, so it's just about a toss-up whether you'd find it easier to build the model right from the plans, paying no attention to the names of the different parts, or to identify the parts by name. If you don't know a topping lift from a peak halyard, you're not alone, but don't let it stop you. We'll use some of the names, but you can rest assured there'll be plenty left unused.

For that reason, and because of the way we'll build her, *We're Here* is about as simple a version of a schooner model as you'll find. Untapered dowels for masts, another dowel for the windlass, screw-eyes for the halyards, and so on—all help with simplicity. Later on, if your skill and patience allow, even this modest try will help you in duplicating the real thing.

Tools Needed

- tablesaw
- bandsaw
- vise
- pin vise
- clamps
- spokeshave
- block plane
- Dremel tool
- rasp
- sanding battens
- 10" mill file
- 3/8" rattail file
- 3/8" #6 brass ribbon pins, 3/4" #12 brass pleating pins
- 6" combination square
- scissors
- #3 pencil
- narrow masking tape

Building the Hull

The plans consist of three sheets, drawn at a scale of 1/4 inch = 1 foot. The waterline lifts, 1 through 7, are all 1/4 inch thick. Note on Sheet 1, showing the lift layout, the pattern for marking the outside of the bottom: this is not a lift, but is used for marking the underside of Lift 1. Note, too, that the bottom pattern and Lifts 1 through 5 and 6 all show the location of *We're Here*'s 3/8-inch dowel masts passing right through flush to the bottom of the hull; this is so you can ream the holes in case of any misalignment in stacking and gluing the lifts.

Lift 5 shows a line drawn across its width about amidships which shows the *great beam*—or *grub beam*, as Erik A. R. Ronnberg, Jr. calls it in his book *Gloucester Clipper Schooners*—where the deck splits into two levels. Look at the hull profile, also shown on Sheet 1, and you'll see that Lift 5 tapers to nothing at the beam, starting from Lift 7 at the stem; and that Lift 4, with its solid midsection under it, provides bearing after the taper is cut. The taper for the

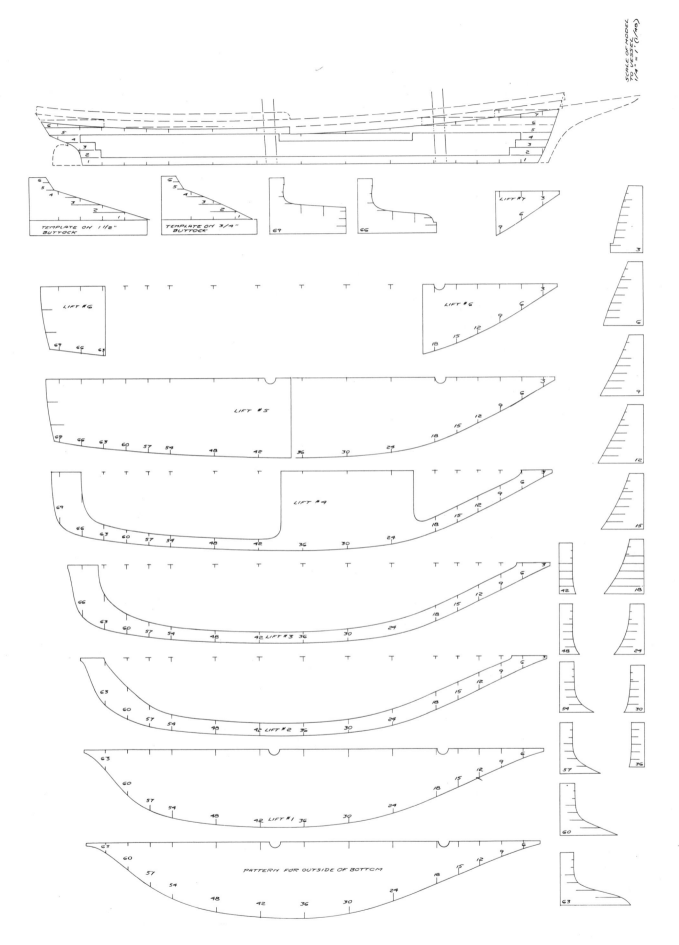

Sheet 1
Enlarge 400 percent for full-size plans.

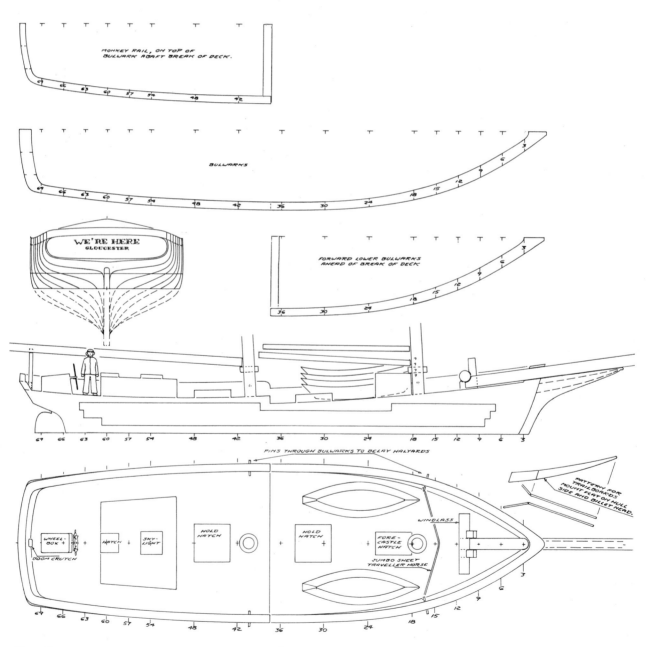

MONKEY RAIL, ON TOP OF
BULWARK ABAFT BREAK OF DECK.

BULWARKS

WE'RE HERE
GLOUCESTER

FORWARD LOWER BULWARKS
AHEAD OF BREAK OF DECK

PINS THROUGH BULWARKS TO BELAY HALYARDS

PATTERN FOR
TRAILBOARDS
MOUNT FLAT ON HULL
SIDE AND BILLET HEAD.

WHEEL-
BOX

BOOM CRUTCH

HATCH

SKY-
LIGHT

HOLD
HATCH

HOLD
HATCH

FORE-
CASTLE
HATCH

WINDLASS

JUMBO SHEET
TRAVELLER HORSE

Sheet 2
Enlarge 400 percent for full-size plans.

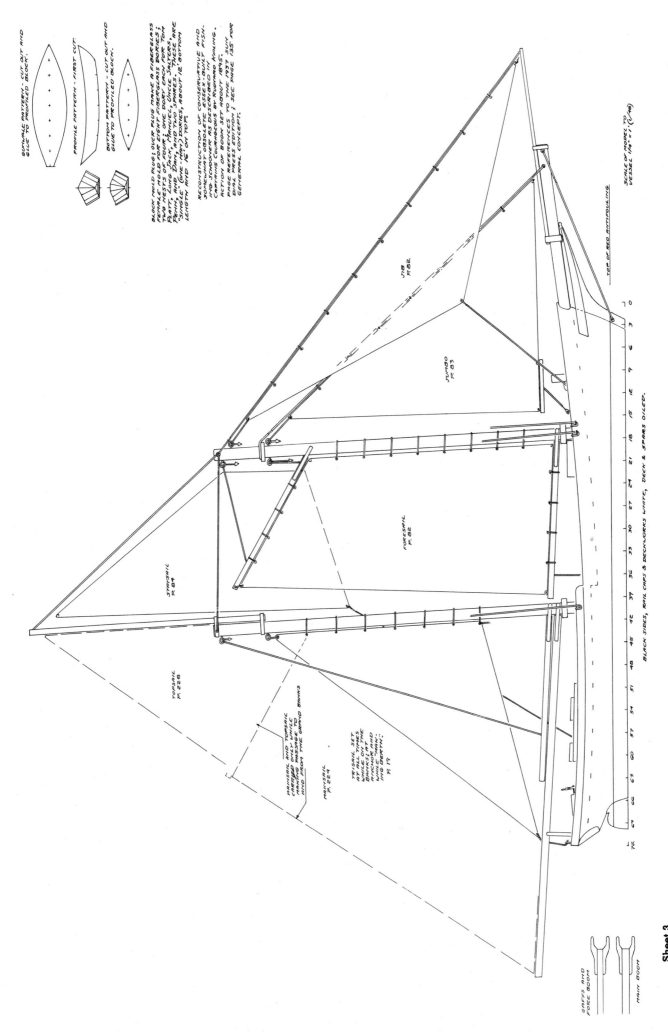

Sheet 3
Enlarge 400 percent for full-size plans.

deck sheer is provided by the hull profile template; you'll also use this for marking the hull's profile shape.

The forward lower bulwark is sprung onto the deck with its aft end butted against the grub beam. The full-length bulwark rests on top of it, and the *monkey rail* sits on top of this, aft of the *break of deck*.

Simple, you say—yup, not bad, but probably enough to offer a slight challenge if this is your first model.

Like most of the other models in this book, *We're Here* is built in halves on a right-angled jig (see the Introduction). Note that the hull profile shows Lift 7 at the bow but not at the stern. When laying up the stack of lifts, you'll need to place (but not glue) a temporary ¼-inch scrap at the stern to correspond to Lift 7's height. In other words, the stack of lifts, laid up upside-down, must be parallel in height to the base of the jig, not tilted, so you have to compensate for the missing sections of the short lifts. As with the rest of these lift models, be sure that the thickness of your lift stock is accurate so that the total height of the stack will match the hull profile.

With the basics of building the hull in mind, let's get back to the lift templates. You can lay them out just as they are on Sheet 1, without cutting them out of the plans, just glue the whole plan on Masonite; the same goes for the body section templates. Cut the sheet right below the hull profile, spray the cutout with glue, and stick it to tempered Masonite. If you want, you could use aluminum newspaper plates for the body section templates; the thin aluminum sheets are easier to use in checking the hull's curve at each station as you carve, because you don't have to watch which side of the hull's section lines you hold the templates. You need to pay attention with ⅛-inch thick Masonite templates, but I still like the stiffness of the Masonite, and these templates won't get bent when they're passed on down to my great-grand-kids.

You'll need four pieces of basswood, pine, or your choice of wood 6 feet × 3 inches × ¼ inch thick to make all of the waterline lifts, bulwarks, and monkey rail. (If you order lumber from a mail-order house, you'd need 18 pieces of 2-foot boards, which would be more costly.) Carefully lay these pieces out and mark all of their section lines, numbering them as you go. Saw them out on a bandsaw, scroll saw, sabersaw, or even by hand with a coping saw if that's all you have.

Staple some waxed paper to your jig to keep the lifts from sticking, and start stacking the lifts upside-down, starting with Lift 7 at the bow and the ¼-inch scrap piece to support Lift 6 at the stern. Put two more ¼-inch support scraps amidships, and another ¼-inch scrap under the bow portion of Lift 6. Stack the lifts dry to begin with, aligning each lift at Station 36 to the jig's plumb line. Trace the outline of each lift onto the lift below to outline the areas to spread glue. Then "butter them up," following the same steps described in Chapter 1, "Laying Up the Lifts." Weldwood dry-powder glue works fine, though you could use epoxy or Franklin Titebond. Before putting on the final lift, Lift 1, glue two pieces of ¼-inch scrap on Lift 4; these will support the deck and the hull's bottom and prevent you from crunching the model when you get to carving the hull, with it held in your vise.

Next, let's mark the hull profile in preparation for cutting the deck sheer, which you'll cut on both hull halves before gluing them together; the deck sheer is cut out at the two deck levels, joining at the grub beam. Also, at the same time, carefully cut out the stem, the billethead which supports the bowsprit, and the rudder. We'll want to glue these on the hull after the hull is carved.

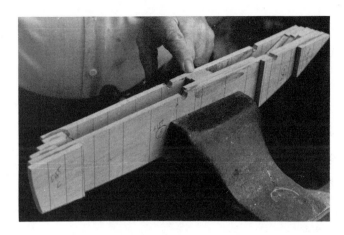

Clockwise, from upper left: Hull in vise and ready for carving, note support. . . . Working sheer down by hand. . . . Checking sheer for flatness across from centerline. . . . Scrap pieces hold hull halves in line for gluing, and strengthen the hull. . . . All bulwarks are on, including monkey rail, being clamped.

One half at a time, put the hull in the vise and lay the profile pattern on, matching waterline to waterline and station to station; then trace the hull profile—at stem and stern, and the deck sheer. Put the half hulls together in the vise, right-side up, and cut through Lift 5 just aft of Station 36 for the grub beam. Next, take them out of the vise and cut the deck sheer on each half. You can remove the excess wood with a bandsaw or use a chisel to work the sheer down by hand to the hull's centerline (later, after the halves are glued together, you'll finish the sheer flat across to the outside of the hull).

Before gluing the halves together, slip three ¼-inch pieces of scrap wood in the aft-section cavity and two in the forward section for additional hull stiffness. Measure their depth so the hull halves will go together, and glue them in; they'll help with alignment as well. Put the whole works in the vise, add pressure until glue squeezes out of the seam, and let everything sit tight until the glue hardens.

After glue sets up, put the hull in the vise right-side up, and finish the deck sheer flat across with spokeshave, mill file, and sandpaper. At this point you might decide the deck doesn't look all that good, with its shingled effect (glue lines) from the tapered lifts. The plans call for an oiled deck, which will make the tapers even more apparent, so I decided to cover both decks with ¹/₆₄-inch plywood. Using the deck template for a pattern, I cut out the two sections and glued them down with epoxy, using ³/₈-inch #6 brass ribbon pins to hold them until the glue hardened. Then I struck a centerline along the deck, and drew the locations for the *deckworks*—the wheelbox, cabin trunk, and hatch aft, and the hold hatch and forecastle hatch forward. Before putting on the bulwarks, I drew caulking seams with a #3 hard pencil and let it go at that. The planks run straight on the main deck and run with the sides of the cabin trunk on the quarter deck, with their forward ends butting against the grub beam. The grub beam's forward face aligns vertically with the ends of the monkey rail.

The reason for putting on the bulwarks now is that in this model they're part of the hull carving (see the stern profile, Sheet 2). Pull the temporary pins and put the forward lower bulwark in place, with its centerline matched to the hull's. Mark its inboard shape along the deck. This is so you can relocate the bulwark precisely after you take ³/₁₆ inch off its bow end to allow for half the thickness of the ³/₈-inch bowsprit you'll be putting in later. It's much easier to make a hole for the bowsprit now than later. The same goes for the full-length bulwarks, except here it's a rabbeted joint: the tops of the bulwarks meet at the centerline, and the bowsprit slides underneath, as you can see on Sheet 2. A ³/₈-inch rattail file is great for this job.

After you've fitted the forward lower bulwark, glue and spring it down in place and fasten it with #12 ³/₄-inch brass pleating pins. Pre-drill holes for the pins, using a .75 drill bit in a Dremel tool or by hand, holding the bulwarks in a pin vise (you can buy these tools at most hobby shops). Without pre-drilling, the pins will bend over, even in soft basswood. The full-length bulwark goes on next, and then the monkey rail on top of it. See the shapes of all three on Sheet 2.

Carving the Hull

By adding the filler pieces before gluing the hulls together, you've strengthened the hull enough so that you can hold *We're Here* sideways in your vise without fear of cracking her. Add a pad of wood so as not to mar the deck, and you're ready to go, carving one side at a time. (If you forgot the filler pieces, you can place the hull on your workbench with wooden stops at the stern and bow to keep the hull from slipping fore-and-aft.)

Before carving the hull, cut out the transom from the plans (Sheet 2) and glue it to thin aluminum or cardboard. The transom template needs to be flexible so it'll bend to the rounded stern of the model.

The bow area is the easiest to shape, so start there to get a feel for what you're doing. The stern area is much harder; take your time, and use the station and buttock templates carefully here. At the stern you'll be giving her underbody quite a bit of shape. To guide you in carving, Lift 5 at the stern shows two buttock lines, ³/₄ inch and 1 ¹/₂ inches out from the centerline. Section templates 66 and 69 show them again, and use the two "buttock templates" in the final shaping of this area. The idea is to flow the lift waterlines into the transom area a little at a time. When the transom shape starts to appear, place the transom template on the hull, matching its centerline to the hull's, and carve a little more. Re-draw the station marks as they get carved off, and number them. It's most important to keep them along the sheer and her bottom's centerline; in between, it doesn't matter that much.

The stem is put on after the hull is carved and faired, the billethead will be put on in a bit.

Deckworks and Spars

After the hull is sanded come the deckworks, starting with the samson post— two bitts at the bow, on either side of the bowsprit, hollowed to fit where the windlass is set into them. You can see two views of this assembly on Sheet 2. Make the two pieces ¹/₄ inch square × 1¹/₂ inches (real measure), and mark their height above the deck from the plans, to scale. Next, you'll need to bore two ¹/₈-inch or larger holes through the deck where the posts go. To locate the holes, slide the ³/₈-inch bowsprit along the deck centerline, place the two posts on either side of the bowsprit, mark around them, then bore for their centers. Below the deck line you marked earlier, whittle the posts round like pegs, and with the ³/₈-inch rattail file shape their aft faces and the end of the bowsprit to catch the windlass. Put some five-minute epoxy on the pegs and plop the samson post in its holes, then put some glue on the deck centerline and slide the bowsprit in place. Glue the windlass on, and you're done here for the moment.

Now on to making the cabin trunk, the hatch and the skylight for it, the wheelbox, the two hold hatches, and the forecastle. Use the plan view on Sheet 2 to get their widths and lengths, and note their heights in profile. Cut these out of basswood, or whatever you're using. Paint them white before gluing them to the deck.

Cut out the billethead, and fit and glue it to the stem and to the underside of the bowsprit. Make it ³/₁₆ inch thick (the thickness of the keel; see the stern view on Sheet 2), and while you're at it make the rudder from wood of the same thickness. Don't forget to cut out the trailboards (¹/₁₆ inch) and the halyard belaying pins to fit through her bulwarks, also shown on Sheet 2. Make your belaying pins from .050-inch brass or thereabouts, cut to ¹¹/₁₆ inch. Glue the rudder to the sternpost.

The masts are simply ³/₈-inch dowels 14¹/₈ inches long, with no taper. You can determine their rake aft by laying the hull on the sail plan, Sheet 3. Note that the rake (angle) of both masts is the same. To get the masts plumb athwartships, level the hull and wedge them plumb while holding a level against them. Glue them in place, flush to the bottom of the hull, with superglue.

The boom crutch measures ¹/₄ inch wide × ¹/₈ inch thick × 1³/₈ inches long, real measure (see Sheet 2). File a groove in it for the ¹/₄-inch-diameter boom, then let the crutch into the bulwark and glue it. To make the two mast saddles, first draw their $5/8$-inch diameters on a scrap of $3/16$-inch wood with a compass, bore $3/8$-inch holes in them, and cut them out with a bandsaw or scroll saw.

Now you're ready to spray the masts, bowsprit, and deck, cabin trunk and all, with Minwax fast-drying clear satin polyurethane. Two coats should do it.

Give the hull a coat of sealer (shellac, varnish, or B-I-N will do just fine), and fill any uglies with putty in preparation for painting. (Be sure to do this before you sand the sealer, so the putty will have a good grip.)

At this point you might as well continue on with the spars. The main and fore booms and gaffs all need to be made, also mast caps for the topmast, and the mast hoops should go on before the topmast is stepped.

Since it's no easy job to make the mast caps, let's start with them first. I made mine from a piece of $1/18$-inch-thick flat brass, after thinking over other ways (glued paper or thin strips of brass). If you go the brass route, bore a $3/8$-inch hole for the mainmast and a $1/4$-inch hole for the topmast, leaving about a $1/16$ inch between them. You'll want a drill press for this job. Lay the brass on a piece of wood and clamp both to the drill table; be sure to do this, since a stuck drill of that size can swing brass and all, hurting or cutting your fingers if held by hand. After drilling the holes in the two caps, trace around them, leaving about $1/16$ inch all around. Saw them out on your bandsaw, nibbling at them to get them near round. Take small nibbles, and be sure to saw the mast caps on a piece of scrap wood; otherwise, the blade is likely to catch and go flying if you try to saw over an open table slot. File the edges of the brass to finish the job. It took me about an hour to make the mast caps, but the results were worth it.

The jibboom is a $3/16$-inch-diameter dowel $6 5/8$ inches long. Glue it to the bowsprit, and fake the bowsprit cap and band out of paper or thin sheet brass. Now's a good time to decide whether you want *We're Here* to be rigged for fishing on the Banks, with her trisail set (shown on Sheet 3), or making passage, with everything set except the trisail (also called *riding sail*).

Clouds of sails look nice, so I decided for making passage, though it would be much easier rigging her as shown with the trisail set. The main and fore booms are $1/4$-inch dowels; their gaffs are $3/16$ inch. Make a template of the jaws (see the lower left corner of Sheet 3) and cut out four of them. I made mine whole from maple, and fitted them into a slot cut in the boom, rather than fitting the jaws around the boom. This shortcut is easier and faster for a model, but it was never done this way on a real schooner.

Mast hoops are next. You can make them from paper, chair caning (using superglue), or house wiring. I make mast hoops from small (about .050 inch) brazing rod because I want a bit of spring to them. If you use brazing rod or some other wire, drill a hole through a dowel (a bit larger than $3/8$ inch) so that when you wrap the wire around it, you'll have hoops that are about a third smaller than the mast. Make a trial run first, then stick the end of the wire in the hole and wrap as many turns of wire as you need hoops. Be careful not to let the wound brazing rod go; let it slowly unwind while hanging onto it to spare your fingers from getting whipped. The hoops will spring to the right size when they unwind. Of course you can make them from any wire you want; hoops for the smaller topmast are about .030 inch.

Put eight hoops on the mainmast, if you're using a mainsail; slip them on the mast, then stick the topmast on and glue it in place for good. If you're using only the trisail, seven hoops will do. The foresail calls for eight hoops; put them on before attaching the springstay and the foremast mastband.

If you haven't done it already, you should paint the inboard sides of the

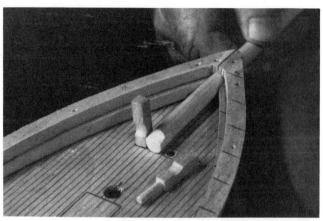

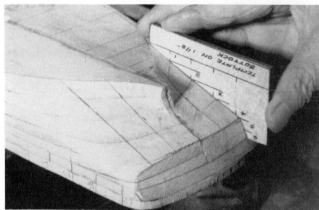

Clockwise, from upper left: Using gouge with inside bevel to carve stern area. . . . Samsom post and bowsprit. . . . Checking shape of transom and rake with buttock template. . . . Mast hoops. . . . Gaff jaws.

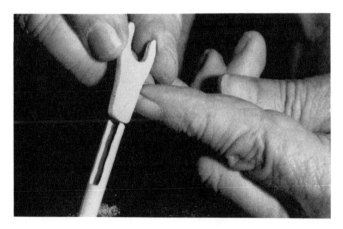

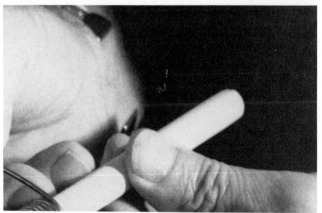

bulwarks (white) before you get too much stuff in the way. Glue the trailboards to the hull, then put a 1/16-inch-square molding around them. Sawing 1/16 inch square or less is easy to do with a good table saw and a sharp hollow-ground planer blade. After you set the fence and the blade very low, run a piece of scrap through the blade to cover the slot so the small stuff you're sawing will have something to bear on other than air. When we get to painting the hull, you'll paint the trailboards flat black, the same as the hull. If you feel artistic, you can decorate them with a white vine.

Dories

While waiting for glue to set up is a good time to build the eight dories, two nests of four each. There are at least two ways to make them. One is to cut two blocks of wood, each large enough to make a solid stack of four dories. Whittle their shape as shown in profile and in plan view as best you can, and hollow the top dory so it looks as if they're all hollow. It's no easy job to do this unless you're a fairly good whittler; on the other hand, once you've carved and painted them, the stack of dories will look plenty good enough for this model.

If you're better at working with fiberglass than at whittling, then go the 'glass route. A nest of fiberglass dories appealed to me—I just plain wanted to see if I could make a plug that small and make fiberglass cloth, cut in one piece, conform to the dory's shape. Both plug and cloth worked as I'd hoped.

If you decide to make your dories from fiberglass, let's start with the plug for the female mold. Cut a block of wood $4^{1/2}$ inches $\times$ $1^{1/4}$ inches wide $\times$ $^{7/8}$ inches deep, and use a combination square to draw eight $^{1/2}$-inch sections across the block. Lay the dory profile on the side of the block, and cut it to shape. Put a centerline on the block fore-and-aft and square the $^{1/2}$-inch sections across the top and bottom; then lay the plan view on the block (that's looking down at the top or bottom), locate the bottom pattern on the block, and trace around it. Cut the plug to shape with your bandsaw or, lacking one, put the block in a small vise and cut it by hand. Sand the plug smooth and wax it with car wax (this works better for me than mold-release). Glue a $^{1/4}$-inch dowel in the plug for holding it in the vise.

For making a female mold (which most boatshops build for laying up a "production run" of boats) as well as the dories themselves, 4-oz glass cloth is what you want—its fine mesh and flexibility will allow you to cover the plug without cutting darts in the cloth while stretching it around the stem or transom. Cut the cloth on a bias for the best flexibility. Six layers of cloth, each about $^{1/32}$-inch thick when cured, will be enough for each dory. For each layer, measure two teaspoons of polyester resin, add three or four drops of hardener (MEKP, methyl ethyl ketone peroxide), stir well, and go to it. Drape the piece of cloth over the plug, and use a $^{3/8}$-inch brush (from an artist's supply or hobby shop) to saturate the cloth completely. Trim each layer, leaving about $^{1/8}$ inch above the sheer, and go on to the next, wetting it and each subsequent layer out; then let the whole thing harden. When you're done wetting out cloth, clean the brush with acetone or lacquer thinner. Just after the mold layup has hardened (about a half hour; keep checking so it doesn't get too hard), trim away the excess cloth along the sheer with a sharp knife, and free the mold from the plug.

I found in actual practice that it was much easier to lay up the dories over the plug than in the female mold. It was difficult at this small scale to get the mold smooth enough in the stem and transom areas so I could break the laid-up hull free. Also, laying up each hull over the plug allowed me to see how much resin was being used; and the layup's being upside down ensured that I got enough resin along her sheer to stiffen it. Of course, this meant the dory was $^{1/16}$ inch longer and wider than it was supposed to be, but who cares? At a scale of $^{1/4}$ inch = 1 foot, translated to real life, the dory would be only about 3 inches longer and 3 inches wider.

For each dory, use six layers of the 4-oz cloth. Mix the resin and lay up the cloth as described above. It took me about 15 minutes to lay up a dory and

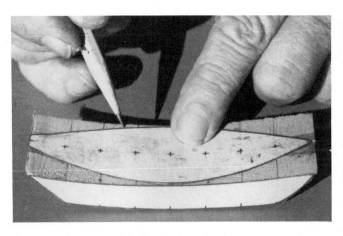

Clockwise, from upper left: Dory's shape has been cut in profile, top shape being marked. . . . Dory plug all waxed; first layer of four-ounce cloth going on. . . . Wetting out first layer of cloth. . . . Trim excess cloth before it gets rock hard. . . . Eight dory offspring from mother plug.

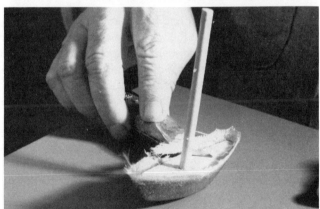

about a half hour at 70 degrees Fahrenheit for the layup to harden enough for trimming. To hasten curing, put the layup near a light bulb or near a warm shop stove. After the resin hardens, trim the cloth around the sheer with a sharp knife or utility knife. Be sure to trim the excess cloth before it gets rock hard. Check the layup every few minutes so you won't get surprised.

After the layup is trimmed, sand along the sheer with a mill file and sandpaper before freeing it from the plug. Remove the layup from the plug by inserting a razor blade between the layup and the plug, working it along carefully on both sides of the hull. After the sides are free, the hull will come free with a bit of rocking motion and leverage with the dowel.

What color to paint the dories seems to be up for grabs. There's a reference on page 67 in *Captains Courageous* of Captain Disko Troop's son Dan's little red dory, named *Hattie S.*, lying astern of the schooner, and there's mention of Dan's Uncle Salter's blue dory on page 44. (The 1896 edition has the same page numbers as the 1937 Sun Dial edition.) It appears that no standard color was used by all of the fishing fleet, but the colors varied from boat to boat. I do remember that, when I was a kid in the early '30s, every trawler I'd see lying at the wharf in Rockland carried an orange dory on top of its pilothouse—and a bright orange at that—so I chose orange with buff interior for this tiny fleet. I flattened the gloss orange by sanding it, making the color more acceptable to the eye. (The risk in bright colors, especially gloss, is that it's hard for your eyes to get past the dories to view the rest of the model, which is all painted flat.)

Once the paint is dry, you can nest the dories as shown in profile on Sheet 2. The six layers of cloth should give the hulls close to the right thickness (about 6/32 inch) to allow nesting as shown; if anything, a nest of four 'glass dories will be slightly shorter in height than shown, but you can bring them to the right height by gluing a chip of wood inside the bottom of each dory. It's much better that the dories nest more closely together, which is easily remedied, than be too tall a stack. Glue one dory to the other, and later glue the nests to the deck, port and starboard.

Finishing, Rigging, and Sails

While we're in the painting business, now's a good time to paint the hull. The first step is to mask off the waterline and paint the topsides and the trailboards flat black. To get the copper color for the bottom antifouling, I mixed Rust-O-Leum rusty-metal primer, which is brown, with Pettit International Orange. You can thin and doctor both of these oil-based paints as you wish with linseed oil, mineral spirits, or turpentine and hasten their drying time with Japan drier if needed. For *We're Here* I went the route of special model paints and found them OK for painting small areas and fittings, but for painting larger areas I prefer to mix my own oil-based paints or use off-the-shelf spraypaints.

You can letter *We're Here*'s name and her port of call (Gloucester) with "instant" 18-point bold white lettering (see the Introduction, "Lettering Transom Names"). Even with the letters all made for you and ready on a transfer sheet, it isn't always easy to get them spaced right, especially when the transom is raked. You must take this into consideration as you lay out the letters so that when viewed from above the stern, they won't look too close together vertically. I used 18-point letters for both her name and port of call because that's all I had; the lettering for "Gloucester" looks a bit large, and I might replace it with smaller letters someday.

If you'd like to paint a fancy scrollwork of some kind on the trailboards, it's not that hard to do, even if you're not an artist. Paint the molding around the trailboards a fairly dark green to set them off from the hull. Pour a tad of white paint in a small container, then dip a pointed toothpick into the paint and make a snake's path from each trailboard's aft end to its forward end, suggesting a

Color Scheme:

Topsides and trailboards, flat black
Trailboard molding, medium green
Bottom, copper
Deck, natural (oiled or varnished), or painted gray
Bulwarks and deckworks, white
Jibboom, white
Mast, oiled or painted buff

vine. At the concave side, midpoint of each curve, draw a very small loop, leaf, or whatever you fancy. My effort is far from being a masterpiece, but that I tried it at all came from looking hard at the artistry of the trailboards my artist friend Frank O'Brien did for me for *Lisa*, the Friendship sloop.

With the trailboards painted, it's time for some finishing touches before tackling the sails and rigging. *We're Here's* $7/8$-inch (rim size) eight-spoke steering wheel from BlueJacket Shipcrafters is the next item to go on. It's slightly large—$5/8$ inch would be better—but $7/8$ inch was all I had on hand, and it was close enough for me.

Sheet 3 shows the jumbo sheet traveler horse and the mainsheet traveler in profile, located on top of the monkey rail, but you can leave these off if you prefer.

Now for more rigging. Look at the sail plan, Sheet 3. We'll start with the bobstay chain, scale is about 18 or 20 links to the inch. It fastens to the stem and to just aft of the bowsprit cap iron. The jumbo stay is next and is made of three-strand tin plated copper wire, item #1673 from BlueJacket; so are the spring-stays and the standing rigging for the jib and the main topmast.

Sails are next. As mentioned before, I wanted to see a cloud of sails on *We're Here*, just for the fun of it. I used $1/32$-inch aircraft plywood to make them since I feel more at home working with wood than with cloth. Wood is much easier to keep dustfree and, painted white with the seams drawn on, looks quite nice. An easy and accurate way to lay out a full suit of sails is to slip a sheet of $1/32$-inch aircraft plywood under the sail plan, Sheet 3, stick an awl through the corners of each sail, pull the plywood out from under the sail plan, and connect all the corners with a straight edge. If you go for the full set, leave off the trisail or riding sail, as it was used only when at anchor or in making port. I used alcohol-based B-I-N primer/sealer for painting the sails because it dries in minutes, allowing three sanded coats in about three hours, depending on humidity and temperature.

Lay each sail on the sail plan and mark the locations for the mast hoops. While you're at it, lay off the 2-foot panels (that's $1/2$ inch at $1/4$-inch scale) with a ruler and draw them in with a #3 or #4 hard pencil. Draw the reef ties freehand. At the top and bottom of the mainsail and the foresail, drill a hole at each panel's seam with a #61 drill bit and lash the booms and gaffs to the sail with nylon twine, size 3, made by Brownell and Co. You may be able to find this at a fishermen's supply store, or use what you can find, which is usually about $1/64$ inch in diameter. My nylon twine is white, which is OK with me—let the purists howl. It's easier to lash the booms and gaffs off the boat than on. Bore holes along the luff for the hoops. Put the main boom in the crutch, and install the mast hoops. Place screw eyes—which you can make by wrapping wire around a dowel—as shown to catch the halyards. Note that the main and foresail gaffs have throat and peak halyards.

Lay off 2-foot panels on the jib and jumbo and with a #8 drill bit bore holes at each panel for the split rings. You can make these in a minute or two by wrapping 24-gauge brass wire around a six-penny nail and cutting them with nippers. As seen on Sheet 3, the sails are sheeted home to the belaying pins shown sticking out through the bulwarks. I sheeted both jib and jumbo to the forward belaying pins on the port side; the main and foresail peak and throat halyards are attached to the pins on the starboard sides. The staysail peak is attached to the main topmast stay, with its throat to the same eye screw as the foresail gaff peak halyard; the clew is fastened to a cleat at midpoint of the main boom. (The tack needs no halyard because the staysail lies OK without it. If you

Setting sail for the Banks.

want one, you can run it to the forward port-side belaying pins.) The topsail has hoops, so can't be sent down. A man would have to go aloft and furl it. The topsail clew belays to the top of the main gaff and the tack to the aft belaying pin.

Add a couple of fishermen, made over from kids' plastic spacemen at ¼-inch scale (I described a sample toy-spaceman make-over in Chapter 4, in the section on *Mite's* pilothouse), glue the nests of dories to the deck, and that about does it.

As I look at the plywood sails of the finished model, I'm glad I stuck to my guns, working with materials I'm used to, rather than trying to deal with cloth. My eye tells me this simple version of a fishing schooner looks better than if I'd tried to make an exact model. This model will probably never live in a glass case; instead, she'll set sail for schools, for the entertainment of kids who might hear the call of the sea.

10

Snow Leopard
A Torpedo-Sterned Launch

"**L**ike its animal namesake, this modern motorboat is poetry in motion"—so the headline reads in the article Phil Bolger wrote about *Snow Leopard* for *Boating World*, August/September 1980.

One of the delights of working with the likes of Phil Bolger is his versatility: you never know what he's going to come up with next. And so it was with this torpedo-sterned launch design.

Phil asked me to build a lift model of *Snow Leopard* and photograph it for the *Boating World* article. As he put it, not only would carving this hull be "an example of buttock lifts, and the use of a model to try a shape that is extremely tricky to design," but he also wanted to see how it would look: "I think she'd look lively reflected from the dark blue car [my Mazda hatchback]. Would a taped 'wake' astern work? Just a streak the breadth of the boat, as if she'd run out over a low swell?"

This wake had me momentarily stumped. After I calmed down from the first reaction of "Impossible," I started sorting things out in a more positive manner. I had the car and the model and even the background scenery of a nearby neighbor's wharf. All that was lacking was the wake and how to do it. I do my own photography, but—trick photography? I remembered seeing a classic Hacker in a high-speed turn gracing the pages of *WoodenBoat* magazine. I copied this by laying a piece of window glass over the page and painting the wake's spray pattern on the glass with "red opaque" (a water-based printer's paint for blocking out light-transparent areas in negatives). Once I'd photographed the model on top of the car, I projected the negative onto an easel so that the glass with its wake silhouette was held between the image and the light, and burned it in. All quite convincing, I'd guess. Bolger, on seeing it, said "Fantastic," a word I'd never heard him use before—or since.

For me, the experience and results were as satisfying as making the model. Fun? You bet!

Materials Needed

- 22 running feet of ³/₈" × 2³/₈" pine or basswood
- 12" × ¹/₈" brass rod
- one-half 4' × 8' sheet of tempered ¹/₈" Masonite (smooth both sides)
- spray adhesive
- epoxy or Weldwood plastic resin glue
- can of chrome spraypaint
- sheet of .030" acetate
- full-size plans

Building the Hull

Tools Needed

- table saw
- bandsaw, scroll saw, sabersaw
- drill press, if you have one
- vise
- clamps
- spokeshave
- chisel
- ⁷/₈" or 1" gouge
- block plane
- 10" mill file
- sandpaper
- sanding battens
- combination square
- scissors
- #3 pencil
- narrow masking tape

The torpedo-sterned *Snow Leopard*, drawn at a scale of ³/₄ inch = 1 foot, goes together a little differently than the other lift models in this book, in that the conventional right-angle jig isn't used. The jig in this case is two 6-inch brass alignment rods which pass through the hull, serving the same purpose. To further help in alignment, each lift template has the outline of its neighbor drawn right on it. Another difference is that this is a buttock lift model, with vertical slices rather than the horizontal waterline lifts of the other models included here. Otherwise, the basic procedure's the same.

Before starting in, take a good, hard look at the *Snow Leopard*'s expected shape; look at each of the body templates (15 of them for good control) and note their shape. You'll see that starting with the Section 7 body template, a hard chine starts to appear and holds right to her pointy stern; the rest of her is pretty curvy.

To make the templates, you'll want a pair of scissors, a can of artist's spray adhesive, and a half sheet of ¹/₈-inch Masonite. Cut out the template patterns from the plans—roughly at first, well outside the lines. Give their backs a shot of spray glue and stick them to the Masonite. (You could use some other tough but thin material, like aluminum plates from a newspaper which you can cut with ordinary scissors, but Masonite is better for the buttock lifts, as you'll see.) Take the template layouts to your bandsaw or scroll saw and cut them out to the line. Then carefully bore holes in the templates for the alignment rods; a drill press, if you have one, is good for this job.

For this model, with the lifts all ³/₈ inch thick I used ³/₄-inch pine boards, cut down to ³/₈-inch thickness with a hollow-ground planer blade on my table saw (this is described more fully in Chapter 1, "Getting Started"). A pine board 12 feet long × 6 inches wide, ripped into 2³/₈-inch strips, will give you 24 running feet, enough to make all the lifts. If you're using ³/₄-inch boards, I'd recommend cutting them to ³/₈-inch thickness before you lay out and trace the lifts; this makes the job of sawing out the lifts much easier. (Or you can use 1-inch-thick rough basswood and get the lifts from half the amount of wood, since you can get two lifts to one.) Make sure to use a set of wooden fingers, for safety and accuracy.

Before sawing the boards to the ³/₈-inch thickness, run some scrap wood through your saw as close to ³/₈ inch as you can get it, make a stack of 14 pieces,

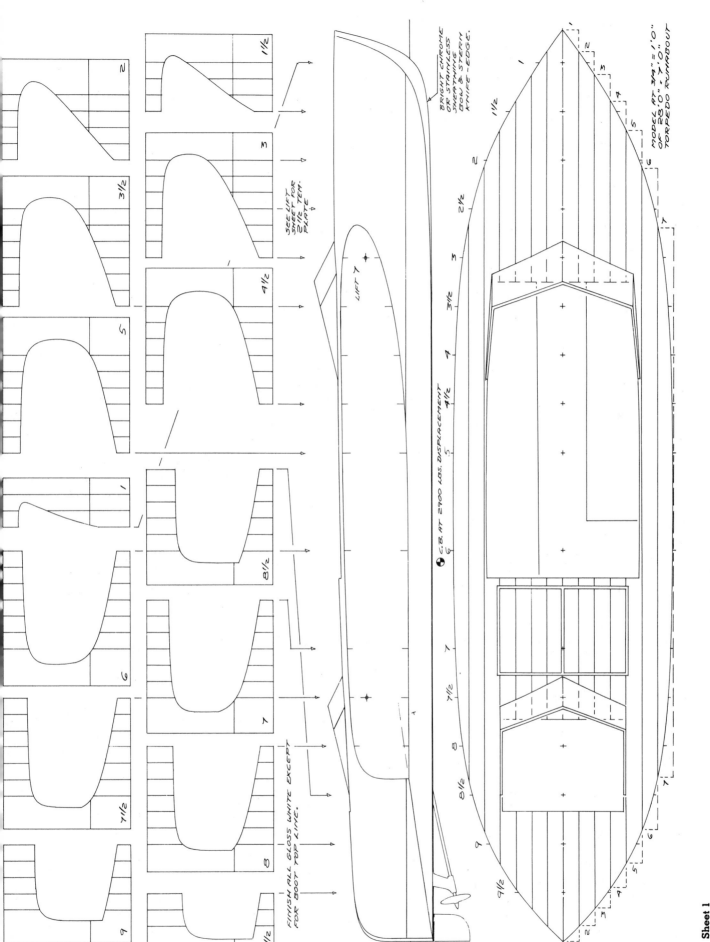

MODEL AT ¾" = 1'0"
OF 28'0" × 7'0"
TORPEDO RUNABOUT.

BRIGHT CHROME
OR STAINLESS
STRETCHING
BOW & STERN
KNIFE-EDGE.

SEE LIFT
SHEET FOR
2½ TEM-
PLATE.

FINISH ALL GLOSS WHITE EXCEPT
FOR BOOT TOP LINE.

C.B. AT 2900 LBS. DISPLACEMENT

LIFT 7

Sheet 1
Enlarge 221 percent for full-size plans.

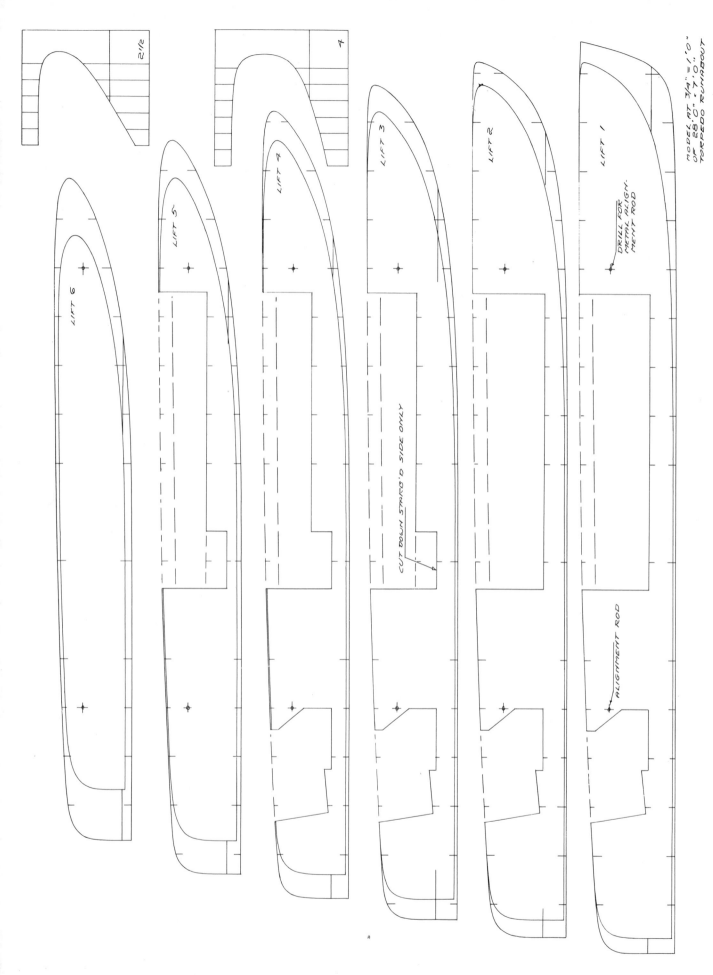

LIFT 6

LIFT 5

LIFT 4

LIFT 3

LIFT 2

LIFT 1

2/12

4

CUT DOWN STARB'D SIDE ONLY

DRILL FOR METAL ALIGN-MENT ROD

ALIGNMENT ROD

MODEL AT 3/4" = 1'0"
OF 28.0" × 7.0"
TORPEDO RUNABOUT

Sheet 2
Enlarge 221 percent for full-size plans.

and try them for size on the deck template to be sure your lift stock thickness is accurate (it's also a good idea to try the actual lifts when they're sawed out). Better to be a hair thicker, which can always be taken off, rather than be on the thin side, which would mean filling out your hull with putty.

Note that the forward cockpit jog is cut on the starboard side only on Lifts 3, 4, and 5. This is where the helmsman stands; there's a seat forward of him and another seat on the port side.

In the deck plan view, you can see that the forward end of the cockpit begins to curve at Lift 5, so it seems easier to cut it out square, as Lift 5 shows, then saw out a curved piece and glue it in to serve as a coaming.

With your 2⅜-inch × ⅜-inch boards ready to go, lay out your lift templates for the least waste. If you're sure you have enough material, it's easiest and fastest just to whack off 14 2-foot lengths and trace each template on the individual pieces. Lay your template on the board and clamp it in place. Trace around its outline—no stations or boottop yet. Without moving the template even a hair, take it to the drill press and bore through the hole in your template into the lift for the alignment rods. It works best to put the drill into the hole of the template first, then start your drill; this avoids making a barnyard pass at the hole from outside, with the risk of wobbling.

After you've bored all the holes, slip Lift 1 onto the rods, then the Lift 1 template, then Lift 2, then its template, and so on through to Lift 7—just like making a shish kebab. This perfectly aligns all the lifts for marking across the stations all at once, rather than marking each one individually while holding its template in place. Also, mark the boottop on each. While you're at it, bore two holes in a board long enough and wide enough for the layup, using one of the templates as a guide for the holes. Cut the two rods long enough to span the hull, stick them in the holes, and tack a piece of scrap over their ends so they won't fall out. Now you're ready to lay up half a hull.

If the weather's cool, Weldwood dry-powder glue is OK because you have time to readjust the lifts before the glue starts to cure. But with 14 lifts, which is a lot, I used a slower setting epoxy because it gives you more time and makes for easier alignment. Whatever you use, mix up some glue, pour some in a container, and apply it to one side of Lift 1, using a roller. Slip the lift over the rods, then glue both sides of Lift 2 and slide it on the rods, and so on through to Lift 7 (gluing only one side of Lift 7). With one half hull laid up, take it off the board, rods and all, and lay up and glue the other half on the rods. Clamp the hull together where needed, and drive the rods out of the hull after you're sure the glue has cured thoroughly enough. Another way, and perhaps better, is to glue all 14 lifts together all strung on the rods at once, using epoxy with a slower cure time. Just be watchful for any twisting of the hull. While waiting for the hull to cure is a good time to cut out the body templates, if you haven't done it already.

If you discover, like I did, that you forgot to draw the station lines on the second half of the hull lifts, no problem—push the rods back through the hull, shove the templates back on them, and line them across.

Putting in the cockpit coamings isn't hard to do. Look at the deck plan and see how the forward cockpit's coamings fit against Lift 6, sweeping inboard at the forward end of the cockpit and very slightly at the rear of the cockpit; the stern cockpit's coamings are straight. Once you put in the forward coamings and work them down to the shape of the hull of templates 3, 3½ and 4, the hull should appear as it looks in profile (if you left them out, you'd see straight lines instead where they're supposed to be). You can make the coamings from a scrap

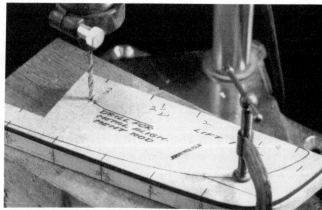

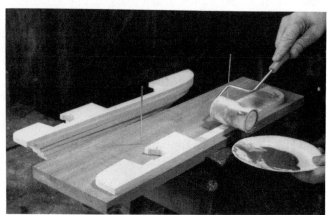

piece of aircraft plywood or most anything. The forward ones need to be about ¼ inch wide at their forward ends in order to saw the required amount of curve out of them. I cut the shape of the forward coamings out of the plans and stuck them to Masonite, as I did with the rest of the templates. The aft coamings need no templates, since they're straight, and they only need to be about ¹⁄₁₆ inch thick.

Clockwise, from upper left: Comparing test lift thickness with that of plan; remember, this is a *buttock* lift model, with *vertical* slices. . . . Drilling lift for alignment rod. . . . Applying glue to lifts with roller. . . . Checking amidships shape with template.

Carving the Hull

Since this hull curves in every direction, finding points of reference to carve to is the key to keeping these curvaceous lines under control. First, for visually aligning the station templates plumb and square to the centerline, let's make a centerline to butt their ends against. Cut a rectangular piece of Masonite measuring 5 inches × 24 inches, stick white paper to both sides, trace the Lift 1 template on it, and cut out its profile. To keep the curve flowing fair at the top of the hull over the cockpit areas, spring a batten along the template. Mark the stations on it, and number them. Slip the profile cutout over the glued-up hull, fitting the hull to the profile cutout precisely along its centerline, then mark the stations on the hull and number them (they disappear often). Now you have three points—a tripod, you might say—for reference in carving: the deck and bottom centerlines, and station lines.

And there's still one more. Center the deck template on the hull and mark around it, top and bottom. It's good to train your eye for a moment before you begin removing the excess wood around the hull sides. You can start this process on the bandsaw, roughly cutting around the deck outline. Keep a healthy margin; make sure you don't cut off the ends of the buttock lifts, thus shortening them where they're glued to each other.

Now put the hull in your vise, clamped on its sides; just a couple of scraps of wood on each side is all you need for protection. Start planing along the straight part of her bottom. This is easy and you're not likely to get into trouble here, but stop short of planing the section marks off.

Begin carving where you feel most comfortable. Avoid bulling into the job. It's easy to take off too much on the outside curves, so beware; go easy on them, and finish them last. You can round the top and bottom of Lift 7 (the hull's two center lifts) slightly. Shift to the bow and work that area, because it's obvious what to remove. The trickiest part is the transition from the hard chine at the stern quarter, from Lift 8 to Lift 7. I saved this until last, only making stabs at working it in as I went along.

Note that the ends of the section templates are cut right to the centerline, so with the hull clamped in the vise on her side, keep working each station down, all the while eyeballing an equal distance from its ends to the centerline. Since all of *Snow Leopard*'s lines fall away outboard from her centerline, each bit of wood taken off—each time you try a section template—shows progress. You might as well finish one side at a time, to avoid re-clamping, but do it to suit. The idea is to gradually work all these stations down almost to the nitty-gritty finish, then stop.

Use edged tools—a chisel, a gouge, and a block plane—only at the start. You won't make many passes at this hull before you put them away and switch to sandpaper and a mill file; it's just plain too easy to remove wood where you don't want to. An ordinary rubber sanding block is no good for this, because the ones you buy are too large and clumsy—you simply don't have the control. Instead, make your own curved sanding block from a piece of wood. Mine is 4¾ inches × 1¾ inches × ¾ inch, curved on its top and rounded across the width of the face on one end for sanding up next to the centerline without hitting it, and for concave sanding where needed. Cut a piece of 60-grit sandpaper to fit, and bring the ends up over the block and thumbtack them where they meet. Wood is much better than rubber because you can feel the wood transmit to your hands what you're taking off, while rubber doesn't communicate as well. You'll keep losing the station marks and their numbers as you work, so slip the profile template on the hull and re-mark them as needed.

Plan on three or four days for carving the hull, with a few breaks thrown in to rest your eyes. Up to this point, carving each station as close as you dared, all you needed was a couple of scraps of wood to hold the model in the vise. Now we're getting down to the fussy work, the final fairing to finish her off. For this we need to be able to work all around the hull, so we'll make a holding device that allows the model to be held in the vise on either side or upside down. A piece of 2 × 4 jammed down on end between the seats in the forward cockpit and a piece of scrap nailed flat across its end will do it. Put a spot of glue on the 2 × 4 to hold it in the hull; you'll knock or chisel it out later when the hull's done. With this holding device in the way, you won't be able to use the profile centerline again, so make sure you aren't going to need it.

Sandpaper glued to long, thin battens are great for final fairing, but before using them draw all the station lines on the hull. When you find high or hard

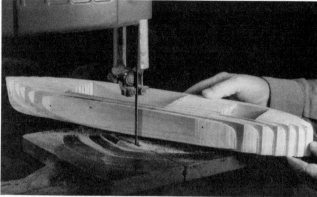

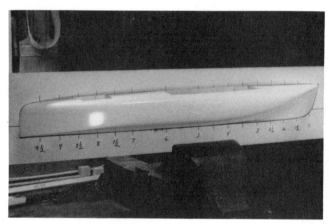

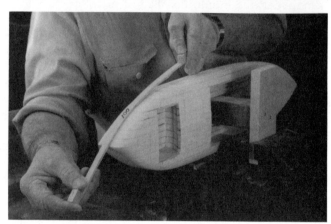

Clockwise, from upper left: Tracing deck pattern as a rough guide for carving . . . then sawing off excess wood from layup. . . . Hull's nearly carved. Note templates at each station to check accuracy. . . . Fairing hull with 100-grit sandpaper glued to fairing batten. . . . Use profile template to mark boottop and check overall accuracy.

spots between them, first take them down slightly with more sanding or filing. Then give the hull a coat of sealer—shellac thinned half-and-half with alcohol or a couple of coats of B-I-N, a shellac/alcohol-based white primer. After the sealer's dried, some more sanding with 100-grit sandpaper stuck to a batten will show up high and low spots. Take the high spots down to bare wood and fill any low spots.

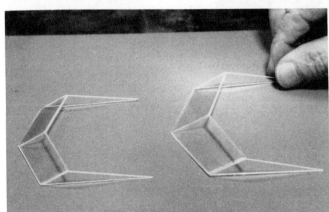 

Clockwise, from upper left: Marking boottop. . . . Marking plug for windshield from deck template. . . . Plug marked; ready to cut rake for windshield. . . . Forward and aft windshields ready to go on.

Finishing

Give the hull another couple of coats of B-I-N, sand them down, and give the hull a final coat of gloss white. I used an airbrush for painting her final coat, but it was more trouble than it was worth, considering the time it took to mix the paint and clean up. A can of spraypaint right off the shelf would've been quite acceptable.

To mark the boottop, lay the hull on your table saw or some flat surface, and mark the ends of the boottop from the profile template. Then level the hull across, tape a pencil to a wooden block and slide it along the table to mark the hull waterline boottop. Saw 3/32 inch from the block, then go around again. Then mask off the boottop and paint it either red or black.

You can ignore the interior of the cockpits or paint them to suit. Should you decide to paint them, it's much easier to line them both with aircraft plywood than it is to try to fill all the unevenness of the rough lifts.

The windshields really add to *Snow Leopard*'s looks. Make a wooden block

Color Scheme:

Hull, gloss white
Boottop, red or black
Bow and stern sheathing plates,
 chrome

Poetry in motion.

template to the plan and profile views of the windshields (don't forget to deduct glass thickness), and wax it or tape waxed paper around it. Cut some acetate of the thickness wanted (.030 inch) and glue the acetate panels together right on the block template with superglue or acrylic solvent cement (this you can buy at a glass-replacement company, made especially for gluing acetate or acrylic plastic together). You have to apply the glue very carefully so as not to get glue where you don't want it. This is where the masking tape comes in. For gluing the windshield to the hull, I used a needle with the tip end of its head ground off (you can't file it off because it is hardened); this acted like a soap-bubble pipe, holding a tiny bit of glue, allowing me to place it exactly where I wanted.

Finally, mask off for the knife-edge sheathing plates at stem and stern (see the hull profile/Lift 7) and paint them with Bumper Chrome spraypaint. I sprayed a little of this into a small container and painted it on with a small paintbrush. It looks quite nice, though it looks more like silver than chrome.

The scale young lady driver? I found her in the kids' toy section of a nearby department store.

A Clear Cut Case

Getting a display case for your model brings out some interesting problems. It's tough to find glass cases the right size, and building one yourself is expensive. Wood for the base and corner supports for a glass case to display a model the size of the sardine carrier *Pauline* would have cost $150. An acrylic case gives an unobstructed view—no wooden corners, nothing to catch your eye, just a nice clear view of your masterpiece. But acrylic is tough to work with, and unless you live in a city with a big glass-replacement store, it's difficult to find someone to build one for you.

I made my own acrylic case for *Pauline*, and while the process led to some frustration, I saved a lot of money and came up with a method to spare you the aggravation. I'll warn you from the start, it is near impossible to build one of these acrylic cases and do it right on the first shot. But if you are as stubborn as I am, don't mind experimenting, and can stand the sting of a few trial failures, then go to it.

Let's look at *Pauline*'s 36-inch × 19-inch × 12¼-inch case. The model is 31 inches long, 7 inches wide, and 17 inches high to the top of her mast, cradle and all. The case leaves about 2 inches' clearance over her mast, 2 inches at the stern, and 3 inches at the bow. With no corner supports, this gives the illusion of more room around her than there really is.

Clockwise, from top: With the two acrylic sheets resting in the jig, rabbeted edges locked, apply the glue starting at the highest spot. Gravity will take care of the rest. . . . Two pieces of cardboard glued ½ inch from the jig's joint will suspend the acrylic . . . A rabbeted joint.

I used ⅛-inch acrylic (the same stuff you would replace a window or glass in your door with) I bought at a local hardware store. That's about as thick a sheet as I'd use; while thicker acrylic is easier to work with, it's also more expensive. I bought a 3-foot × 6-foot sheet for $33. It would have cost $48 if I had had it cut at the store, but since I wanted to try cutting it myself, I chose the cheaper route. At that price you could still make three or four cases, throw them away, and still spend less than a custom-made case would cost. Not to mention the learning experience.

I spent about two weeks making trial boxes out of scrap acrylic and screwed up every one of them before I got courage to try the full-size case. The first full-size case, which I gave up on, had an unacceptable number of blemishes that weren't worth the time to take out. I gave it away as a planter. By the time I made the second one, I got a little smarter and made a case that I could still see minor faults in quick enough, but it is quite acceptable. If I don't count the hours experimenting, this case is still cheaper than the store-bought kit, but more than that, it is exactly what I wanted—and I made it.

Cutting

Determining the size of case you want is the easy part. Once you've done so, lay out your cuts on the acrylic sheet and mark them with a pencil and a straightedge, leaving on the protective plastic. You'll be using a portable electric handsaw to cut the acrylic; remember to add the width of the saw's shoe when you lay out and mark the cuts. Remember also that the case will fit *outside* your base. Leave the protective plastic on when cutting, and set the electric hand-saw's planer blade just deep enough to cut through the acrylic. And be sure the saw's blade is hollow-ground, with no set to the teeth.

To ease gluing and to lock the joints, I rabbeted out the sides and top edges of the side panels and the tops of the end panels—eight in all. The rabbeting is easily done on your table saw. Support the edge of the acrylic while you're sawing, you don't want an open saw slot where you would get a lot of bounce or chatter. Clamp a piece of wood to the rip guide, and with a planer blade saw the acrylic on top of a piece of Masonite or something smooth. Set this on the saw table and bring the blade up through it so the saw slot is covered. For me this worked great.

Gluing

Now comes the tricky part. Most any glass replacement store sells acrylic solvent cement, a liquid that bonds acrylic. The cement I used was made by Craftics, Inc., Chicago, IL, 60639. You squirt this liquid in the joint, capillary action spreads the cement, and the acrylic bonds quickly. You need only wait a few minutes before you can move the joint, so the actual process of gluing the case proceeds almost without interruption.

Joining the case's corners and holding them in the right position while getting the cement exactly where you want is the real job. The cement comes in a small plastic squeeze bottle with a built-in self-draining reservoir, and is applied through the bottle's fine, hollow snout. You are supposed to squirt this stuff out at a controlled rate along the joint, since a spilled drop spoils the job by etching itself in the acrylic.

I found that if you follow the very scanty directions on using this liquid, you can be about a 100 percent sure of certain failure. You are told to peel back the protective plastic layer a ½ inch. This makes sense, because the cement's capillary action follows anything in it's way—even uphill—in a horrifying instant. This I found out the hard way.

The instructions also tell you to hold the glass together with masking tape while applying the liquid. Naturally, you'd assume they are referring to the case's corners, since the corners are what you would join. But how are you going to tape the corners without the cement following the tape's edges? Certain disaster again. The cement passes through the joint and onto the masking tape, etching a perfect pattern of the tape in your prized case. And it doesn't matter whether the joint is vertical or horizontal.

The Jig

You can lick this problem easily, using gravity to your advantage. Find two chunks of plywood; size isn't that important but you'll use the plywood to support the acrylic while the glue dries, so don't make them too small. Join the plywood to form a 90-degree corner, creating an L-shaped jig on which you lay the acrylic sheets for gluing. Take pains to make sure the inside of the joint is smooth. Support the jig at an angle so any cement placed in the acrylic joint

Pauline at home in her case. Note how the case fits over the 1/2-inch plywood base, which I painted a darker shade of gray than her deck. The contrast shows off her underbody.

flows both down and away, unobstructed. To further ease the flow of the cement, suspend the joint slightly by gluing lengths of thin cardboard back about 1/2 inch from the jig's joint. Gravity will hold the acrylic joint together, and any excess glue will simply run through the joint and drop to the plywood.

I first laid one end and one side in the jig, locked the rabbeted edges, applied the glue in a smooth continuous motion starting at the higher edges, then cut some cardboard gussets and taped them to the acrylic to support the joint. When the joint has set, turn the case around, set up the other end and side, glue them, then use the jig to finish the final two joints.

The Top

Putting on the top isn't so easy. I didn't want to apply the glue from the outside and chance the cement running down the sides of the case, and I didn't want to experiment. I did it from inside, and this is where the applicator's reservoir came in handy. Lay the top on your workbench and fit the case to it, making sure the rabeted edges lock. Apply the liquid halfway along the joint, then tip up the snout and the excess liquid runs into reservoir and back into the bottle. The trick is not to panic when you shift directions; hold the snout directly over the joint while the excess runs back in the bottle, then finish the joint from the opposite side.

With a deeper case, where it's awkward to apply the cement, there is a simpler way. Place the case top in the rabbet, and mask the top and side of the case along the joint, leaving the joint itself open. With some quick-setting epoxy and a customized putty knife made from a razor blade (half a blade or smaller is better) inserted in a wooden handle, fill the joint. Let it harden, then sand the joint, working your way from 100-grit paper the 320-grit or finer. Don't use superglue; you'd just be asking for trouble.

You can remove tiny scratches and other minor imperfections with very fine sandpaper (five mic.) from a fiberglass boatbuilding shop and two kinds of polish made especially for acrylic, Novus 1 and Novus 2. Novus 1 removes the static electricity—or at least 95 percent of it—and Novus 2 takes out minor scratches and clears the glass again. A La Cross "high shine" three-step fingernail buffer did the job best of all for removing fine scratches.

Was all the trouble of making the case worth it? You bet. Despite acrylic's vulnerability to scratching, I have a lightweight case that gives me an unobstructed view of my model. Just what I wanted.

Making *Pauline*'s acrylic home ended many years of modeling—and the learning that goes with it—that's been a privilege and joy to share. If I've inspired someone to have a try, then I've been rewarded for writing this book. As old-time boatbuilder Pete Culler once said, "Experience starts when you begin." So begin—and have fun.

Aft. Toward the stern.

After. Closer to the stern.

Amidships. In the middle portion of a boat. As an adjective, "midships."

Athwartships. Running across the hull. As an adjective, "thwartship."

Baseline. A line, usually parallel to the waterline, drawn on boat plans and used as a reference for all vertical measurements when lofting the lines of a hull.

Batten. A thin, flat length of wood that can be sprung through a series of reference points and thereby used to determine and draw a fair curve through the points.

Belaying Pin. A rod or pin used in making fast running rigging.

Bevel. An angle cut along the edge of a timber or across its end to produce an exact fit between parts of a hull.

Bilge. The lower internal region of a hull, or (often as "turn of the bilge") the region of maximum curvature between the bottom and sides in a cross-sectional view of a round-bottomed boat.

Billethead. A carved wooden scroll at the upper end or top of the stem, with the carving turning inboard. If the carving turns outboard, it is a fiddlehead.

Bobstay. A stay from the lower stem of the boat to the end of the bowsprit that counteracts the upward pull of the forestay.

Boom Crutch. A notched board or X-shaped frame that supports the main boom when the sail is lowered.

Bowsprit. A spar that projects from the bow and extends the sail plan by allowing headsails to be secured forward of the bow.

Bowsprit Cap. An iron band at the outboard end of the bowsprit that secures the inboard end of the jibboom.

Breasthook. A thwartship structural member near the stem.

Bulkhead. A thwartship panel dividing a hull into sections.

Butt. To join end-to-end or edge-to-edge. As a noun, a butt strap or butt block fastened across such a joint to hold the two elements together. Also, the lower end of a mast.

Buttock. The rounded overhang of the lower stern forward of the rudder.

Carvel Planking. A method of planking in which the strakes or planks are fastened to the frames of a hull edge to edge.

Centerboard. A short, hinged, retractable keel used to reduce leeway in a sailboat. It is raised and lowered through a watertight case, or trunk.

Centerline. On boat plans, a line dividing a hull into two identical fore-and-aft sections, and used as a base for establishing thwartship measurements when lofting. Also, a vertical line on thwartship members used to align them during assembly.

Chine. A longitudinal joint where panel edges meet in a hull constructed of a sheet material such as plywood. Most commonly, the joint between sides and bottom in a flat- or V-bottom boat.

Chine Log. A reinforcing strip of wood along the inside or outside of a chine, to which the joining panels are fastened.

Cleat. A fitting to which a line can be made fast. Any short length of small dimensional lumber used for miscellaneous framing needs.

Clew. The lower, aftermost corner of a triangular fore-and-aft sail. Also the lower outboard corners of a squaresail.

Cringle. A reinforced aperture in a sail, such as a metal grommet, through which a line can be passed.

Deadrise. The upward slant of the bottom of a hull to the chine in a V-bottom hull, or from the keel to the turn of the bilge in a round-bottom hull.

Dory. A flat-bottomed craft that has flaring sides and a narrow stern. It is capable of carrying heavy loads but is very tender when light.

Double-ended. Having a sharp end at both bow and stern (e.g., a canoe or a peapod).

Edge-nailed. A method of planking in which successive narrow strakes, usually square or nearly so, are fastened together with nails and generally glued as well.

Edge-set. In a carvel-planked boat, to drive one plank down forcibly to meet the plank below despite irregularities in the planks.

Face. The flat, broad surface of a board or timber.

Fair. Said of a graceful curve that changes gradually and has no bumps, hollows, or flat places. Used also as a verb.

Fid. A pointed, tapering spike used for opening the strands of rope when splicing.

Flare. The outward angle of a boat's sides between waterline and sheer when viewed in cross section.

Flush. Even or level with, not protruding.

Foot. The bottom edge of a sail. Also, the butt of a mast.

Frame or Frame Mold. A thwartship member to which planking is fastened.

Framing Piece. A strengthening member fastened to the edge of a bulkhead or transom to add rigidity.

Freeboard. At any given point along a hull, the height of the sheer above the waterline.

Gaff. The spar to which the head of a gaff sail is lashed. It has a set of jaws that run up or down the mast when the sail is hoisted or lowered.

Gaff-headed. Describing a sailing rig consisting of a quadrilateral fore-and-aft sail fitted with a gaff.

Garboard. In a carvel-planked boat, the plank next to the keel, either port or starboard.

Grommet. A round, metal eyelet or a ring of rope sewn into a sail or other piece of cloth.

Gudgeon. A metal eye or other aperture installed on the keel, skeg, or transom of a boat, into which the rudder pintles fit when the rudder is shipped or installed.

Gunwale. The longitudinal strengthening strip that runs along the sheer of a hull from bow to stern. (Pronounced gunn'l)

Gusset. A stiffening bracket fastened to any two structural members where they meet at an angle near 90 degrees.

Halyard. The line, reeved through a block or similar device, with which the sail is raised.

Head. The top corner of a jibheaded sail or the top edge of a quadrilateral sail. In a gaff rig, the head of the sail is attached to the gaff.

Heel. The foot or butt of the mast or the end of a frame at the keel. As a verb, the tendency of a sailboat to lean from the vertical in response to the pressure of the wind on the sails.

Horse. Athwartships iron rod along which the traveler slides.

Inboard. Within the limits of the hull area.

Jaws. A U-shaped fitting on the inboard end of a boom or gaff that allows the spar to swing around the mast.

Jibboom. An extension of the bowsprit.

Jig. A wooden structure on a fixed base on which the parts of a boat can be assembled. A jig determines the shape of the part.

Keel. The main structural member and longitudinal backbone of a hull; it usually extends below the hull to help keep the boat on a heading and reduce leeway.

Knee. A strengthening timber that is fastened to two angled members and distributes stress to both.

Lapstrake. A method of planking in which each strake slightly overlaps the one below it, giving the appearance of clapboards.

Leech. The after edge of a fore-and-aft sail.

Limber Holes. Apertures in bulkheads that allow water in the bilge to move from one section of the hull to another.

Lofting. The process of laying out the patterns of the parts of a hull full size, working from plans drawn to scale.

Luff. As a noun, the forward edge of a fore-and-aft sail. As a verb, to head up into the wind so much that the forward edge of the sail begins to shake.

Mast. The vertical spar that is the main support column of the sailing rig.

Mast Partner. A transverse member located at a height just below the sheerline of a boat, through which the mast passes to acquire steadiness and bearing.

Mold. A pattern of a transverse section of a hull, set up in construction but removed when the hull nears completion. A frame mold acts as a mold but remains in the finished hull.

Monkey Rail. A light, decorative wooden fence above the main deck in the after part of a sailing ship.

Offsets. A table of measurements from the baseline and centerline that establish points defining the shape of a hull. Offsets are used to loft and lay down the lines of a boat full size.

Outboard. Outside the limits of the hull, or in a direction away from the centerline.

Peak. In a sprit or gaff sail, the after upper corner of the quadrilateral.

Peak Halyards. The lines to hoist the peak of a quadrilateral sail.

Pintle. A vertical pin or rod used to hang or hinge a rudder. Pintles are attached to the forward or leading edge of the rudder and slide into gudgeons fixed to the stern of a boat. (See Gudgeon.)

Prebore. To bore a hole in wood that a nail or other fastening will be driven into. Preboring reduces the danger of breaking out or splitting. The holes should be slightly smaller than the wire diameter of the shank of the fastening.

Quarter. One of the two outboard quadrants of a boat's stern.

Rabbet. A beveled recess cut into the stem to receive the forward, or hood, ends of the planking and into the keel to receive the lower edge of the garboard strake.

Rake. A departure from the vertical of any member of a boat, such as the stem, transom, or mast.

Reef Points. Short lengths of rope made fast to a sail at the reef band that when tied allow a sail to be taken in, or "shortened."

Run. The curve of the bottom of a hull as it rises from a point near amidships toward the stern. If the rise is gentle, with little rocker, the boat is said to have a flat run.

Saddle. A piece of timber having a rounded notch in which a boom or spar is stowed.

Samson Post. A strong vertical post or bitt onto which lines or rodes can be secured.

Scarf. As a verb, to glue two beveled pieces of wood end to end or edge to edge; beveling allows the pieces to overlap without an increase in thickness. As a noun, describes a joint so made.

Seam. The joint between two planks or strakes, rendered watertight by caulking.

Seize. To bind together; or, to put a stopper on a line. Line for seizing is always smaller and lighter than the line to which it is applied.

Sheer. The uppermost line of a hull viewed in profile, also called the sheerline. The top plank, or strake, on a hull is the sheerstrake.

Sheet. A line used to control the positioning of a sail in relation to the wind. On a sail attached to a boom, the sheet is made fast to the boom near its outboard end; on a loose-footed sail, it is attached to the clew.

Shim. To wedge up or fill out with thin sheets of metal or wood.

Shutter. The strake that closes in a hull that has been planked both up from the keel and down from the sheer.

Snotter. A line that bears on or near the butt of a sprit to maintain its thrust against either the clew of a jibheaded sail or the peak of a quadrilateral sail.

Spanish Windlass. A length of line looped around the planks or side panels of a hull to pull them into place, usually by means of a lever that twists the line and constricts the loop. In action it resembles a tourniquet.

Spar. Any timber (mast, boom, gaff, or sprit) used to support a sailing rig.

Spile. To determine and scribe a line that defines the shape of any element in a hull so that it will exactly fit an adjoining element as required. Most frequently, to transfer the shape of the upper edge of a plank or strake onto the bottom edge of the plank to be fastened immediately above it.

Sprit. A spar used to set a spritsail by extending the clew of a triangular sail or the peak of a quadrilateral sail.

Spritsail. Any sail set by means of a sprit.

Spring Stay. On a two-masted vessel, standing rigging extending from masthead to masthead.

Stay. A fixed line to support a mast in a fore-and-aft direction.

Staysail. Traditionally, any fore-and-aft sail, except a jib, that is set on a stay.

Stem. The foremost vertical or nearly vertical structural member of a boat's hull; sometimes called a cutwater.

Stemcap. External fairing piece that overlays the planking joint at the stem.

Strake. A single unit of the planking that closes in a boat's hull.

Tack. The forward lower corner of any fore-and-aft sail.

Template. A pattern cut from wood, metal, or paper and used to scribe lines on building stock.

Throat. The forward upper corner of a quadrilateral fore-and-aft sail.

Thwart. A transverse member, often a seat for crew or passengers.

Topmast. The mast rigged above a lower or principal mast.

Topping Lift. A wire, rope, or chain used to take weight off, for example, a yard, boom, or sail, enabling it to be topped or raised to the desired level.

Trailboard. A carved plank on each side of the stem near the deck edge where the bowsprit starts, originally used as a brace for the ship's figurehead.

Transom. The after face of the stern of a boat; often, the entire stern.

Traveler. An iron fitting, to which a sheet block is attached, that slides along the traveler. The horse and traveler provide for better sheeting angles off the wind.

Trunk. A narrow boxlike structure, open to the sea at the bottom of the boat, through which a centerboard or daggerboard can be lowered to extend below the bottom; also called a case.

Trysail. A triangular, loose-footed sail fitted aft of the mast and used to replace the mainsail in heavy weather.

Tumblehome. The inward curve of the upper sides of a hull toward the centerline.

V-bottom Boat. A chine boat whose deadrise is flat between the keel and the chine; sometimes called a deadrise boat.

Wale. The strip of planking running beneath the gunwale, parallel to the sheer.

Waterline. Any horizontal line on a boat's profile generated by a plane parallel to the surface of the water. The LWL, load waterline, is the upper limit of a boat's draft under normal conditions with the designed load.

Windlass. A drum with a vertical axis around which an anchor rode is wound.

Build the New Instant Boats

by Harold "Dynamite" Payson

Harold H. Payson—known to his associates, friends, and his wife as Dynamite—thinks *you* can build a boat. In fact, if you can saw a penciled line, apply glue, drive nails, and bring a modest measure of patience to the task, you can build and launch a smart and able craft in as few as 40 man-hours. You need not be driven by lack of tools, materials, skills, or time to abandon in frustration a project you conceived in a spirit of pleasurable anticipation.

Years ago, when Dynamite began supplementing his boatbuilding work by selling boat plans, he got feedback from a number of customers who found the boats too difficult to build. Many of these would-be boatbuilders had never heard of lofting and were intimidated and discouraged by the necessity of building a jig before building the boat itself. Many of them, too, couldn't find local suppliers of the lumber and other materials called for in the plans.

Selling plans for boats that never got built went against Dynamite's Down East grain, and it was also, he figured, a "straight road to bankruptcy in the long run." He discussed the problem with designer Phil Bolger, who agreed, on one condition, to design a series of boats that would require no lofting, no jig, and no lumber that could not be obtained at any local building-supplies store. Boats that would not require a great investment of time to cut out and button up. In short, boats for the inexperienced builder whose desire is to get out on the water. The one condition was that Dynamite, a member of *Small Boat Journal*'s Hall of Fame, build and test each prototype to wring out every bug before offering the plans for sale. The result was a fleet of six boats described in his first book, *Instant Boats*.

Here are eleven new instant boats to choose from, including a 15-foot, double-chine rowing and sailing boat; an 8-foot sailing pram; a 15-foot, double-chine outboard speed boat; and a 16-foot, double-ended, lug-rigged sharpie. Three of the new boats are built with a new "tack-and-tape" method that eliminates most of the beveling and results in a very shapely and spritely craft. Dynamite writes of everything you'll need to know to build one of his boats with common sense and uncommon good humor. Then you can start right in.

Pleasant sailing.

160 pages, 92 photos, 33 plans, $19.95, Book No 60230

Skiffs & Schooners

R.D. "Pete" Culler

There is nothing else quite like *Skiffs & Schooners*, and there never will be. This book offers the chance to sit for a while with a master shipbuilder and soak up his knowledge and wisdom on every facet of small boats and boatbuilding: how to choose and work wood, what boats serve what purpose, how to finish a boat, how to fit her out, how to build oars, how to design and fashion a small-boat rig. First published in 1974, *Skiffs & Schooners* galvanized the renaissance of small craft that was then in its infancy.

Skiffs & Schooners lapsed from print in 1985, another victim of a decade of self-indulgences and instant gratification on a scale Pete Culler could never have countenanced. Now that guzzling gas and borrowing from the future are once again passing from fashion, perhaps some small corner of our collective imagination will turn again to gracing our waterways with simple, stout boats that arrest the gaze, soothe the soul, and dissipate rather than fulfill the restive urge to always be somewhere else doing some other things.

The simple things are still the best. May this book enrich your boating, and your decade.

"The author has rendered a profound service to wooden boat enthusiasts and students of wooden boat building arts by sharing with us a knowledge that is rapidly become extinct. This book is a must for anyone who takes the subject seriously."

—*Yachting*

208 pages, 180 illustrations, $19.95, Book No. 60186

**Look for These and Other International Marine Books
at Your Local Bookstore**

To Order, Call Toll Free 1-800-822-8158
(outside the U.S., call 717-794-2191)

or write to International Marine, A Division of TAB Books,
Blue Ridge Summit, PA 17294-0840.

Title	Product No.	Quantity	Price
_____	_____	_____	_____
_____	_____	_____	_____
_____	_____	_____	_____
_____	_____	_____	_____

Subtotal: $_____

Postage and Handling
($3.00 in U.S., $5.00 outside U.S.): $_____

Add applicable state and local sales tax: $_____

TOTAL: $_____

❑ Check or money order made payable to TAB Books

Charge my   ❑ VISA   ❑ MasterCard   ❑ American Express

Acct. No. _____ Exp. _____

Signature: _____

Name: _____

Address: _____

City: _____

State: _____ Zip: _____

International Marine catalog free with purchase; otherwise send $1.00 in check or
money order and receive $1.00 credit on your next purchase.

Orders outside U.S. must pay with international money order in U.S. dollars.

If for any reason you are not satisfied with the book(s) you order, simply return it (them)
within 15 days and receive a full refund.